THE FALSE HEALER: A TRILOGY

BASED ON TRUE EVENTS

PAULA SEVESTRE

CONTENTS

Part I
THE FALSE HEALER (2020)

Preface ... 3
1. The Opening ... 5
2. The Way ... 16
3. God Speed ... 22
4. In the Quiet Lull ... 32
5. The Grace ... 43
6. The One ... 52
7. The Way of the Soul ... 63
8. In the End ... 70
9. The Telling ... 79
10. The Verdict ... 95
11. The Reckoning ... 99
12. The False Healer ... 107
13. The Truth ... 114
14. The End ... 117

Part II
HEAVEN'S WAIT (2014)

Preface ... 123
Introduction ... 125
1. Our First Meeting ... 127
2. The Early Years ... 134
3. A Creative Path ... 141
4. Bound by Fear ... 147
5. An Adolescent View ... 154
6. A Spirit Connection ... 163
7. The Healer's Influence ... 170
8. Journey to Adulthood ... 176
9. Higher Understanding ... 185
10. The Dream Connection ... 190

11. Past Recollections	194
12. Angers' Hold	203
13. The Healing Begins	209
14. A Last Look Back	213
15. A Mother's Legacy	222
Afterword	225

Part III
OUT FROM BENEATH YOUR WINGS (2016)

Preface	231
Introduction	233
1. The Unveiling	237
2. A Child's Love	246
3. Sojourns to the Past	255
4. A Tangled Web	263
5. What went Before	271
6. When Angels Beckon	278
7. The Last Stand	285
8. To Know Thyself	292
9. Understanding the Unknown	300
10. Taking Flight	313
11. Concepts for Living	319
12. Living in Harmony	328
13. Endings and Beginnings	340
Afterword	343

Copyright@2020 Paula Sevestre

All rights reserved. No part of this book may be used or reproduced by any means, graphs, electronic or mechanical, including photocopying, recording, taping or by any information storage retrieval system without the written permission of the author, except in the case of brief quotations embodied in critical articles and reviews. Because of the dynamic nature of the Internet, any web addresses or links contained in this book may have changed since publication and may no longer be valid.

The author of this book does not dispense medical advice or prescribe the use of any techniques as a form of treatment for physical, emotional, or medical problems without the advice of a physician, either directly or indirectly. The intent of the author is only to offer information of a general nature to help you on your quest for emotional and spiritual well-being.

Any images depicted in stock imagery provided by Shutterstock are models, and such images are used for illustrative purposes only.

ISBN: 978-1-7772829-0-5 (sc)

ISBN: 978-1-7772829-1-2 (e)

The False Healer: A Trilogy contains Book 1 (*The False Healer* 2020), Book 2 (*Heaven's Wait*, 2014) and Book 3 (*Out From Beneath Your Wings*, 2016). The trilogy details an entanglement with a deceptive spiritual healer and the author's journey to a personal and legal resolution.

To the soul that whispers Truth.

I

THE FALSE HEALER (2020)

If you could reimagine your suffering, what would it look like? In *The False Healer*, Paula draws on Joseph Campbell's "The Hero's Journey" to help tell her story. Faced with a sexual assault trial and its damaging impacts on her well-being, Paula weaves her story to reflect how she reimagined her suffering through the telling of her own "Hero's Journey." A once-daunting emotional trauma shifted in the light of a new perspective.

"*I opened the door. It was the detective who had emailed me about a sexual assault case he was investigating. He wanted to ask me a few questions about a book I had written in 2014 titled Heaven's Wait...As I came to learn, disclosure was just the first of many steps, and the fight to reveal the truth would be an exhausting battle.*"

PREFACE

In all the times I have been asked "What do you do?" not once did I feel qualified to say, "I'm a writer." Writers, I thought, are professionals who are trained in their art. I, on the other hand, was thrown into writing by Spirit. However, I now understand that I was born to fulfill a mission and within that mission I would need to write, so when the opportune time emerged so did the ability. In this story, I share the *why*.

Why did what happened to me with the False Healer need to happen? What brought me to this realization? How has my life changed as a result? How does what happened to me compare with other stories of healing? Why does it matter?

A new person came out of this experience. In this story, I want to share this transformation with you and the tremendous joy it has brought to my life. My heart is your heart, and I want you to know that you too can reimagine suffering.

1

THE OPENING

In Light so bright my soul shines
Deep, deep into nowhere and everywhere
I smile a knowing pleasure
Of the treasure
That exists
Not alone, but ever as one
Keep your faith oh lover of mine
For the joy of one is sublime

I will tell my story the best way I can within the confines of a publicity ban that exists for my court case. In 2010, I met a False Healer. I did not go to him; he was introduced to me via a close friend and confidant who told me that he had a message for me. As she was my friend, I trusted her. This introduction led to a nine-month entanglement with a deceitful spiritual healer. In these sessions, I was sexually assaulted, manipulated, humiliated, and left in ruins physically, emotionally, mentally, and spiritually. Here is my story and journey to my personal and legal resolution.

There was a knock on my door. I took a deep breath and braced myself for what I knew was going to be a difficult conversation. I peeked out the kitchen window to confirm that it was the visitor I was expecting. I opened the door. It was the detective who had emailed me about a sexual assault case he was investigating. He wanted to ask me a few questions about a book I had written in 2014 titled *Heaven's Wait*.

I was nervous, as I didn't know if the purpose for the detective's visit was to challenge the facts of my book or ask for my help. I was aware that a criminal investigation had been opened two months earlier regarding the False Healer because I had seen a post about it on Facebook, but I was still in the dark as to his motivation for reaching out to me. I invited the detective to take a seat at the kitchen table, and we made small talk while we got ourselves settled. I held onto my tea to keep my hands occupied, as I was sure they would shake.

The detective explained that he had been given my name by someone who gave him my book, but he was not at liberty to share their name. He further explained that some of the information and practices the False Healer utilized during our sessions together, which I had wrote about in my book, were similar to the complaints he was investigating. He was here on this day to confirm that it was the same individual and to get the facts of my story firsthand.

I can see now why I was nervous. The facts of my story I had written about in *Heaven's Wait* were not complete. When I wrote *Heaven's Wait*, I was not yet healed enough from my experience to share the details of the sexual assault I experienced. I left that entirely out of the book, and I wasn't sure in the moments when I was speaking to the detective if I wanted to reveal that side of the story. I worked hard to find a sense of peace with everything that had happened with the False Healer, and I was protective of the health of my whole body. I watched the detective closely as he talked, trying to get a sense of who he was as a person. Could he be trusted? Perhaps I had read too many bad news stories about investigations gone wrong and women being re-assaulted by the justice system, and I wondered if opening up this can of worms was worth it.

By the time the investigation started, I was already well on my healing journey. I had written two books and was doing workshops and public speaking events related to healing and expanding awareness. I didn't feel any need to delve into criminal justice as a means to find closure. I was up front with the detective about this, and he understood my position. However, there were other people involved that did not have that same level of awareness – they didn't feel safe, protected or free from their experiences with the False Healer. What was I going to do?

The detective informed me that he wasn't going to take any notes or record our conversation. He was only interested in confirming what I had written in my book. I believe he had highlighted certain sections in the book that he wanted to confirm, clarify or expand upon where appropriate. I don't remember much about this exchange. When his questions were done, the detective asked me if anything had happened with the False Healer (my words) that I felt was inappropriate. Here it was, the question…what was I going to say? I had never been asked that question before, and I knew in my heart I had to tell the whole story because I was now dealing with a criminal investigation. Yes, I said, there were incidents that occurred that were inappropriate.

The detective asked me to describe what happened. It took me a few seconds to shift my thought process – just a few minutes ago I was a potential witness, and now I was a potential victim. But it was my choice to tell. I would be the one to decide whether or not to step into the ring. As I came to learn, disclosure was just the first of many steps, and the fight to reveal the truth would be an exhausting battle.

I described to the detective what the False Healer did to me. He listened intently and asked some questions. However, at this point, my disclosure was not an official statement. It was still up to me if I wanted to proceed with criminal charges against the False Healer. I told the detective that I would need some time to think things through and talk to my husband before making any decisions. The detective gave me his card and asked me to contact him when I made a decision one way or the other.

My life was good. I was not looking to upend the peace in which I now lived. I went over everything in my head, trying to make sense of what I was feeling. Did I really want to go down the road of a possible trial? It was really just my word against the False Healer's. Plus, I had a past that was not so pretty, though it had been more than 30 years since I lived that life. I wasn't hiding anything, as I had written all about it in my second book *Out From Beneath Your Wings*. But still, in that long-ago past, I was not always an honest person, and I wasn't sure if I could withstand the scrutiny, given that it was out there for all to read. I didn't bring it up with my husband right away, as I needed to process all the information first. I told him about the conversation with the detective, but not yet about the potential sexual assault charges. There were at least five instances of sexual assault, and each instance would be a separate criminal offence.

It was a few days before I connected again with the detective. In that time, I finally spoke to my husband about considering filing charges against the False Healer. He said it was up to me, though I know it was difficult for him to speak about the False Healer. My husband still had a lot of animosity against him, and this was opening old wounds that he was trying hard to close. After all, the False Healer had decimated our lives, and he witnessed firsthand the devastating effects this had on me. I know he was being protective while at the same time trying to provide me with guidance. Ultimately, it would be my choice.

After reviewing all the pros and cons of a potential trial, I decided not to proceed with criminal charges. I went over in my head what I would say to the detective. I called him just before lunch and told him of my decision. I recounted to him the hard work I had put into healing myself after enduring nine painful months with the False Healer, and I didn't want to open old wounds. He understood my position, though in my heart I felt his disappointment not for himself but for the other victims who needed support. I wasn't even sure now if I could be a potential witness and share what I had written in my book; I forgot to ask.

When I hung up the phone, I sat down on my couch and cried. I didn't cry for myself but for the other victims who were still so profoundly impacted by the False Healer's actions. In that moment of tearful compassion, I experienced a flash of clarity and higher guidance – I knew immediately what I needed to do. Without a moment's hesitation, I again called the detective, and this time let him know that I was ready to file charges. He was elated. I informed the detective that I wanted him to take my statement that same day. He said he would be over in an hour. I called my husband to tell him the news. He asked if I wanted him there, but I knew in my heart it would be better if he remained distant from the case. I could at least spare him the details. This was my opportunity to help others and to heal my own heart.

I have no idea what my thoughts were before the detective arrived. I remember letting him in and once again settling in at the kitchen table. He took out a small recorder and notepad. We made small talk while he prepared the recorder, making sure it was in proper working order. I was a bit anxious but not emotional. I wanted the statement over and done with so I could have it on record what the False Healer did to me. The detective asked if I was ready, and when I gave him the okay he turned on the recorder.

The detective started off by stating the date, the time, and the case he was investigating. He introduced me, and I stated my name and spelled out my last name. I started to give my address, but the detective stopped me and advised that I not include any personal information like my address, phone number, children's names, etc., for my own protection and safety. He went over some of the ground rules; for example, he said that he would talk, then he would have me talk, and once he saw that I was finished, he would ask questions. He would also take notes to help him understand my statement. Before I began, he wanted me to know that if there was anything I felt uncomfortable talking about, that I could say that I was uncomfortable. I'd like to note that from the start the detective was very sensitive to the nature of my statement, and for that I am very appreciative.

Once the detective said I could begin, my thoughts went into hyper-drive. The experience was daunting. *Where do I start? What is relevant to the investigation?* Fortunately, I had written about my experience with the False Healer in *Heaven's Wait*, so I tried to follow that timeline. I explained how I met the False Healer and how our connection was made. This differed from what I stated in *Heaven's Wait* because I was aware when I wrote the book that I needed to protect the identity of the False Healer and explaining how I really knew him would identify his family and thus the False Healer. Not that I cared about protecting the False Healer's identity or my supposed friend, but at the time I hadn't taken any legal action, so I had to be mindful of what I wrote.

Even now in this account, I cannot provide information on how we met or who was there due to the publicity ban. However, most of my story follows *Heaven's Wait,* aside from the sexual assaults and certain patterns and specific words the False Healer used during our sessions together. I explained to the detective the exact location where the sessions with the False Healer took place and provided in detail the setup/layout of the building. I also went into detail on the nature of the sessions, payment, and common practices the False Healer employed in each of our sessions.

I want to recap a few things about myself and my experience with the False Healer. However, I'm not going to go into the whole story of *Heaven's Wait* because that book has its own energy, as does *Out From Beneath Your Wings*. I am Indigenous and was raised on a First Nation community on Canada's east coast. I grew up in a home that was loving, but it could get tumultuous when my parents drank. Their drinking increased in frequency as I grew into a young teenager, and the fighting that erupted between my parents could become explosive. It was sometimes a hard life for our big family as it was for many in our community. My mother quit drinking when I entered grade eight, which stabilized our home life, though my father continued to binge drink off and on for the next ten years, which put considerable stress on the family. My brother, who was a year older than me, died when I was fifteen, which greatly impacted our family. He had cancer, though his official cause of death was a blood clot that entered his heart following surgery to amputate his leg. I finished high school and attended university. After a couple of years at university, I decided to move to Toronto. Though it was fun living in the big city, it came with many hardships, which I shared in *Out From Beneath Your Wings*. I didn't make very good choices during this time. I moved back to the east coast and met my husband when I was 29. We married nine months later. He, too, is Indigenous, but he is from the Ontario region. We moved back to Ontario and lived in a few different locations for work before settling into a small town in southern Ontario. We have twin boys who are now in high school. In the years before I met the False Healer, my mother and two sisters were all diagnosed with breast cancer. This is important because it would play an important role in the decisions I made with the False Healer.

For a long time, I had dreams that I could not quite figure out the meaning of. They were like messages and gave me a feeling that I was actually living the dream in real life. I could clearly recall everything when I woke from these dreams or what I sometimes called "visitations". Three or four months before I met the False Healer, I had a vivid dream. In that dream, I had a conversation with my eldest brother, who is very tuned in metaphysically. My brother told me that I would get cancer in seven years and that when I did, I was to travel home and they would help me (though I don't know who he meant by "they'). He then breathed a white light into me and told me everything would be okay. I woke from the dream and wrote down what had happened. I emailed my brother and asked him if he remembered visiting me. He said he didn't know, as the night before he was exhausted from a long drive and immediately fell into a deep sleep. I shared this dream with my close friend and confidant who introduced me to the False Healer, and they would also become relevant to my story.

The other components that figure into my story are fear, guilt and shame. Fear was ingrained into me as a small child while I would wait for the violent outbursts that would inevitably ensue when my parents drank. I would lie in bed waiting for the first scream or bang of furniture being knocked over. Also, the fear of death was etched into my psyche every time I visited a home in our community where a wake was being held. We all waked our deceased family members in our homes, usually in the living room and sometimes in a bedroom if the space was too small. I grew up with this experience and from the time I could remember it was common for children to roam in and out of wakes. It was also quite normal to hear of hauntings and supernatural happenings on our reserve and on others. I heard of things like forerunners, which I actually believe were four-runners – devil-like beasts with four legs. Then, of course, the movie *The Exorcist* was released, and though many of us had not seen the movie, it was enough to hear about it. So much energy went into thinking about how I would protect myself from such beings.

Then there was the guilt and shame – guilt for all the wrong I had done to others and shame for who I was and where I came from. These two potent perceived character flaws would drive many of my decisions with the False Healer. I knew I had done wrong, but what could I do to atone for it? I knew I was ashamed of my heritage and upbringing, but how could I fix it? I knew I was not where I needed to be, but how could I get there? At the time, I felt that by living a better life, doing good deeds, and being kind and compassionate that I could atone for the not-so-good things that had happened in my life, but the False Healer had a different take on atonement.

I had not been involved with Indigenous traditional healers prior to my experience with the False Healer. I was raised Catholic, and though I was not a practicing church member, I still tried to follow church doctrine. I had a family doctor who looked after any medical concerns, plus we didn't grow up in a community with medicine people or shamans. Certainly there were those that knew medicine and traditional ways, but not any that I would have known about as a child or even later in my life. I want to reiterate here that I did not go to the False Healer – he came to me with a message.

Getting back to my statement with the detective, I spent time filling in how I came to be a client of the False Healer. This happened when my friend invited me to have lunch with her and her close acquaintance, the False Healer. She informed me that morning that the False Healer had a message for me and asked if I would be interested in meeting with him. The message had to do with a trip I was soon going to take to help with my mother's care and to provide respite for my brothers and sisters who had been helping out with around-the-clock care. The False Healer told me my brothers and sisters would turn on me and make me stay with my mother, and as a result I would suffer a mental breakdown. I write this now and cringe because I was always and still am very close to my family. This action marked the first step in the False Healer's attempt to separate me from those I love and those who love and support me. I asked the False Healer how I could remedy the situation, and he said he would tell me more, but I had to agree to meet with him at his place. I agreed and went later that day when I finished work.

It was at this initial meeting that the False Healer said that I would need medicine, which he would prepare, to cleanse and protect me for my trip home. This soon turned into a session in which I was told I was a bad person and that I had only lived my life for myself. He said my grandmother's spirit was with us, and she was disappointed with the way I looked (I had blond highlights and wore makeup). He told me I had to quit drinking any alcohol and make a promise to the Creator to commit to a year-long healing journey, which he would facilitate. With all that I had expressed earlier about fear, guilt, and shame, in that moment, I felt I had no other choice but to agree. Very soon after agreeing to the year-long healing commitment, the False Healer told me I would die if I didn't complete the journey. He said my husband was going to die if he didn't agree to join me or if he tried to prevent me from fulfilling my year-long commitment. He said he had dreams about my children that showed they were going to be kidnapped and would not survive. These are just a few of the things the False Healer used against me. But the main theme was cancer. I had it, I was getting it, and I would die from it. Over and over, the False Healer stated this throughout our sessions together.

Whenever I think about the False Healer today, it is mostly in the context of my work. The separation of emotion from the experience has allowed me to take a more expansive view of what occurred. I recognize that he had no superpowers. He got his information in three ways: first, from the personal information I willingly and blindly provided; second, from my close friend and confidant, with whom he had a close relationship; and third, from methods he gleaned from past experiences with other victims in terms of what worked best to lower our defenses and create uncertainty, fear, and dependence on his counsel. I do not feel unsafe or unprotected from the False Healer. I see him as a broken, weak, shell of a man who tried his best to yield power and control by utilizing spiritual tools in a manner offensive to the Creator.

However, when I was an initiate, for lack of a better word, the False Healer was all-powerful in my mind. When he told me I had to pay $900 or more for each "release session", I paid. When he told me I needed to pay and use medicine for myself and my family, I agreed. When he told me to convince my husband to join in the year-long healing journey, I did so. When he told me I had to participate in ceremonies that cost $650, I was honoured. When he told me I had to move, sell my house and build a new one based on his specifications, I did. When he told me not to tell anyone about our sessions, I didn't. When he told me things about other people, I believed him. When he told me I would get cancer if I didn't allow him to use medicine on me, I allowed him.

So you see, I was a victim first of his perceived knowledge and awareness, then I was a victim of his sexual desire. In the very first session with him, I made a promise to the Creator that I would complete the year-long healing journey. I did everything in my power to keep that promise until it became evident that I no longer could, because if I continued I would have been lost to God forever. A colleague once told me that I was one of the most focused people they knew when it came to completing work assignments; multiply that by 10, and that is the strength and focus with which I entered this year-long commitment until it became untenable. However, this was this same strength and focus that I put into healing myself and enduring the three-year judicial process. I truly don't think the False Healer knew that about me.

When I finished my statement, the detective asked a few clarifying questions on how the False Healer applied the medicine that was meant to protect or cure me of cancer. Unfortunately, these details cannot be disclosed in this book due to the limitations of the publicity ban. The detective also did a detailed sketch of the property where the sessions with the False Healer took place. We went over a timeline of events and how they compared to what I had written about the False Healer in *Heaven's Wait*. In all, the statement took about 90 minutes. I was exhausted by the experience. I asked the detective about the next steps and when the False Healer would be formally charged with my complaint. The detective said he wasn't exactly sure, but he would get back to me with all the details once he processed the statement. I walked him to the door and wished him luck with everything. Little did I know that it was only the beginning of a very long process that would test my will and determination to succeed!

2

THE WAY

> Into the eyes of the future
> We cannot see our unfolding
> But of the future
> Our mind's eye sees all
> Nay a warning comes
> As we cross
> The threshold
> Hold tight, will you fight

The possibility of writing a book did not come into my awareness until I received guidance in meditation to write about my life. Now, you may ask who gave me this guidance! It was my higher self. The higher self is also referred to as the higher mind, higher consciousness, Buddha, etc. The higher self knows everything about me in this lifetime and my prior lifetimes, and it is the keeper of my purpose. It is like somebody narrating a story to you that they have already read. The higher mind didn't ask of me anything I didn't already possess the skills to do.

When I wrote my first book, it seemed as if the skills and ability to inscribe my story emerged out of thin air. However, I must ask myself: Did they emerge out of thin air, or were they dormant until I was ready to use them? For example, could they have been embedded in my DNA at birth? Perhaps I was a writer in a previous incarnation, and this skill carried over through my DNA. Did I somehow tap into universal knowledge and when the time emerged to inscribe my story, I had access to this knowledge? Perhaps it was downloaded during sleep. Did the talent to write become cultivated over time, and as a voracious reader did I subliminally understand how to craft a story? I think it's all of the above. I think we are just discovering how our physical, emotional, mental and spiritual bodies align to intuit our higher consciousness.

That brings me to the story I was asked to write about. Was it preordained that I would meet the False Healer and did everything happen just as it was supposed to? Did the False Healer and I write a contract before our incarnation to help fulfill a portion of our respective missions in this lifetime? Was it just an unlucky choice on my part? Was it karmic? Again, all of this plays a role. However, in the end, it was the False Healer's choice to commit illegal acts against me, and that is his path. How I reacted to it and sought a personal and legal resolution is my own. My higher self in all its love and awareness would not have put me into the battle unless it was known that I had the skills to overcome and create new energy out of the old.

What did I learn from this entanglement with the False Healer? For me, it was a step across a threshold that would lead to my spiritual awakening. From what I can surmise at this time in my life, I was put on the False Healer's path for three reasons: 1) To tell the story and unmask the False Healer, 2) To help heal others who were victimized by the False Healer and others like him and, 3) To heal a split I had created in my energy. The False Healer mirrored to me what I already felt about myself. I had to learn how to live with all of who I am or else the shadow would cast a dark pall over the light that was trying to emerge. The split needed to be sealed in order for me to become whole. This is called Wholeness Medicine. A friend recently shared with me a phrase I am learning to embrace: "We master what we will teach. And we teach what we are mastering."

We often seek out opportunities or inspiration to help us understand our journey. One day, out of the blue, I happened upon information about a seminar that was scheduled for the upcoming weekend in Philadelphia, Pennsylvania, which is about an eight-hour drive from where I live. Without any hesitation, I bought a ticket for the two-day seminar. The presenters were well known to me, and I had attended a couple of other seminars they had hosted in Buffalo and Toronto. However, it was my first time doing a two-day seminar, as it was usually out of my price range, especially with the US/CAN exchange rate. I informed my husband that same evening that I was going to drive to Philadelphia the next day to attend the seminar. When I purchased the tickets, there was absolutely no question in my mind that I had to attend. The agenda didn't specify what the seminar was about, but I knew it was a teaching seminar.

The drive to Philadelphia was uneventful and very scenic in a lot of areas. The tolls roads were abundant, and I paid more than $20 in tolls each way. I guess there may have been ways around them, but it would have added time to my trip, and the GPS selected the toll routes. I noticed though that many of the toll routes were newly set up and had probably been established in the last couple of years. I arrived at my destination early in the evening and was exhausted from the drive. I had an appointment scheduled the morning of my departure, so my start time was delayed. When I arrived at the hotel, there were a lot of people milling about, with many talking about the upcoming seminar. I peeked into the conference room and recognized some familiar faces from previous events; they were in the middle of the setup for the event. I settled into my room and made it an early night. Registration opened at 9 am, and I wanted to get a good seat.

THE FALSE HEALER: A TRILOGY

I attend a lot of events on my own, so walking into the conference room alone was not a problem. I found a seat with a good view and waited for things to begin. As usual, the topic of the seminar was well presented. In this case, there was a focus on evolution, the Akash, and the Hero's Journey. Everything was very interesting and enlightening, but I wasn't sure if I had gotten what I needed at that time. I was searching out a new beginning and inspiration to achieve it. I knew there was something I was missing, but what?

I bought a beautiful ring from a vendor at a break in the morning session. She was one of only a few vendors that are invited to sell items at the events. The ring caught my eye immediately. It is very rare that I will purchase jewelry. However, this particular ring was different. I put the ring on, and I could not get it off. I asked the vendor if she would allow me to wear the ring while I retrieved my handbag from my room. When I paid for the ring and sat again at my chair, the ring came off easily. It had the colours of the waters of the Caribbean and the sky infused as one.

The next day, I left the session during a lunch break to start my journey home. I had learned some new techniques for expanding my awareness, which was great, but I felt a little deflated. A couple months later as my knowledge was growing in leaps and bounds, I was drawn to a video on YouTube. After listening to the video, I reached out to the woman who had channelled the Divine message. We spoke for over 90 minutes. It felt so liberating speaking with her about her work and our paths to where we were. It was like we buzzed with the same energy. I could use language that I hesitate to use in everyday conversation and talk about my spiritual truths without feeling that they might be misunderstood. A part of the work she does includes Soul Readings. Although she didn't feel that I needed one, it was my intent to have one done.

I won't go into much about the reading, but the reason I am discussing it here is that the Soul Reading indicated the following: "The final bend, or 3rd phase of the Hero's Core Journey, always involves a kind of sharing of the wisdom derived from walking that journey. It is the Hero's Return. Where they bring the gifts and the gems of all of that hardship, all of those initiations, all of those struggles, searches, trails and tears…back to the people in their community, back to their families, and back to the world, to share the riches of this journey with others."

This was incredible. The primary focus of the seminar I attended in Philadelphia was the Hero's Journey. I did not mention this to her in our conversation. In addition, she informed me that my primary soul colour is cobalt/royal blue and aqua blue, just like the colours in the ring I had bought.

At the seminar in Philadelphia, they talked about the Hero's Journey, citing a book by Joseph Campbell, *The Hero with a Thousand Faces* (1949). Campbell says that every single one of us has the Hero's Journey inside of us. Using mythology, he helps define the human experience. In his book, Campbell itemizes and labels sections of the journey we all undertake. The following is an abbreviated list that over time has come to represent the Hero's Journey:

1) Call to Adventure (there has to be a reason for the journey)
2) Supernatural Aid
3) Threshold (the threshold across to the unknown)
4) Gather Helpers (you don't do this alone)
5) Challenges and Temptations
6) Revelation (that which is going to change your life)
7) Transformation (you come through challenge and you are transformed)
8) Atonement (looking backward to who you used to be)
9) The Return

It is through this journey that I will relay my story, for it is within the storytelling that the wisdom of the journey is revealed. I'm not going to say it was all seen as wisdom, as I was in the midst of its mud-soaked entanglements, but when I cleaned myself off there lay the hidden gem of all my foibles – Ascension.

There are many definitions of Ascension. Google defines "Ascension" as "The ascent of Christ into heaven on the fortieth day after the Resurrection." However, spiritual ascension is defined more broadly; for example, Learning Mind, *7 Ascension Symptoms that Show You Are Awakening* (www.learning-mind.com) defines Ascension as follows: "Ascension is the process of spiritual awakening that moves you into a high level of consciousness."

For me, I have pieced together my own understanding of Ascension from various videos, blogs and books. They all appear to provide the same key elements. Ascension is a call from our soul to higher spiritual learning. In this learning, there are periods that require us to study, grow, and expand our awareness; then there are periods in which we must rest and take time to assimilate what we have learned. Rest helps us integrate what we have learned and clear out anything that no longer fits into our new energy or awareness (it's like we climb one mountain, then rest in the valley before we climb another). These never-ending cycles help us gain knowledge and wisdom so we can graduate and move on to the next level of spiritual awareness.

I answered the soul's call.

3

GOD SPEED

In the thunderous roar
A dove speaks
Quiet little one
There is peace
No more will you rage
In the quietness of your cage

For the purpose of this story, I'm going to use the trial and its ensuing madness to highlight the Hero's Journey. It is not *Lord of the Rings* or King Arthur, but it easily connects with the labels used by Joseph Campbell in *The Hero with a Thousand Faces*. Yes, I could have used only the incidents with the False Healer, but that story has already been told. It is refreshing to share another side of the story, one that involves real-life heroes. This is my Hero's Journey.

So, as you can surmise, my "Call to Adventure" was the day I agreed to speak to the detective about my book and then disclosed to him that the False Healer had inappropriately touched me. The

"Supernatural Aid" in this case was the intuitive prompting to participate and file criminal charges against the False Healer. The "Threshold" is when I agreed to file criminal charges and proceed with the statement, thus casting me from what was "known" into the "unknown" of not only the judicial system, but also as a victim of sexual assault. The decision to participate was one I made with complete honour and understanding of its true Divine origin. I did not have to be coaxed into the decision by fear, manipulation, or threats to my life. I felt the decision, just as one would feel love, happiness, or joy. The deal was sealed, and I was prepared to walk the path.

Now, the term "Supernatural Aid" will be sprinkled throughout this story. This refers to the intuitive insights I received in the form of direct guidance from spirit. What is spirit? Spirit is the Divine Intelligence that inhabits all things. Your higher self or soul is the direct conduit for spirit. When I was with the False Healer for nine months, I received many messages in dreams that warned me of his deception, but I was not yet able to interpret my dreams. Dream interpretation was left to the False Healer. I relied on him to for guidance through these dreams, but he always put the focus on other men, saying certain men would get to me by using bad medicine. What he meant by this was that they (the men) could put bad medicine on me, or even on my coat, to get me to fall in love with them or for them to use me sexually. He said it had been used on him before, and he was trying to protect me.

About a year before I filed criminal charges and was "called to adventure", I had a supernatural experience. My husband was away on a business trip, and I had just gone to bed. I closed my eyes to say my prayers, and no sooner than I had closed them I felt like I was being pulled out of my body. There was a loud sound like that of a waterfall all around me. I felt like I was flying and falling all at the same time. I was very frightened as I flailed my arms and legs trying to steady myself. I was aware of what was happening, but I couldn't stop it. I honestly thought I was possessed, so I started to pray. I fought hard to get out of it, and then as quickly as it started it just stopped. I lay in bed frozen with fear. I instantly realized I had had an out-of-body experience. I later recounted the story to my husband and told him I wished I had not fought so hard because I was curious about it now, though it truly did frighten me at the time. He advised me to just "go with it" when it happened next. Of course it did happen again. I first heard that swooshing sound, and I thought to myself, *This is it!* However, again I was frightened. I fought against it and flailed again, but this time I was able to steady my flight. I was still scared, but I went with it. I was taken to a courtroom and suspended over the witness box. I could see three or four women crammed into the box as I was lowered into it. I could hear talking, and I was waiting my turn. Then, as quickly as I was taken to this scenario, I was whisked back and was again fully aware of my body. Little did I know at this time that I would move forward a year later with criminal charges against the False Healer and actually testify from the witness box. Today, when I feel an out-of-body experience about to occur, I still flail when it initially occurs, but I'm not as frightened. Uncertain, yes, but not frightened.

Six weeks went by before the False Healer was officially charged and arrested for my complaint. There was a change in Crown prosecutors within that time and a pressing police investigation that was time sensitive. The detective kept me up to date on any new developments. When I got the call saying that the False Healer was in custody, I breathed a deep sigh of relief. In a way it felt like it was over, but in reality it was just the beginning. The False Healer was arrested on a Friday. I was told he would likely stay in custody throughout the weekend, but he was arraigned that Saturday and released on bail the same day. Fortunately, this didn't come as a surprise. I was advised by the detective that he could make bail, though I didn't think it would be so fast. There was a part of me that wanted him to stay in custody. I knew he was guilty. I knew exactly what he had done to me. However, that is not how the justice system works; it was my word against his, and he entered a plea of not guilty.

The hardest and most challenging aspect of this experience was allowing the justice system to run its course and being patient and kind to all those who play a role in its delivery. Whenever it became too overwhelming, I reached out to those closest to me who helped me refocus on the greater good of what I was doing. A part of me also knew that at any time I could withdraw the charges against the False Healer. When these thoughts came, I would light up inside and feel like a warrior ready for battle. There was a constant inner struggle to stay on the path. There were so many times when I wanted to turn back because I would get caught up in the unknown. This too is part of the Hero's Journey. In *The Hero with a Thousand Faces,* Joseph Campbell identified this as the "Threshold" of the "Known and Unknown" where the rules and limits are unknown. Campbell writes, "…Beyond them is darkness, the unknown and danger; just as beyond the parental watch is danger to the infant…" Also in the unknown are aspects of yourself that you must reconcile. These can often manifest themselves in dreams. Upon stepping over the threshold, the "hero must survive a succession of trials" notes Campbell. It is a "purification of the self," or, in simple terms, overcoming our past. Further, Campbell explains that in our dreams, "…we may see reflected not only the whole picture of our present case, but also the clue to what we must do to be saved."

One particular dream I like to recount happened when I was still under the influence of the False Healer. I shared it in Heaven's Wait, but I'll quickly describe it again because it has significance to the Unknown element. It happened around the third month with the False Healer. I dreamt I was at my mother's house and I was afraid to go upstairs. I kept repeating that I didn't want to go, but a force pushed me up the stairs. I was not walking but more like gliding. At the top of the stairs, I stood still and would not proceed down the hallway to the two back bedrooms. But again, I was forced to move forward as I glided down the hallway. I closed my eyes. I knew I was in the spot between the two bedrooms when the voice said to open the door. I was shaking, but I reached out my arm while keeping my eyes closed and opened the door. A voice said to open my eyes. I was hesitant and frightened, but I eventually did as I was asked. There, standing in the room, was a little boy that looked like a monk. He showed me my father, who was cradling someone with an illness. He was comforting this person – "This is compassion," he said. Then, he moved over into the other bedroom. There were babies under the cover – babies who had recently passed but needed to be cared for and loved. This represented a doorway – a doorway to Heaven. In my youth, these two rooms represented the fear of ghosts or supernatural events. It seemed that whenever anything supernatural happened in our house it originated in these two rooms. Though I later slept in these rooms as an adult, I always had a sense of unease about them until after this dream. It was as though I was forced to face my fear, not only of ghosts but of evil. A psychoanalyst might say it was the evil I harboured inside of me about my past wrongdoings. I didn't want to look at them. In being forced to examine my shadow or "evil" side, I had to show myself compassion. I was being shown how to save myself.

In this phase of the "Unknown" or the "Road of Trials", Joseph Campbell explains that for the hero…"it may be that he here discovers for the first time that there is a benign power everywhere supporting him in his superhuman passage". To me, "Benign Power" could refer to spirit, guides, angels, spiritual helpers, entourages, etc. You can use whatever term resonates most with your heart. In my earlier journey with the False Healer, I came to the conclusion that I had spiritual helpers, and without these helpers I would not have made it through the experience or the healing that took place afterward. I went into this Hero's Journey fully aware that I had spiritual helpers. I just had to listen.

There had been a recent sexual assault trial in Toronto that had been highly publicized in which the defense counsel had eviscerated the alleged victims during their testimony, and the defendant was found not guilty. Though many in that case believed the victims were telling the truth about the sexual assault, their actions following the alleged offenses were determined by the judge to be suspect and not in keeping with a person that had been assaulted. This played in my head, and I was nervous at the thought of going to trial and having my story dissected.

The path to trial was a slow process. I was first contacted by Victim Witness Assistance. They serve as a go-between with the Crown prosecutor's office to help keep victims and witnesses abreast of charges and court proceedings until the court case is over. This service is not available for all offenses, and it is mainly used in sensitive cases such as those that involve sexual assault, child physical and sexual assault, domestic violence, human trafficking, and more. The initial contact was via telephone. The first purpose was to introduce me to my case worker, determine a contact schedule and schedule counselling services if any were needed. I didn't feel that I needed any counselling services, as my healing journey had been well underway for a number of years prior to filing official charges. The other purpose was to determine the level of contact. I could choose to be contacted every time the False Healer and his defense council made an appearance in court, met with a judge, or filed any type of motion. I could also choose to be contacted only when it was necessary for me to know information or appear in court. I chose the latter. I didn't want to be bombarded with information about the False Healer's every move. I'm happy I chose this route because the False Healer's defense counsel filed many motions throughout the duration of the judicial process. Surely I would have been angered with this ploy.

It was always my hope that the False Healer would accept a plea deal, but that didn't happen. After the charges were filed, my contact with the detective was limited. If I had any questions about the judicial proceedings, I would contact Victim Witness Services.

About six months after the charges were filed, I received information on the status of my case. I was informed by Victim Witness Services that the False Healer was going to plead guilty and accept responsibility for the offences in my case. I was given the option of providing a victim impact statement and reading it in court the next month. I was overjoyed! I excitedly called my husband and gave him the good news. I was so thankful that I wouldn't need to go to trial. However, something nagged at me...what about the others?

I called my case worker at Victim Witness and asked her about the other victims. She didn't understand my question. She could only talk with me about my case. I hung up the phone and called the detective. He had no idea what I was talking about. He hadn't heard anything about the False Healer's decision to plead guilty in my case or the others. He said he would look into things and get back to me. I felt a little worried; what if it was a mistake?

The detective called me back in a couple of days. Unfortunately, my case was mistakenly sent to another district and was not linked with the other victims' case files in a nearby district. The detective told me that he had to get my case file moved to the district where the others were filed. With the case files all together, the False Healer could not plead guilty to just one; it was all or nothing. I was disappointed, but I couldn't think just about myself. That was not the reason I had entered into this journey. My actions had to be altruistic, and I had to show a selfless concern for others.

There are virtues we must abide by in spiritual life. These virtues include **Altruism, Right Action, Clarity, Humility, Love, Happiness for Others, and Temperance**. As we walk our spiritual path, we are given opportunities to embody these virtues of the soul. They are reflections of God and aide in our ascension. I demonstrated **Clarity** when the intuitive guidance to participate came through, and I recognized it as higher prompting. Then, based on this intuitive prompting, I took **Right Action**. The Right Action was the act of calling the detective and agreeing to move forward with criminal charges against the False Healer. Now, there have been times over the past few years when I have received intuitive messages and taken action immediately, but not all intuitive promptings are meant to be executed right away. Divine timing requires patience, and sometimes we're impatient with moving forward. I had to learn to recognize the difference between when intuitive promptings were just seeds that spirit was planting for future use and when immediate action was required. By further developing my intuition, I came to understand the subtlety in the difference. I am still learning today.

It was another few months before I heard about the case again. I learned that the False Healer's legal counsel had put forward legal motions in that period, though I didn't know their exact purpose. However, I was aware that the False Healer wanted to separate my case from the others and perhaps even plead guilty to my case alone. I was informed that they had met with the Judge and Crown Prosecutor to discuss the matter. In the end, the cases were kept together. It was now coming up to a year from when I had first initiated criminal proceedings against the False Healer. In all that time, it was the Crown Prosecutor's hope that the False Healer would accept a plea deal; it was the hope of all of us that he would accept a plea deal. But that was not to be.

Fourteen months after I filed charges, I received notice from the detective that the False Healer had requested a preliminary hearing. It was scheduled for the following month. This hurt. A week later, I received a phone call from my case worker at Victim Witness, who informed me that the Crown Prosecutor had requested a meeting with me to discuss the preliminary hearing. The case worker would attend the meeting with the prosecutor as well. The detective dropped by my home to serve me with a summons to appear at the preliminary hearing. We talked briefly, and he said he would be there to support me. However, I couldn't help but feel like I was the criminal. It was all so formal.

I had no idea what to expect, so I researched as much as I could about preliminary hearings. The definition provided on Google says, "A Preliminary Hearing is an initial inquiry that occurs at the demand of an accused wherein a judge screens the proposed criminal charge against the available evidence. A preliminary inquiry is often used by the Crown to test or challenge the Crown's case."

Basically, the Crown wants to determine if their evidence/witnesses can stand up to the scrutiny and legal challenge of a trial. Did our stories match our statement? And could we adequately defend our statements while in the formal setting of a courtroom?

We as victims would be tested yet again.

It was a beautiful sunny day when I finally got to meet another of my "Gather Helpers" as described by Joseph Campbell in *The Hero with a Thousand Faces*. The first Gather Helpers were my husband, sister, and friend. They kept me balanced and in the game. The second was the detective. The third were the fabulous staff at Victim Witness and the Crown prosecutor. Many of my Gather Helpers humbly stated they were just doing their job, but there are those who do their job and others who do their jobs with compassion and grace. Fortunately, I encountered the latter.

The Crown prosecutor's office was located in one of the area's courthouses. I had to go through security similar to that at an airport to enter the building. The case worker from Victim Witness was waiting for me inside. It was my first time meeting her in person. The Crown prosecutor's office was located on the second floor. We went in together, and I was warmly greeted by the prosecutor responsible for my case. I had been informed earlier by Victim Witness that the meeting was to help prepare me for the preliminary hearing and to tour the courtroom where the hearing would take place. At this point, the prosecutor knew me only by the statement I had filed more than a year ago. He didn't know anything about me personally or if my story had what it takes to withstand the scrutiny of a trial.

As I was trying to get a read on him, he was trying to get a read on me. He began by explaining the purpose of the preliminary hearing and the activity to date on the case (they were holding out hope for a plea deal, but at this point it was not on the table). He asked me questions about the circumstances surrounding my case and in particular about my statement. I felt at ease answering his questions and asked a few in return, mostly to clarify the research I had done on preliminary hearings. I asked him what the defense counsel could bring up in questioning, in particular about my background. He said that if you are shining a spotlight on the accused, you too must be able to withstand the spotlight. I had to admit that this was fair; after all, in the eyes of the law, the False Healer is innocent until proven guilty. Though I knew he was guilty.

The prosecutor let me know that he believed I would be a good witness. He walked through the proceedings for the preliminary hearing and then we went to view the courtroom. He showed me where I would sit and where everyone else would be seated. He informed me that I could ask for a break during questioning if I needed it, and if I didn't understand a question, I could ask for it to be repeated or clarified. The courtroom was smaller than I had imagined. Perhaps I had watched too many crime dramas on TV where the courtrooms look more expansive and intimidating. He explained that when it was time for my case to be heard, I would be summoned to the assigned courtroom via the courthouse speaker system. The courtroom assignment would be made available to me upon my arrival on the day of the preliminary hearing. I asked about media members and would they be allowed in the courtroom? He said they were allowed to attend, but there was a publication ban on the case, so any information such as my name or the details of the case could not be reported. The meeting lasted just over an hour. The prosecutor informed me that Victim Witness would schedule a date to review my statement prior to the preliminary hearing. Then, the meeting ended.

I was emotionally drained from the experience. I had a lot to think about and wrap my mind around. It is said that walking the unknown takes courage, but when you're in the midst of it, it doesn't feel like courage at all – it feels like gut-wrenching confusion. My only thought was that I had to get through to the next step in one piece and not make a mess of everything.

4

IN THE QUIET LULL

In the light of my light
There is only heaven
We search for you in vain
Why are the heavens
Choked at the gate
Suffering, it makes us wait

*J*oseph Campbell in *The Hero with a Thousand Faces* describes the fifth element or label as "Challenges and Temptations." I believe the nine sections Campbell describes can overlap. For the purpose of this book, I am following them in somewhat of an orderly fashion as presented by Campbell in his book. Two significant events happened to me before the preliminary hearing. First, I was diagnosed with cancer a few months after filing criminal charges against the False Healer. Second, my beautiful, funny and much beloved nephew died suddenly.

In the book *The Impersonal Life* written by Joseph Benner and published in 1914, Benner stated that he believed the words contained in his book were directly from God. He believed it to be of the same Divine inspiration as the words spoken by Moses and Jesus. It is truly a profound read. An excerpt from the book in the chapter titled Finding Me says, "…You must be capable of withstanding every attack from without before you can fully manifest all My Divine Powers pushing forth from within…Know that I AM manifesting these powers in you as fast as you can bear it and be strong…The mistake you make is in trying to grow yourself…I AM the Tree of Life within you, My life will and must push forth, but it will do it by gradual and steady growth. You cannot come into your fruitage before you have grown in it."

A free PDF version can be found online at StillnessSpeaks.com.

In *The Hero with a Thousand Faces*, Joseph Campbell writes of the Navaho myth of the Twin War Gods, who go out in search of their father, the Sun god. This myth depicts all the elements of the Hero's Journey. It describes their journey along the holy trail; their meeting with the Spider Woman, who provides them with a charm in the form of a feather to help them pass four places of danger; arriving at the house of the sun, where they are greeted by a woman; and meeting the bearer of the Sun, who puts the twin warriors to certain tests to disprove that they are his sons. In these tests, they are "flung at sharp spikes on a wall in the east," "turquoise spikes in the south," "haliotis in the west," and "black rock in the north". During these tests, the boys hold on to their feathers and survive, and then the father tries to steam them to death in a sweat lodge, but they are "aided by the wind". Then, the father gives them a "smoking pipe filled with poison," but "a spiny caterpillar warned the boys and gave them something to put in their mouths." Finally, the Twin Gods win the confidence of their father, the Sun. Campbell writes that, "The twin Heroes are tested against the symbols of the four directions, to discover whether they partake of the faults and limitations of any one of the quarters."

Further, he explains, there is "the need for great care on the part of the father, admitting to his house only those who have been thoroughly tested."

When I was diagnosed with cancer, it didn't come as a shock. As you may recall, I wrote earlier that my brother told me in a dream that I would get cancer in seven years. This was before I had even met the False Healer or my friend and confidant, whom he also had a close relationship with. I am 100 percent certain that the False Healer was informed of this dream and my family's cancer history by this mutual acquaintance. When I received the cancer diagnosis, I didn't cry or get angry, as it was something that I already knew would happen. An abnormality was detected in my regularly scheduled pap tests, and further testing indicated a tumor in my uterus. I only asked what next steps were required. The doctor said I would be referred to a gynecologic oncologist for further examination and treatment; however, the prognosis was good. It was anticipated that the tumor would be removed and no further treatment would be required. I went alone to the appointment, so when I got back to my car I called my husband. "It's cancer" I told him. He was shocked, but I wasn't. I had even warned him before I left for my appointment, but I know he didn't want to think it could be cancer.

For the previous six years, I had been eliminating many things from my diet. It felt very natural, though it wasn't done all at once. First it was alcohol, then meat, caffeine, sugary treats, chicken/fish, and dairy. It was like my body was preparing me for the diagnosis and protecting me until the cancer was discovered. To this day, my food choices are selective, though I may occasionally indulge in a sugary treat, especially a slice of lemon meringue pie or blueberry cake, both of which remind me of my mother.

The oncologist who performed my surgery said I was an ideal candidate for the type of surgery I would undergo, a laparoscopic hysterectomy. I was in good shape and didn't have any other medical issues. I was prepped for surgery on a cold February morning. My husband helped entertain me while I waited to go into surgery. It was early in the morning, and I was one of the first on the surgical schedule. It was a cancer hospital, so there were at least 10 other patients waiting for surgery. When my name was called, I felt a flash of terror in my gut. I had been calm up to that point, but the realization then set in that I was about to undergo a serious surgical procedure. My husband helped me relax and walked with me as far as he could. It was cold in the operating room, and I tried not to shake, but at this point I was cold and fighting against the growing anxiety I was feeling. I remember counting backwards then someone calling my name. I opened my eyes to the nurse asking me questions. "Is it over?" I asked. "Yes," the nurse replied. "It all went well." It was 11 am. I spent the day recovering and was on my way home by 4 pm. I even dressed myself to go home, though my husband helped with my shoes. The full recovery period was six weeks. I was able to do most things on my own after the first week.

The only other matter we had to wait on was the pathology report. At my six-week follow-up, I received the good news. The pathology report indicated that the cancer had not spread beyond the uterine wall. It had grown 50% into the uterine wall but hadn't spread to other areas. No further treatment was required. I would have checkups with the oncologist every six months for the next three years. I feel in my heart that had I continued with my normal diet the tumour may have been more aggressive.

Throughout the time I was diagnosed, had surgery, and received post-surgical care, I never once thought I would die. I knew from the beginning that I would be well. I continued meditating, researching, and expanding my spiritual awareness. My calm helped keep my husband calm…and his calm helped keep me calm. Our boys were not told of the cancer diagnosis until after I received the pathology report. It made no sense to me to stress them unnecessarily. They were relieved that all was okay. However, I did have a bit of a setback a couple of weeks later, when I required emergency surgery to repair some stitches. I required another six to eight weeks of rest to heal from the second surgery.

It was after all the medical issues had been resolved and I was truly on the mend that I received the previously mentioned call from Victim Witness telling me that the False Healer was going to plead guilty to my criminal accusations. It felt like a blessing after all the months of recovery. But you already know the story – my case file was accidently separated from the other complainants, and the False Healer was no longer able to plead out for just one case; it was all or none.

From my vantage point, I am now so happy that the earlier guilty plea didn't happen because without the trial experience I would not be the "whole" person I am today.

However, I cannot say the same for the tragic death of my beloved nephew. It was indeed a spear to the heart. He died just a couple months before the preliminary hearing at the young age of 32. The loss was devastating to his young family and our family as a whole. I will only share one thing about that day because I know this story belongs to his sister, who one day will write her own Hero's Journey. As I woke from a dream on the day we learned of his death, I was unsettled. In my dream, I was looking at some items on a glass display case in a shop. I picked up a stone and asked the lady what the stone meant. She gently rubbed the stone down my face, and in a soft voice said it meant someone had died. I went over to another display case, and I started playing a game. It was like a mini swordfight, but I noticed that we were swordfighting crabs. My nephew was a fisherman, and he fished snow crab in particular. He was soon to go out fishing when suddenly he stepped up into his spirit journey. We love you gwi's. (In our language this means "son", "boy", or "little brother".)

There were other challenges that presented themselves as well, but they are not my story to tell, as they were not directed at me, though I was impacted nonetheless. I guess one could use the phrase "collateral damage" in regard to them. In these times, I was tempted to lash out on behalf of my loved one involved, but that would not have solved anything. Fortunately, I had dreams in which I received a heads-up on the trouble ahead, but the hurt still stung. The temptation or animalistic urge to protect my loved one by causing hurt in return was strong. I knew there were things I could say that would cause considerable pain, but I fought to restrain myself. I had to come to terms with the fact that I didn't need to fight anyone else's battle. That was their path and karmic entanglement. I could offer advice, which I did, but I didn't put myself in the middle of the situation. I came to understand that people reveal their long-held and repressed wounds in different ways. I will not judge the circumstances that God puts anyone in. I am here only to offer a helping hand in love and compassion when called upon.

Throughout that year, I didn't do much work in the area of spiritual development. I tried at one point to host a workshop, but I cancelled it almost as soon as I posted the information on my website. I decided to close down my website as well as most of my social media sites. I didn't feel that I was in the right headspace to teach or facilitate. A friend called to ask if I was still consulting. It was just what I needed, a new research project. It helped that I started the project before the preliminary hearing because it took my mind off what lay ahead.

There were a few days when the temptation to pull out of the criminal proceedings was strong. I actually called Victim Witness to inform my case worker that I was going to drop the charges against the False Healer. Fortunately for the case, my case worker was away from the office that week. By the time my call was returned, a meeting with the Crown prosecutor's office was scheduled. I decided I would move forward as planned. It's funny how things work out.

As mentioned at the start of this chapter, "Challenges and Temptation" are all part of the Hero's Journey. In the face of these obstacles, we have the free will to do whatever we choose. Do we choose what is good for ourselves, our family, or humanity? I believe it's a little bit of everything. Maintaining a place of love within yourself helps when all else feels disjointed. Making wise choices comes with experience. I came across a quote that I believe sums it up nicely, "You can't make the same mistake twice. The second time you make it, it's no longer a mistake, it's a choice."

Love is one of the hardest Soul Virtues to attain and maintain, but it is the foundation for all the others. Why would I say it's the hardest? Because we start from a point of believing we know what love is. After all, we love our parents, family, children, pets, spouse, friend, and even pizza if that's your comfort food of choice. We say it casually to each other, on social media posts, and watch portrayals of it constantly in movies. We are bombarded with all things love on multiple platforms meant to capture our interest and dollar. So yes, we know what love is…or do we?

Do you love yourself? Maybe you've never had to answer this question before and you may even laugh it off. But until you're asked to love yourself, your sojourn into understanding what love really means cannot begin. Love means loving yourself in spite of everything you have been through, experienced, done to others, said to others, the perceived flaws you 'hate' about yourself, your actions/inaction, or the internal words that you tell yourself. Saying you love yourself on a superficial level is like saying to a brand-new car, "I'd like to love you, but you're the wrong colour." If you ever say to yourself, "I love everything about myself except my nose, my skin, my weight, my height, my hair, etc.," isn't that like treating yourself like a car – I'd like to love you, BUT!!!

In that moment of "saying yes, but" you have just given permission to others to treat you like a car. If we can't even love ourselves completely without "fixing" some perceived flaw about ourselves, then how can we expect others to respond in kind? I'm not saying that we can never do things that boost our self-confidence, but if taking that action brings only external gratification, then improving or boosting anything about ourselves will never be enough if love is not present.

Unfortunately, from the beginning of relationships, there are conditions, including the relationship we have with ourselves. Think about the conditions you put on yourself, a loved one, a spouse, a parent or a child. For myself, I know there were many times when I didn't share things with people because I was afraid they wouldn't love me if they knew my truth. In turn, I know people didn't tell me things because they feared I would not love them if they expressed their true feelings. When this happened, I would express astonishment that they had thought I wouldn't love them for one reason or another. But that fear still sits with us because of perceived conditions on love we have all learned. Take some time to think about times when your perceived conditions of love stopped you from being or doing what touched your heart. Be honest with yourself, but don't beat yourself up. Recognize that it is learned behaviour and can be unlearned.

It is not easy to extract yourself from this way of expressing love. But acknowledging your choice to learn about love is a first step. The way I walked my way through this was by expanding my knowledge. If I didn't understand how to love myself, then I would learn. I mentioned in *Heaven's Wait* that I was able to forgive everybody else for what they did to me, but I couldn't forgive myself for allowing it to happen. I was especially hard on myself for what I did to others, and it took a long time to forgive myself for my actions. But for me, my journey to love began with forgiveness. Once I was able to clear the slate on the big things, I started on the little things: the resentment I carried, the perceived conditions I felt others had put on me, the love/hate relationship I had with my own body, and my feelings of being stuck and placing blame on others or the universe. There were many steps on this journey to forgiveness, but it was needed to open the door to love.

The reason I had a hard time understanding love is because I didn't know that love is energy. As energy, we can attract and repel love, and that includes love for ourselves. We probably are all familiar with the warning on an airplane to put on your own oxygen mask before helping others; well, this is the same concept. Before you go and tell someone else that they don't understand love or know how to love, look in the mirror. You have shown them how to love you.

This is energy in its purest form; it will find the path of least resistance. This is one of the Universal Laws: What you put out, so shall you receive. I recommend familiarizing yourself with the Universal Laws if you haven't already. I'm not saying we deserve what we get, but if we don't like what we get, then we should do something about it. Reach out to someone who might help bring a new perspective to your situation. This is often necessary to step out of your friend/family circle because you want a higher perspective, not reassurance. What's the difference? The difference is that reassurance tells you that you're right, and it's not your fault, whereas a higher perspective shows you different ways of looking at the situation while taking everyone and everything into consideration, even if this means it's not what you want to hear.

So, if love is energy, then how do we sustain it? Quite simply, through practice. This practice can be done by means of meditation, prayer, affirmations, studying, or anything else that clears the way for the flow of energy. Then, in these moments of clarity, you can ask love to fill the space you have cleared. In the beginning, it might be just a few moments of intense energy, but in time you can sustain it for longer periods. I shared some of these exercises in *Out From Beneath Your Wings*. I'm not saying your goal is to walk around in a constant state of bliss, because that would be nearly impossible and unproductive. You are here to align with your greater purpose of ascension and help others along the way in whatever way your unique soul intends.

Even with daily practice, I sometimes slip up. I might quickly judge someone or feel a pang of jealousy or envy. In these times, I sometimes don't want to acknowledge or accept these feelings because I know it means I need to do more work on myself and the emotions were mirrored to me for a reason. We must always be willing to get at the root of our emotions. I attended a talk not long ago at which the speaker talked a little about this. He compared our emotions to a tree. We can cut off a branch and we may feel better for a while, but the branch had deep roots, and that is where we must travel to find any real and lasting solutions.

It has to start with love, because the love you bring into your physical being through practice will flow out to those who surround you. I learned that we have what's called a Merkabah. Leo Carroll, who channels Kryon, explains that <u>our DNA creates a field</u> called the Merkabah (Live Kryon Channelling, "The Energy of the Future", New Port, California, Dec 7, 2014). The Merkabah is a circular energy field of up to eight metres that surrounds us at all times.

When you are within another's Merkabah or energy field, you may be able to feel their energy; it may feel good or not so good. The degree to which you feel energy may depend on how clear your own energetic field is. If your energy is muddied, you may not feel anything different. When I learned about the Merkabah, it made sense to me. Over the past few years, I have started having a hard time at the movies. I would change seats three or four times because something didn't feel right; it was like I was sensing too much, and it was annoying. I now attend movies at times when I know it won't be packed, and I sit in a location where it is unlikely that others will sit near me. I think I may have frustrated my friend because I attend a lot of movies by myself now.

So think about it. When you are sitting on the couch watching a movie with your family, depending on how many of you there are, the Merkabahs are all overlapping. That is why when one is not in the mood to participate, it brings down the whole group. It's the same with anything you undertake. That person in the cubicle next to you at work is in your Merkabah, and yours is in theirs. For the whole day, you are overlapping and picking up each other's energy. It's no wonder we are so tired when we leave work. What can you do about it? Strengthen your own Merkabah or make different choices. As you begin to flow more freely with the energy of love, then the person in the cubicle next to yours may also be inspired to transform. So, as with every change, it begins with you. Love that you love!

In time, you will begin to understand that you live in two different, yet synchronized, worlds: one where you must remain grounded and do the work that is needed for humanity to ascend and another where you explore your higher consciousness and begin to understand the "Way of the Soul."

5

THE GRACE

You are our voice
Let us be heard
So many are not hearing
The calls
Ring
Will you, answer
The call that love brings
For joy will be yours
Exquisitely

I looked in the mirror and asked, "Are you ready?" It was the morning of the preliminary hearing, and I had to be at the Victim Witness office at 9 am to review my statement. The detective was going to meet me at the courthouse at 10:45 am. I had spent a couple of days preparing myself through meditation and pre-trial research. I wanted to ensure that I understood what was expected of me at the preliminary hearing. I also wanted to review the do's and don'ts of giving testimony and how to dress for a court appearance. Most of the information was directed at defendants, but I adjusted it for my purpose.

Some things in the do's and don'ts were obvious, like be calm and avoid answering questions in a hostile manner, stand-up and sit-up straight, speak frankly/naturally, speak loud enough to be heard, and be confident. While other things, like trying to avoid language that can be misinterpreted or unclear and can lead to misunderstandings was worrisome to me. I wanted to speak naturally in my testimony, but I worried about overediting what I would say. I didn't want to give the defense counsel anything that could be used against me or volunteer more information than was required. In addition, listening carefully to the question was also a worry. The prosecutor said that two or three questions were often rolled into one long question. If this happened, I was to ask him or the defense counsel to repeat it or break it down for me.

I'm somewhat willful and stubborn, so I knew that when asked simple questions I should just provide a one-word answer: yes or no. Not every question had to be challenged, and this could actually annoy the judge. If it was relevant, I could even answer with "I don't know." I knew I had a right to stand up for myself. However, sometimes when I feel disrespected or challenged on the veracity of my answer I can really push back. It was going to be an interesting day. As for my clothing, it was to be conservative. This was easy for me because I felt comfortable in business attire. The clothes shouldn't have been overly trendy or with a lot of big jewelry.

Nervousness started to creep in by the time I arrived at the Victim Witness office to review my statement. It would be the first and only time I would review my statement before my testimony. I was placed in an office where a computer was set up to play my audio statement. My case worker left me alone to work the laptop. She was scheduled to be at the courthouse for another client who was testifying earlier in the day. I cringed at the sound of my own voice. It had been more than a year since I had given the statement. I listened intently as I wove through the story. I realized there were a few little things I left out, though I think that is relatively common. My statement was the first time I had ever talked in detail about the sexual assault, so having it on record was unsettling. I wondered how many people had listened to it. My statement was close to 90 minutes. It was a lot to absorb in the time I was allotted. Time seemed to pass quickly. The detective texted to ask me when I would be at the courthouse! I quickly wrapped things up and hurried over to meet him. He was waiting outside for me. We went through security together, and he prepared me to see the False Healer; it would be the first time in many years.

I walked beside the detective as we made our way to the waiting area outside the courtrooms on the second floor. I was initially scheduled to take the stand at 11 am; however, there was a delay. I caught a glimpse of the False Healer as I walked off the elevators. He looked the same but older and had put on even more weight. He was dressed in the same clothes he always wore, nothing special for his court appearance. He was not alone. He had his supporters with him.

I chose on that day to attend the preliminary hearing on my own. My sister said she could fly out to attend with me, and my friend was willing to take a day off work, but I reassured them that I would be fine. I had already discussed with my husband that it was better that he not attend. I wasn't completely alone, as I had my case worker and the detective to support me.

I would never meet the other victims involved in the case. We were kept apart from each other throughout the whole judicial process.

The delay turned into hours. There were other non-related court cases like bail hearings being heard in the same courtroom. People were in and out of the courtroom throughout the day. I thought the courtroom was set aside for the week for our specific case, but obviously that was not the case. Court proceedings broke for lunch at 1 pm. I brought my own lunch and snacks since my food choices are somewhat limiting, and I didn't know if there would be any place nearby where I could eat. The detective and case worker left for lunch, and I stayed around the area outside the courtroom. The waiting area had cleared out, so it was quiet. For the first 45 minutes, it was very peaceful. I had a chance to talk to my sister, and she helped calm my anxiety. Then, the False Healer and the individuals with him returned. They were seated at the other end of the waiting area. I was in an area where I couldn't see the False Healer directly, but I could hear them because the waiting area was like a backwards L shape. The False Healer and his family were talking and laughing like nothing important was happening at all. I'm not sure if it was a show because they knew I was alone in the waiting area or if they really were having a good time. Who knows!

Slowly, other people started to congregate again. There were lawyers talking to their clients in rooms provided for conferences and all kinds of people on their phones. Soon, the detective was back from his break as well. I saw the False Healer's defense counsel for the first time, and he reminded me of someone from my long-ago past who I genuinely disliked. This was going to be interesting. The court was called back into session, and I prepped myself to take the stand. I went to the washroom to get a few moments of quiet and settle my nerves. However, when I returned, I was informed yet again that my testimony was delayed. The detective couldn't stay with me, as he needed to be in the courtroom. I kept myself busy watching a movie that was downloaded on my phone. At least the False Healer and his supporters were inside the courtroom.

Finally, at about 3 pm, I was called into the courtroom. My name went out over the courthouse speaker system to report to the courtroom, though I was sitting right outside. I guess that's just standard protocol. A court officer walked me to my seat that was situated just below the judge's bench but above floor level. I placed my handbag at my feet and sat down. My nerves were shaking as I was asked to stand and swear an oath. All the research in the world couldn't prepare me for the overwhelming sense that I was the one on trial. I asked for a glass of water and tried desperately to calm myself down. I glanced around at all the people in the courtroom, trying to establish a sense of security. Fortunately, most of the people in attendance were officers of the court. All the other cases on the court docket had been cleared. There was no one in the courtroom that was not connected with the case. The prosecutor asked me if everything was okay, and when I replied it was, he began his questioning.

For obvious reasons, I cannot write anything about my testimony. The prosecution's questioning went on for about 90 minutes. I didn't need a break, though I did request more water. I held up during the questioning, even though I started out quite nervous. When I was finished, it was time for the defense counsel to ask questions.

When the False Healer's lawyer stood up, I braced myself for the cross-examination. It had been a long day, and I wanted the questioning over and done with. However, when the lawyer spoke, it wasn't to ask me a question but to address the lateness of the time and to ask the court for a continuance. If the court could have heard my thoughts, they would have been offended by what laid beneath my calm facade. The judge granted the continuance, and I was scheduled to return a few days later. The judge noted that on the day of my return, my case would be the first one scheduled on the docket. In my head, I was screaming *please just get this over with... today*! But I politely acknowledged the judge's decision, stepped down from the witness stand and departed from the courtroom.

I walked out into the waiting area and took a seat. The detective soon joined me and gave me an update on the day's testimony. He said I had done well as did the case worker, but I knew I had stumbled in a few areas. I had studied public relations and was somewhat comfortable with answering uncomfortable questions but being in the courtroom was completely different. I think I had read my statement too close to my testimony. As such, I wanted to answer each question exactly as was in the statement. Plus, all I could think about was the information I had left out of my statement and immediately focused on it in my testimony. I wanted to control the flow of information much like I did in my book. I'm hard on myself, so if I thought I did okay then it was a good day.

I worked long hours on my project over the next couple of days, as it helped take my mind off of the impending cross-examination. The fact that I had an instant dislike for the defense counsel didn't help. This was war, and it was up to me to defend myself. I knew what happened, and I knew what the False Healer had done to me. No one else could tell my story except me. I had to trust that I would be guided through the process.

I arrived at the courthouse around 9:30 am on the morning the preliminary hearing was scheduled to reconvene. The detective awaited my arrival and escorted me up the stairs because the False Healer was seated near the elevators, talking with his lawyer. We went back to the area where we sat the previous time and joined the Victim Witness case worker. Every fibre of my being didn't want to be there. It was hard for me to stay focused because I wanted things to be over. When I passed the False Healer, I noticed that he had tidied up his appearance somewhat, probably something his lawyer had asked him to do.

Bells started chiming, indicating court was in session. Since I was scheduled to be first on the docket, I quickly ran into the washroom to tidy myself up. The prosecutor stopped by to fill us in on the schedule. He expected that I would begin soon. The False Healer's lawyer sat near us at the courtroom door while we were waiting to enter. I forced myself to continue talking with the detective about mundane things like the weather to keep myself in control. I said a quick prayer when I saw the prosecutor approach us. *It's time*, I thought.

We stood up in anticipation of moving into the courtroom, but the prosecutor had some bad news. One of the judges had called in sick so the judge that was overseeing our case would need to clear the docket for both courtrooms before we could proceed. The prosecutor said it was better if the docket was cleared so the people waiting for their cases to be heard would not interrupt our hearing by walking in and out of the courtroom, as is common. Due to the sensitivity of my testimony, the prosecutor didn't want any interruptions. He thought it would take an hour to clear the docket and then we would begin.

Let's just say the first word that came to my head was not "puck". I looked at the detective, who was clearly disappointed, and shook my head. At this point, I had no choice but to wait. The three of us sat around talking for the next hour. It was a friendly conversation, not about the case, but just things about our families, travels, etc. I noticed that even an hour later there were still a lot of people milling about the waiting area. I was getting hungry because I hadn't brought any snacks with me since I thought I would be done that morning. It was approaching 11:30 am when we got another update from the prosecutor.

The prosecutor was talking to some people near the entrance to the courtroom. He made his way over to us and apologetically said it looked like I wouldn't take the stand until after lunch, maybe 2 pm. This news was upsetting. The prosecutor walked away to report the same news to the defense counsel. I could hear the False Healer's lawyer expressing his disappointment and arguing that he had another matter to attend to that afternoon. The detective walked over to the prosecutor while he was talking with the defense counsel and requested that I be allowed to go home for lunch and return at 1:30 pm. Usually, the court asks that witnesses stay close by in case they are called earlier, but the detective mentioned that I hadn't brought any food for lunch and there were no restaurants close by that could accommodate my diet. I was allowed to return home, which turned out to be a blessing in disguise.

I got home and changed into a sweatsuit. I made myself some lunch and sat in the quiet of my home. It felt so good to be out of the courthouse and that frenetic energy. I updated those close to me about the delay and decided to meditate. By the time I was ready to return to the courthouse I felt rejuvenated. I returned just before 1:30 pm. The detective went to get a coffee and asked if he could bring me anything. I said a tea would be nice. I felt like I was in a totally different head space. My nerves were calm, and my stomach wasn't doing summersaults. It was like the serenity I felt from my home had erased all the anxiety of the unknown. I didn't even feel bad when 2 pm came and went.

It was 2:45 pm by the time I walked into the courtroom for the second time. I'm not certain if I was sworn in again or if my oath had carried over from a few days prior. I believe it was the latter. The judge was set to begin when a lawyer not connected to the case asked the Crown prosecutor for a moment of the court's time. The lawyer informed the court that his client had been waiting all morning and is from out of town, so could they quickly deal with his case before our case proceeded. The judge agreed. I got up to leave, but the judge said it was okay to stay seated. This took about another 15 minutes. When all was finished, the judge apologized to me for the interruption and then indicated to the defense counsel that he could begin.

The cross-examination lasted about 90 minutes. It seemed the defense counsel had a stack of foolscap questions. I remember distinctly that the paper was yellow. He kept flipping the pages as he worked through his questions. However, this time on the stand I was not as nervous. I answered all his questions, and, as I thought I would, I defended myself vigorously. It's odd really; here I was on the stand defending myself against a lawyer that looked like a man that had physically assaulted me many years ago…and he was defending a man that had sexually assaulted me. What are the odds of that! I didn't tell anyone about the similarity of the defense lawyer's physical appearance with that of the man who assaulted me. It even seemed weird to me.

I recalled that night when the man who looked like the False Healer's lawyer physically assaulted me. He held my neck while he angrily pushed me towards the edge of his balcony. His apartment was located on one of the higher floors of his apartment building. He had also burnt my leg with a cigarette. I fortunately slipped out of his grasp and made my way to the door, but I shudder to think of what might have happened if I didn't get away. He was angry that I had stood him up at a party where he was waiting to introduce me to his friends. Some of his friends were police officers so there was no way I was going to report him to the police. I never saw him again; that is, until his doppelganger showed up.

    I was excused from the witness stand and made my way out of the courtroom. I knew I had done a good job. I was speaking to the detective and my Victim Witness case worker when the prosecutor hurried over to us. He had a big smile on his face as he expressed his surprise with how well the cross-examination went. He joked that I could train others to be a witness. I was pleased with his praise. It felt good to hear positive feedback after such a stress-filled day. He also informed us that the judge ruled that there was enough evidence to move on to trial. We had won the first battle.

    It felt like a huge weight was taken off my shoulders. We had done what we set out to do, and it was now time to move forward. I knew I had faced my fears and didn't understand how I had ever allowed myself to be manipulated by someone like the False Healer. His mysticism evaporated. He was now just someone fighting for his freedom. The detective walked with me past security as the False Healer and his crew were also getting ready to leave. I don't know what we talked about as we left, but I know we were both jubilant. I waved goodbye to him as I crossed into the parking lot where I had left my car. Behind me, I could hear the False Healer and his crew talking and kind of laughing. I thought to myself, *Why are they so upbeat?* I put it out of my mind and got in my car, but their upbeat nature would come back to me later when I prepared for trial.

    I called my husband and sister immediately to let them know the highlights of the cross-examination. They were both happy for me and were proud of the way I handled myself. I think I smiled all the way home.

6

THE ONE

>Last, but not least
>You come to me in pain
>On bended knee perhaps
>For definitely there is one
>Always one or none
>I await the one

Freedom calls out to us, it splays its beautiful wings, full of vigour and hope, we grab it wings. If you could see what I see, you will know you are the wings.

Why is it we seek freedom? Freedom from what exactly? Let's take a look at the word that so holds us in its embrace.

Freedom is defined by Google as "the power or right to act, speak, or think as one wants without hindrance or restraint." Now, we know that this definition doesn't quite always mirror our experience. If you look at things biblically, humankind has been restrained and hindered from experiencing their surroundings in the manner of their choosing from the very beginning of recorded history. I would go so far as to say that humankind has never experienced life in the manner of their choosing in any society or culture, unless one lived alone, completely cut off from civilization. Individualism has been hindered and restrained for the greater good of society and humankind for eons. So why do so many engage in the ever-losing battle for perceived individual freedom.

In my mind, whoever defined the word in the first place did so with a lack of insight, for as long as there is society there will be no individual freedom. Society leads people to battle in all manner of ways, from the way their neighbourhood looks, to how their children are schooled, to the type of employment one can achieve, to what one can or can't wear. On and on it goes; it's truly never ending. If you put on paper every rule from every category that is defined by the law in every society, culture, city, country, etc., I'm sure the list would stretch around the globe several times over. We are not free and will never be free as long as we perceive our freedom as outward.

Thinking about freedom "outwardly" leads one to believe that we can do whatever we want when we want without consideration for others. Isn't that what "without hindrance and restraint" implies in the definition. Even the most avid freedom-fighter lives by rules. If they have a family, they must be responsible for feeding and clothing them. If they live in a home, they must pay bills to sustain it. Even if they are in a freedom-fighter group living outside of society somewhere, they must abide by the often-unspoken rules of the group. Then, of course, there is the necessity to feed the body in order to sustain life, so we must stay close to food sources. When you think about it, how free are we?

What is driving humankind to seek freedom? Could it be that we know and have experienced freedom beyond that which we experience in this world? If you continue to see freedom as something to attain rather than something you already have, then your quest will be futile. Perhaps a new definition of freedom should be, "That which is within; an embodiment of Divine intelligence." The old definition should be relegated to the heap pile because it is false advertising and glorified by those in positions of power; they have it, and we want it. Nelson Mandela (1918–2013), the former South African President, anti-apartheid revolutionary and political prisoner, during his 25-year imprisonment was notably inspired by a poem written by William Ernest Henley (1875) titled *"Invictus"* that includes the line, "**I am the master of my fate, I am the captain of my soul.**" Does this not more accurately reflect true freedom than the one we've been spoonfed all our lives. How on earth are we to achieve freedom to have the power or right to act, speak, or think as one wants without hindrance or restraint? If I act in a manner that is deemed to be suspicious by another, will I not be arrested? If I speak words that threaten another, will I not be investigated? If I think anything different than what is proclaimed as right and proper, will I not be shunned? Where does freedom fit into this paradigm? Perhaps it should be "freedon't." You are free as long as you don't do…whatever it is you're doing.

I am not one to rail against rules. But I am one to suggest to stop fighting for something that is deeply flawed. Stop using the word as a reason for whatever it is you're doing because when you take a deep breath and examine whatever it is you're doing in the name of freedom, it does not fit. At some point, you will be hindering or resisting another person's personal "freedoms" to do whatever it is they want to do. It's like a dog chasing his own tail and going around in circles until he's tired. But that darn dog will get up again and do the same thing over and over to no end. It's like that idiom, "Same Shit, Different Day." At some point, we must acquiesce.

When we accept that the only true freedom is found *within*, suddenly the fervour of the search is rendered null and void. Yes, there are times when we must stand up against tyranny, abuse, the encroachment of sovereignty, and many other factors that plague our world and take up space in our collective consciousness, but freedom is used in such a blasé manner that it is rendered null and void. It is no longer language that is understood in its purity, for it has gone rogue.

Everyone is fighting for freedom, so why should I care about you or them.

So how do we take back the terminology without joining the hoard of freedom usurpers? We add something to it…freedom consciousness.

Freedom consciousness becomes a separating point between the two worlds I spoke about in an earlier chapter. In one world, we must remain grounded on earth to do that which will help humanity ascend in whatever way our unique talents portend, and in the other, we explore our higher consciousness and learn the ways of the soul. What greater gift of freedom can we receive?

How do we do this? Through one individual at a time recognizing that freedom consciousness is their birthright. It was imbued in our soul at the time of our creation. We have the freedom to create whatever world it is we want in the consciousness of our higher mind. Like love, freedom too is energy. It wraps around us like an invisible cloak waiting for our acknowledgement so it can reveal itself. What does it feel like? It feels like the love of God.

I know you're probably saying to yourself, "How the heck can I live in freedom consciousness when my world is falling apart around me and struggle is a part of my daily reality? How can I possibly imagine another way of living when this one is so hard?" To that, I can't say anything other than freedom consciousness exists; it is for real, and you will get there. It took me nine years of beating the bushes to know its truth, and I wasn't looking for it specifically. But now you do know about it; you are reading it here, and in that understanding you are aligning yourself with the consciousness of Divine Intelligence. That is how it starts – with a little prompt and a little knowledge.

It's like this. Each time you come across something new, you gain a new key that opens another door. That is why expanding awareness is so much fun. One moment, you believe yourself to be one way, and the next you're shaking your head about how you believed such a thing. Everything that you need to know comes to you in the time that you need to know it. This is called Divine timing. You can't define the time because the Universe doesn't know the time. There are too many unknowns due to free will. Here is an example.

Let's say that you set your sights on a new job. All indicators say that you will likely be successful. Your intuition tells you to go for it, as it's the right time. You speak to Human Resources, and you hit it off with the person in charge of hiring. That person also feels that you're the right person for the job. Your interview goes well, and you expect to be offered the position. Then, you don't receive an offer. Instead, the position goes to the owner's nephew. You are crushed. You thought the universe had it all aligned for you. But the universe cannot control the boss, who has free will to intervene and hire his nephew. However, three weeks later, you receive a call from the same HR person who wants to offer you a different job with more pay and greater autonomy. This is Divine timing in its simplest form.

Freedom consciousness allows you to move on with your purpose without needing permission from another to do so.

You might ask, "How are we to serve in the manner that our soul indicates when we do not feel we have the freedom to take up the mission?" This is always the obstacle that presents itself throughout our Hero's Journey. How can I do what I know I need to do for my soul's purpose when I feel stuck? Many are in the thought process that everything has to happen in one great action. They might say, "Okay, today I must quit my job because it doesn't fit with my higher or soul's purpose," but then they suffer in their confusion because they know they have no other means to support themselves. What I learned through many missteps is this: **When you get the feeling to serve, it is real, and it is all-consuming, but understand that it is also just a seed**. This beautiful seed is being planted in your consciousness and will eventually become the tree from which you will harvest delicious fruit. But know that right now, it is just a seed. You're not being called to quit your job immediately but to start exploring ways you can nourish the growth of the seed. There are many ways we can explore to nourish the growth of the seed. Perhaps it's taking an evening or weekend course of interest to you or that you feel a special connection to. Perhaps it's volunteering at some place you have never thought to before. Perhaps it's developing a new skill that reflects your growing awareness like tarot reading, numerology, channeling, intuitive writing, etc. Perhaps it's just joining a new group. There are many things we can do to enhance our energy to attract that which will launch us on our path. But the one thing we cannot do is keep doing the same thing. I have met some of the nicest and most knowledgeable people and teachers by stepping out of my routine. It starts with you, and it often doesn't start with one big action like quitting a job, divorcing your spouse, or moving to another country because in all that external change, you will still be you.

As I mentioned earlier, self-reflection is not always a pretty process. But to live in freedom consciousness, it is a necessary tool. For me, the worst thing that used to happen was when someone would tell me something I didn't want to hear. I would launch into self-defense mode immediately because it evoked in me strong feelings of not being good enough. I thank those brave souls now for their courage to tell it like it is, but in those moments I was riled and wanted vengeance. Even still today, I must take out the proverbial mirror of self-reflection and examine the truth and origin of my feelings. Without this practice, I can become mean-hearted and say things that don't reflect the way of the soul.

For example, just recently, my husband was telling me of some updates with his work, and there was one in particular that seemed to set me off. I felt justified in my anger because in my view I was defending him and his kind nature against those who might try to undermine his position. He was taken aback by my anger. I recognized what I had done, and in the moment I made a statement like, "Perhaps I'm not the best person to talk to about work stuff; I'm too close to you and will always come to your defense." He agreed and said he was just trying to get a higher perspective on the issue, not for me to fix it. Still, I went to bed unsettled. The next day, I engaged in some self-reflection. I knew the moment it came into my heart that it was true. I was jealous. I was jealous of someone else's success whom he had spoken about. But I turned it around to cover for that jealousy, and it came out as anger – how dare this person usurp his position!

Being honest with myself and with him was needed to repair and heal the damage I had done. Traveling to the root of your emotions will always free your soul.

That same day, I had come across a video that helped me cognate what it was that I needed to see. It was about the Soul Virtues I discussed in an earlier chapter: Altruism, Right Action, Clarity, Humility, Love, Happiness for Others and Temperance. You see, I had written about Principles for Living in *"Out From Beneath Your Wings"* that include virtues like Expectation, Intention, Compassion, Forgiveness, Gratitude, Tolerance, Humility, and Moderation. However, one of these Soul Virtues got me thinking.

The one that stood out was **Happiness for Others**. It stood out because in that moment, I understood that I was often not happy for others' success or happiness. Deep in my heart, I knew it was because I wasn't where I wanted to be in my life. I would give myself permission to think things like, "Where is my recognition for all the hard work I've put into expanding my awareness and helping others? Why do I not receive a reward when I have done so much?" It is even present with little things like when my niece told me she was getting a puppy. Instead of wishing her happiness, I told her of all the potential pitfalls of bringing a puppy into her home. It would have been more the way of the soul to wish her much happiness and send her the energy of my love to help her puppy transition into its new home.

As this was all coming into my consciousness, I felt heavy. There was so much to learn that it exhausted my heart. I questioned if I was the right person to share the light of God. Even now as I write this, my eyes well up with tears. The anguish of not feeling good enough weighed heavy on my soul, and I needed respite from my own cage. I decided to head out for a long walk on my own.

I chose a nature conservation area not far from my home. When I arrived, I decided to drive into the park close to where the trail began, though I had to pay for the privilege. I drove up the long road to the parking area and readied myself for my walk. I brought along a few snacks, water and bug spray in a small backpack. It had rained earlier so I also brought along a rain jacket. The conservation park is beautiful. Although it's surrounded on all sides by a township, it still feels very remote. I connected with one of the main trails and leisurely made my way to see all the highlights of the park like the waterfalls, historical sites, and the many areas to observe the flora and fauna. I stopped at a couple of areas to sit and relax and even to meditate for a little while. About an hour into my walk, it started to rain. I decided to make my way back to my vehicle; however, I wasn't in a big hurry because I had a rain jacket.

I picked up a park map at the start of my walk and looked at it to ensure I was going in the right direction. The rain really started to pick up. I walked faster, but in my haste I missed the trail that led back to my car. I hadn't really noticed that I had gotten turned around until I didn't recognize any of the markers. In all the times I had been to the conservation park, I had never been on that particular trail. I walked for about one kilometre before looking at the map. To my chagrin, the map didn't really sync up with the trail. I found an information stand that provides an historical overview of the area, but it too didn't direct me back to the main trail. I decided to select one of the trails and take my chances. I happened across a waterfall I had never seen before, so I took some pictures before continuing my walk. The path was getting slippery from the rain, which really slowed my pace. I hoped I would run into other people. I walked for another two kilometres before I realized I had circled back to the information stand. By this point, a lot of time had passed. I ate some snacks and decided on my next move.

Throughout all this time, I was not upset at all. Actually, I was laughing really hard, like busting my gut laughing at my predicament. In my mind, I pictured when I was about eight or nine and I got lost in the woods with my friends. We were all quite hysterical before finding the path to our reserve. It was like my childhood friends kept me company. I walked about another two kilometres before finally walking out of the conservation park. I recognized the area because it was the parking lot of a well-known restaurant. I spotted a couple parking their car and walked in their direction. When they exited their vehicle, I asked them if they could help direct me to the main conservation gate. The map was soaked by this time but still legible. The guy used Google Maps. I laughed out loud. I hadn't even thought about that! As it turned out, I was on the opposite side of where I parked my car to enter the conservation trails. It was going to be a long walk back. I wasn't even sure if I could find my way back through the woods using Google Maps, as pathways were not highlighted in the same way as streets. It was just a general direction. I could have walked around the park, but many of the roadways are not safe for pedestrians. I thanked the couple and walked back into the woods. As I reached the pathway, the young woman yelled out to me to get my attention. She asked if I would like a ride to my vehicle. I almost started to cry with relief and happily accepted her offer. When we arrived at the main gate, the lady at the gatehouse saw me get out of the car and asked where I had come from. "You came in here hours ago," she said. I told her I had gotten lost, and we had a good laugh together. I walked up the long half-kilometre path to the car. Again, I was busting a gut laughing, and when I reached my car I felt such relief when I sat down. *What a crazy day*, I thought. When I arrived home, I recounted my story to my husband and two sons. They had no trouble believing my story because I had found myself in that predicament one too many times. I guess maps and I just don't go together. I asked them when they would have called out a search party, and my husband said 6 pm. They knew I was alright.

The next day during my meditation, I was still giggling about my walk. Even though I had been lost for a little while, I felt uplifted afterwards. In meditation, spirit told me that I was not lost. I had to walk until all the energy that needed to be transmuted in my body was absorbed into Mother Earth and replenished with her own. Spirit told me that I walked and walked and then when the process was finished, they had a ride ready to return me to my car. How amazing is that!

Everything that has come to me has been a result of hard work, tenaciousness, and a lot of patience. Walking the spiritual path or the way of the soul brings great joy, but it requires daily commitment and the intent to live in higher consciousness. We must be on guard to ensure that the duality we carry within us is tempered. What do I mean by duality? Duality can best be explained by imagining the depiction in cartoons of the good little angel and the bad little devil sitting on the shoulders of the main character. Both are trying to influence the thoughts and actions of the main character. This happens in us by allowing the shadow side (the bad little devil) to influence our decisions or thoughts. The shadow side is all the hurt, anger, fear, jealousy, humiliation, abuse, and negative experiences we have encountered in our lifetime. It resides within us, but it doesn't have to control us. Many make the mistake of believing that they have to completely rid themselves of all these negative aspects and live joyfully all the time. That's not the case. We learn some powerful lessons through these negative experiences. We only need to learn to separate the emotion from the experience so that we don't make decisions from a place of pain or fear. There will be times when we need to draw on these experiences to help others (like through these stories). This requires us to heal that which holds us hostage. This takes time. Every time you heal an aspect of yourself, good energy takes its place. Eventually, the good energy will replace enough of the not-so-good energy to create a sense of balance within your being. No longer is the shadow side having a lopsided effect on your bodies (emotional body, mental body, physical body and etheric body). You have established what is known as **Temperance** or balance. But just because you have established balance doesn't mean your work is done. Maintaining balance involves the constant realigning and adjustment of your bodies. That is what I was called to do when I went for a walk in the woods. I created a misalignment in my bodies by giving my shadow side a bigger platform than usual, and it left a stain on my energy field. Every day is an important day because every new day brings an opportunity to learn from yesterday and do it better today.

So say yes to freedom consciousness. Say yes to love consciousness. Say yes to walking the way of the soul. Your dreams are waiting to come to you.

7

THE WAY OF THE SOUL

Whispers of joy
That bring a grin
A slight touch
Heavenly sent
We know you
We are you

At first, I didn't know the direction this book would take. When I sat down at my computer to write, I trusted that the words and order would come. That is what living the way of the soul is like. You are allowing yourself to be guided by unseen forces that immerse you in the game of life. I know using the word "game" trivializes the deep trauma and painful experiences we endure, but nonetheless it is a game of sorts. If you have ever seen the movie *Clash of the Titans*, you would have been introduced to the concept of life as a game. In this depiction, the gods such as Zeus, Poseidon, Hades, Apollo, Aphrodite, Ares, Hephaestus, and Artemis move around their human pawns like a game of chess. The human pawns are put in peril in all manner of ways to test their skills, ingenuity, and virtue. The gods gain and maintain power through the virtuous acts of the humans and the humans' gratitude and praise of them. But it is Hades who learns that he can gain great power through another avenue – the negative thoughts and actions of humankind because in suffering these attributes abound. This is a perfect example of living life in duality.

We have the free will to choose the path of the proverbial good little angel or the bad little devil perched on our shoulders. It's not so much that we are haphazardly thrown into a game, it's that we are ready to be put in the game because we have been training for some time. In *Clash of the Titans,* the gods all know the skills of their human pawns because they (the gods) have a higher perspective, trust, and knowledge of their charges' attributes – the same is true for your soul.

The way of the soul is a conscious decision to ascend. Through this ascension, we are actively engaged in the game. We no longer sit at board-level, waiting to be moved. Through higher consciousness, we are able view the layout of the board and intuit our next move. Yes, these moves may come with surprises and developments we weren't quite prepared for, but now we have the ability to recalibrate. The ability to recalibrate or refocus comes faster and faster so our movements become almost seamless. From the outside looking in, people may not be aware of the obstacles we encounter because we quickly refocus our energy and move in another direction.

The soul is a conduit for Divine Intelligence. It is the "spark of God." The soul works in tandem with our higher consciousness or higher mind to steer our ship and guide us to our passion, purpose and promise of ascension. It is not that which communicates with you as thoughts – that is your higher mind. The soul is you. It is not separate from you – EVER! We are all moving towards the full embodiment of the soul. In other words, we are constantly in the process of clearing all of our bodies (physical, mental, emotional, etheric) so the soul can radiate its magnificence! The soul is the spark of God that glints in our eyes and fills our hearts with joy. It knows where we are going and where we have been, not only in this life but in all our existences, even those yet to be experienced. For this reason, trust is imperative in walking the way of the soul.

We have become inured to questioning everything around us because our trust in humanity has been eroded. How many times have we heard the idiom "but I'm only human". This idiom is used to excuse all manner of transgressions, from cheating, stealing, racism, laziness, and so much more. It's like people choose to give away their power to what they see as a lack of human ability to be anything other than what they are. I could use the term "lack of faith" here, but faith assumes you have some sense of higher consciousness or awareness in the first place. Trust helps us take the first step into the unknown. Trust gets us up at 6 am to do whatever it is we need to do to keep the momentum going. Trust tells us we are on the right path when difficult choices need to be made. Trust is knowing that we will succeed.

No, you're not going to wake up one morning and declare that your trust in the universe and all will be okay. It takes time. Just as you lost trust a little at a time from when you were a child to now, it takes time to rebuild trust. It starts with you trusting yourself to make the best decisions for you when you are called to do so. You cannot learn how to trust by first learning to trust another because that person has free will and you cannot control their actions. You can only control yours. So, trust-building must start with you.

I remember the first time when trust came into my awareness as something tangible and required me to relearn how I listened. The first incident was during meditation when I was prompted to go for a bike ride. In my mind, I said, "What about the dogs?" I heard, "Don't worry, you will be safe." The ride was pleasurable and uneventful. The next meditation, I was again prompted to go out on a bike ride. I heard something like, "Drive over the bridge to (a location they showed me) and bike from that spot." However, I said to myself, "Paula, that's just being lazy." So I started out from my home. Not too far down the road, a dog chased me and nearly knocked me off the bike. I was terrified. When I finished my bike ride, I called my husband to pick me up from the location that was given to me in meditation. In another incident, I walked out of a Walmart pushing a small shopping cart, and I clearly heard, "Paula, carry the groceries to the car." I didn't have many and could have easily carried them, but the orange juice was awkward, so I proceeded walking to my car with the cart. It was a sunny spring day, and I was really happy, humming along to a song that was in my head. Then, the wheel of my cart hit a pothole and because it was a light load the cart stopped dead in its tracks. As a result, I went flying over the cart and everything tumbled to the pavement, including me. I quickly jumped up, though I had hurt my leg. I gathered my things and quickly scanned the area to see if anyone had seen what happened. I didn't think anyone had. I got to my car and quickly put the items in the trunk. I limped to the driver-side door. When I sat in the quietness of my vehicle, I burst into tears. I had really hurt my leg in the fall, and I was quite angry. I said out loud, "What the heck was that all about – I really got hurt!" I heard, "Paula, if you can't learn to listen to the small things, how are you going to listen to the big things?" I stopped crying because my pain and anger quickly dissipated. I was humbled.

I know now that it is incumbent upon me to trust the little things because in walking the way of the soul, the little things add up to help us meet the big things head on.

When you think about it, how many times have you overridden intuitive prompts from your higher self? Remember, the higher self or mind is different from the soul, though they work in tandem. The higher self is like a registry of sorts; it holds the Akash (all of the experiences you've had in this lifetime and any other lifetime. More importantly, it knows how you think, act, perceive, etc.). It knows how best to help you fulfill your mission in this lifetime. So ignore it at your own peril. For me, even when I did express the intent to trust in divine guidance, I was still shown areas for improvement, as my cart and bike stories indicate. Every day is an exercise in trust. I am trusting right now that the words I am sharing with you will make sense to you and touch your consciousness. Walking the way of the soul means you never have to walk alone. It is important to know this because you will backslide. The shadow side knows your weaknesses and will bring energies to you that stir these weaknesses up. It is your choice and your choice alone whether you accept the bait. If you don't take the bait, the energy redirects back out into the universe. If you do take the bait, the energy attaches itself to you and will feed off your upset or ego self. It takes great strength and courage to redirect the energy of the shadow side; you are basically shielding yourself from your former self. You are not shielding yourself from evil or darkness – it is only that which used to live in you. Once you recognize this, you can say to your shadow side, "I see what you're doing. Nice try, but I'm not biting!"

This really works. I have used it many times. It could be a thought that takes hold or is trying to take form, and you say out loud or in your mind, "I see what you're doing. Nice try, but I'm not biting." In order to fight the good fight, we must arm ourselves with whatever tools will get us through the moment, whether that's using affirmations that touch our heart, or special prayers. I use whatever tool is brought into my awareness at the time.

Not everyone will feel comfortable with these tools so select what works for you. The point of the tool is to redirect the energy your shadow side is presenting. If this is a person who drives you crazy, walk away and out of their Merkabah or energy field. If it's someone who's calling to rant or unload on you, tell them you're not available right now and you will have to call them back. After some time, they'll stop calling on you because you're no longer giving them what they desire – affirmation that they are right. And before you pick up your phone to text or rant to somebody else, think about what that does to you. Think about how much it drains your energy to talk someone off the ledge. If it is a true crisis, a referral to a counselor would be a better solution for you and the individual involved. If you believe you are the only one that can fix or help them, that is more your ego than your soul. We all want to be helpful, but we must first help ourselves.

There is a lot we have to heal in ourselves, so how can we do that when we're running all over the place giving first aid to others.

The choice is ours. We can die a martyr believing that we were there whenever anyone needed us, or we can leave this world knowing that we left another with the tools to solve their own problems. The legacy we leave behind will be determined by our actions. If we decide to heal ourselves, we show others how to heal by example; in this way, we can heal many. If we try to heal others without first healing ourselves, the wisdom of our actions is lost. In this case, we will be eulogized as "someone who was always there for me", instead of "someone who helped change my life".

Captured within our hearts is the soul's pulsating life force. It beats, pulsating the essence of its true divinity. It aligns with the heartbeat for us to feel, hear, touch, and see a physical manifestation of the spark of God. With each breath, it calls to us. It assigns to us the heart of all matters – the reason for our being. Not once will it deprive us of its true nature, its true origin as a creation of Divinity or Divine Source. This is what our soul wants us to know – that we are Divine. We are God Source energy. If you can imagine the soul as a sphere and through that sphere is a beam of light that illuminates the sphere, then that is Divine energy or God Source energy. Without illumination, the sphere is just a sphere. This is the same concept as with our human form. Without illumination, we are just a form. Our craving to experience fulfillment is tied to our need to light up that within ourselves that has gone dark. It is not truly dark because we are a constant illumination of God Source energy, but our ability to perceive the light has dimmed. When we walk the way of the soul, it's like we step onto the path of illumination or a beam of God Source energy. All it takes is that initial spark within us to generate enough light to see the path clearly. For me, that initial spark was asking the question *why*, and a whole journey opened up before me.

When speaking with an acquaintance one day, she brought up recent changes in her spiritual development. I don't usually engage in such discussions because I believe it's important for individuals to learn at their own pace; however, at some point in the conversation, she said something to the effect of, "I know I'm God...I know all of that." While I don't challenge what she said as untrue, I did say to her that her personality was expressing this knowledge more than her Real Self. "What's a Real Self?" she asked. I replied to her that it is the God within. Then, she asked "Who is God?" I answered her as best as I could, but when I got home I thought there had to be a way of answering that question in a more concise manner.

In meditation that evening, the following came to me – **God is the silence in you that speaks volumes**.

Essentially, when we align with the presence of God Within there is no need for words, loud discussions, or debate because the God Within shines outward with such force that others need only to be in your presence to feel God's energy. The debate of "Who is God?" no longer resonates – I AM.

8

IN THE END

In the dead of the night he chases
I run but my strides weaken
He turns, I turn
It seems backward, or is it
I seem to lose him
But the fright
Of the night resumes

It is with trust that I resume the tale of my Hero's Journey. I have talked so far about five components of Joseph Campbell's the Hero's Journey: Call to Adventure, Supernatural Aid, Threshold, Gather Helpers, and Challenges and Temptation. The next is Revelation (that which is going to change your life).

In his book *The Hero with a Thousand Faces*, Joseph Campbell does not label the nine sections in the same way as they are labelled in this outline. The 17 stages he identifies are intertwined in a section titled "Part 1 - The Adventure of the Hero". Within this section are sub-headings titled <u>Departure</u>, <u>Initiation</u>, <u>Return</u>, and <u>The Keys</u>. Each of these sub-headings is defined through mythological stories, and it is through these stories that knowledge is conveyed. I believe the shorter outline of nine sections was used to more easily identify the real-life stages of the Hero's Journey for everyday use, though I am not certain where it originated. The Hero's Journey is known as a **monomyth**. Wikipedia's description is as follows: "Monomyth is the common template of a broad category of tales and lore that involves a hero who goes on an adventure, and in a decisive crisis wins a victory, and then comes home changed or transformed." Joseph Campbell, in his diagram or monomyth of the Hero's Journey, does not use the word "Revelation" as is provided in my outline. The closest description is Father Atonement or Sacred Marriage. In some drawings found on the internet of the monomyth, I have seen the word "revelation" situated near or at the point of the "Abyss or Death and Rebirth." But none of these descriptions were used in the original version of The Hero's Journey provided by Joseph Campbell in *The Hero with a Thousand Faces*. These could have later been added for the ease of interpretation either by Campbell himself or other followers of his work.

Google defines "revelation" in two ways: 1) a surprising and previously unknown fact, especially one that is made known in a dramatic way, and 2) the divine or supernatural disclosure to humans of something relating to human existence or the world. Joseph Campbell artfully relays these divine or supernatural disclosures in his tales. While both of these definitions apply to this chapter, I will utilize the first definition more for the purpose of telling my story.

In the past, I have had revelations or epiphanies following my time with the False Healer and during my healing journey. These usually happened after I had stepped into some new information. This type of information some may refer to as esoteric. Google defines "esoteric" as, "intended for or likely to be understood by a small number of people with a specialized knowledge or interest." For some time, my deep interest in the metaphysical and expanding spirituality has led me to consume large volumes on subjects that interest me. I take copious amounts of notes so I can refer back to the information when needed. I interpret my dreams, meditate and channel daily. There is always information coming into my awareness, some more extraordinary than others. I have had many "ah-ha" moments or revelations, and in these times, it's like I receive another piece of the great puzzle of life. These revelations are meant to keep us going and to help maintain our interest in our soul's journey. However, the revelation I received regarding my case was different.

Months passed without any word about a potential plea deal. It was the prosecutor's hope that the False Healer would opt for a plea deal when the case was approved by the judge to move to trial after the preliminary hearing. I received a call from Victim Witness saying that the prosecutor wanted to schedule a meeting to discuss the case. By this time, it had been 10 months since I last saw the prosecutor. I believe I may have called my case worker for an update at least once during this time, but it was more of the same thing, with the False Healer's lawyer filing motions on his behalf for one thing or another. Most of the motions filed consisted of closed hearings limited to the judge, prosecutor and defense counsel; neither I nor the False Healer were allowed to attend these hearings. There were times when the False Healer appeared in court in regard to other court filings, but I was not interested in attending these hearings.

When I next met with the prosecutor, two years had passed since I had filed charges against the False Healer. This was not a surprise to me because I understood the nature of the judicial system, but it was tedious nonetheless. The prosecution was getting close to the 30-month mark of when offenses needed to be dealt with or they could face dismissal by the court. I asked the prosecutor about this. He explained that due to "Jordan's Law", which had been passed in 2016, Superior Court cases now have up to 30 months to be completed from the time the charge is laid to the conclusion of the trial. However, he said, there were special circumstances that had led to delays in our case, and these would be taken into consideration by the judge. Our discussion that day primarily focused on a potential plea deal. The prosecutor thought they were close and didn't understand why the False Healer was delaying. He explained what the plea deal could look like and what his reasoning was for putting it forward. I agreed with him that I would rather see a conclusion through a plea deal than a trial. He was essentially looking for my approval to move forward with a plea deal. I unequivocally said yes.

I returned home happy in the knowledge that this process could be over soon. I didn't expect to hear anything right away. I knew a deal could take time. I looked up Jordan's Law and found the following: "If the Supreme Court time frames are missed, the onus is on the Crown to argue that the delays were caused by exceptional circumstances that were either reasonably unforeseen or beyond the Crown's control – like a medical or family emergency." I believe that in our situation the delay was necessitated by both parties.

A few weeks after my meeting with the prosecutor, I called Victim Witness for an update. There was still no news about a plea deal, but I was told they would stay in touch. A few days later, my case worker reported back to me that a trial had been scheduled for the following year; it was scheduled in Superior Court for 10 days. My heart sank. The case worker said it was probably due to Jordan's Law and that the Crown needed to get the trial date in the books to satisfy the Supreme Court finding; she would get more information for me. The court date was seven months away, and the dates scheduled in the timetable included my birthday. How depressing! My case worker got back to me the next day. Unfortunately, a plea deal could not be worked out and the Crown was moving forward with trial. For some reason, the False Healer felt he had a chance at trial and wanted to proceed. She said the prosecutor was not sure what the False Healer thinks he has, but it's going to trial.

I can't even begin to tell you what this news meant to me. The thought of taking the stand again made me want to cry. I simply didn't want to do it. I felt the weight of another trial in every fibre of my being. I also knew that this time it wasn't going to be the judge alone, as it was going to be a jury as well. Believe me when I tell you, the temptation to drop out was more real than ever. But after going so far…could I just give up?

After much deliberation, I decided that the best thing to do was put it out of my head. There was absolutely nothing I could do right now. No matter what scenario I came up with, there was little that I actually had control over. I couldn't will things to happen. Things were going to play out as the Universe intended, with or without all my worry. So I went on with my life and decided I would think about the trial when the time came to think about it again. I admit, though, that the impending trial was never far from my awareness.

Time went by fast. Before I knew it, I was being contacted by Victim Witness to begin preparations for the trial. There were matters that required my attention like information on the trial process, the role of Victim Witness, and my testimony review. It would also be necessary to meet again with the Crown Prosecutor to review the trial proceedings. This is a common practice to prep witnesses for trial. I was somewhat discouraged to learn that the detective in charge of the investigation could not provide me with any updates or procedural information during the trial. In addition, he was not allowed in the courtroom during my testimony nor could he accompany me to the courthouse or sit with me while I waited to give testimony. This information was upsetting because the detective championed for me and helped keep me safe during the preliminary hearing. I believe this was to ensure that we didn't corroborate our testimony in case he was called as a witness. Still, it was upsetting.

I scheduled the review of my statement and preliminary hearing testimony two weeks before the trial was scheduled to begin. I learned a hard lesson in the preliminary hearing that scheduling my review too close to my testimony rattled my nerves and didn't give me enough time to synthesize all the information. The last review was scheduled the morning of my testimony. I felt hurried to listen to the 90-minute statement before rushing out to meet the detective at the courthouse. When I finally took the stand that day, I stumbled a few times because I thought the wording and order of events had to exactly match my statement, and I focused on information I forgot to include. I didn't allow my story to naturally flow. I knew my truth, and I couldn't block its unfolding.

Though the judge ruled in our favour with the preliminary hearing, a thought came back into my awareness. As you may recall, on the day of the ruling, I was confused by the upbeat banter of the False Healer and his supporters as they walked to their vehicle. I thought I even heard them laugh. I remember clearly asking myself if I had said anything in court that was favourable to their defense. I wracked my brain but could not think of anything. The False Healer's lawyer's questioning was strange, but I thought that was just part of the show.

A few days before I was scheduled to meet with Victim Witness and the prosecutor to review my statement and preliminary hearing transcripts, I heard a message from Spirit saying, "Paula, pay attention, we're going to show you something." Over and over this message was brought into my awareness by different means. I was straining to pay attention to everything around me because the message didn't indicate what exactly I was to pay attention to – "Paula, pay attention. We're going to show you something." It could be anything. It was frustrating. I felt like I was in a spy movie preparing for an unexpected attack – "Paula, pay attention. We're going to show you something."

The day finally came for my review. I was scheduled to begin at 3 pm. Not a great time, but my case worker said she would stay late if needed. My husband was away so I had to arrange for one of my sons to be picked up. My other son was home from school following a minor surgical procedure on his foot the day prior. I promised I would pick up my son at his friend's house before 6 pm.

The first item on the schedule was to review my initial statement given almost three years earlier. I listened carefully and took notes, which I hadn't done on my previous review. I wanted to ensure there wasn't anything in there I had overlooked. There wasn't. I then went on to my preliminary hearing testimony. I was not allowed to review the testimony in private as I did with the audio statement. I was required to sit with my case worker for the review because the folder included more than just my testimony. It included testimony for the entirety of the preliminary hearing. I reviewed the Crown's questions first, then went on to the defense counsel's questions. I took notes to help me follow what was being asked and how I replied. I didn't really see anything out of the ordinary. Then, out of the blue, I had a vision. It was a vision of the very first meeting I had with the False Healer and who was there. I didn't think too much about it and continued my review. I was nearing the end of the testimony when the prosecutor joined us.

It was now after 5 pm. I remained cognizant of the time. I knew my son wanted to be picked up before 6 pm. We talked for a while about the trial process, and the prosecutor covered material provided by the justice system to help witnesses understand what is expected of them during the trial. We then toured the courthouse. The building was different than the last one. It was older and had a more formal feel to it. Perhaps one could even say intimidating. I sat in the witness seat as well as a jurist seat. I walked over to where the False Healer would be seated and then sat in one of the seats in the spectator galley. I would have liked to stay longer, but my son then texted me. He was waiting. We finished the meeting, and I quickly ran out to my car. I was about to put the car in drive when a revelation overwhelmed me, and I realized what the vision I had earlier was about. *Oh my God*, I thought. *I perjured myself!*

During the cross-examination, I was baffled and even a little amused by the defense counsel's line of questioning. I thought to myself, *Where is he going with this?* I would not have even given it a second thought if it hadn't been for the False Healer and his supporters' lighthearted banter when they walked behind me on their way to their vehicle after the preliminary hearing. But now it all came to light. In fact, I believe my testimony may have played a part in the Crown's inability to reach a plea deal with the False Healer, though I don't know that conclusively. Earlier in the day and before I left for my review, the detective dropped by my house to serve me with a subpoena to appear at trial. It was a short visit because I had just gotten out of the shower. In an off-the-cuff manner, the detective said something like, "I don't know what he (the False Healer) thinks he has, but he wants to take his chances at trial."

Damn it, I thought, I was facing potential perjury charges because I had protected the False Healer's identity in my book and the identity of our mutual friend who introduced us. I can't reveal to you how this happened because I would need to include the defense counsel's line of questioning, so you will need to trust me when I say it was completely unintentional.

I picked up my son and drove home. Throughout the 25-minute drive, I went over in my head what to do with this new information. When I arrived home, I immediately sent a text to the detective. In the text, I informed him that I would need to amend my statement. I cannot go into detail as to the reasons, but the False Healer's lawyer was clever in the way he asked me certain questions. It was information that neither I, the detective, nor prosecution even thought to take into consideration. But the important thing now was that I remembered and could still fix it. The detective asked me to call him in the morning. He would check in with the Crown prosecutor's office as to the next steps.

That evening, I quickly scanned my book and found another part in which a case for perjury could be assigned. It was a part that I had omitted in the book but included in my statement. At the time when I wrote *Heaven's Wait,* I felt that if I had written the part in question in my book the way it had truly happened, it would have given cause to question if there was more to the story than I was willing to tell at the time. As I mentioned before, I didn't feel healed enough to share the sexual assault part of my story in *Heaven's Wait.* Unfortunately, the way the defense counsel asked his line of questions made me look like I had perjured myself in my answers to the court. I didn't even think to read my book before the preliminary hearing. I figured I had written it, so I knew it inside out. Actually, truth be told, I didn't even really think there would be many questions at the preliminary hearing about my book, as it didn't detail the sexual assault. I don't think I slept at all that night.

If you knew me, you would know that I am very detail oriented. To overlook such an obvious ploy by the defense counsel to undermine my testimony was embarrassing. However, the "revelation" of what had happened during the preliminary hearing came to me just as I was foretold by Spirit: "Paula, pay attention. We're going to show you something." I believe I became stronger as a result of this supernatural aid.

I met the detective at the police station the next day. This time, he wanted my statement on video and audio. He led me to one of the interview rooms and briefly discussed the process before we began as my last statement was audio-only. He left the room briefly to turn on the camera, and when he returned he commenced the interview process. My amended statement took a little over five minutes to record. Basically, it was to explain what I had omitted from my book and the reason for my omissions. When I finished, the detective apologized because he didn't know to even ask me why a couple of the points in the book didn't match my statement. I explained that I was somewhat aware of the rules around libel, and I didn't want a fight or to be sued by the False Healer. I only wanted to tell my story, and I realized I could do that without identifying the False Healer or our mutual friend. I was relieved it was over.

My amended statement was filed with the court and was sent to both the Crown prosecutor and defense counsel a week before the trial was slated to begin. It was out of my hands, but I was nervous as to how it would impact the cross-examination. Did I just piss off the defense counsel even more? I didn't know what to expect.

9

THE TELLING

> Walk with us a little while
> Know and remember the feeling of joy
> For it will carry you
> It will light your way in the dark
> Remember always, oh child of mine
> To forgive every time

The knocking persisted. It is time they said to step into the light. It is time for people to know you. You have grieved your old way, and now you have risen from the shambles – let us light the way. No more will you roll in the dirt to hide your pain. The spirit of the Lord has wiped you clean.

At the start of the trial, nine years had passed since I first met the False Healer. It was almost three years since the first charges of sexual assault were filed. The gap in time was somewhat worrisome to me. I realized from the preliminary hearing that providing testimony requires much more detail than I could have ever imagined. However, we never forget the painful incidents that leave deep scar tissue on our memory. For most of us who have experienced trauma or painful events, those details seem to have an instant recall button in our mind. Sometimes, though, little details can get mixed up or forgotten all together. For example, during the trial, there were two small gaps in my testimony where I couldn't recall certain information. Based on this, the defense council actually accused me of lying. As I drove home afterwards, the answers came into my awareness. I was relaxed, and the answers were right there. I wanted to drive back, walk into the courtroom, and yell to the defense counsel, "I know the answer! You see, you fool, I'm not lying!" I laughed at my thought. Oh, the drama we can dream up.

Scenarios like these are some of the things we allow ourselves to play out in our minds, usually to relieve stress. Generally, it's okay to play the "what if" game if you can maintain your sensibilities. If you get a chuckle from playing out a different scenario to help ease your stress, then go for it. But, if you are simply beating yourself up over what you did or didn't do, then you are walking on dangerous ground. It's like walking on quicksand – the more you play the game, the deeper you sink. This could mean sinking into depression, self-loathing, or even revenge. Some turn to harmful or addictive behaviours in an attempt to quiet the game master – the mind. We're not programmed to be perfect. We can be pretty darn good, but perfection is God's purview. So be pretty darn good, or pretty darn decent, but please don't put perfection in your mindset. How can we be perfect at something we can't study for or know nothing of its motives or reasons? This can apply to life in general or anything else in which the unknown presents itself. This was the way with the trial and my testimony. I did my best to respond to what I was presented with in the time I was presented with it. All the game-playing in the world will never change that. It just is and always will be the past.

Every second, we are making our "new now." We must not crowd out our _new now_ with _not now_ because we're preoccupied with thoughts of the past. Our mind needs to be free to walk into our future, unburdened by history. I'm not saying our history doesn't count; it just can't impair the unfolding of our new now. In this book, my history is taken into account, but it does not impair my new now. I have placed my history in the "learned file." This has allowed me to extract that which I need to continue on my journey, and any excess is relegated to the burn pile. The lessons have already been learned so its purpose has been served.

Eckhart Tolle, a spiritual teacher and author, answered the following when asked by an audience member, "How do I balance living in the present moment with being able to plan for the future?" (Eckhart Tolle, YouTube - How Do I Balance Presence and Planning? Published Jan. 10, 2015.)

"Sometimes you need to plan for your future, like retirement, travel, etc. This is when we use what's called **Applied Thinking**," explains Eckhart Tolle. In one part, Tolle says, "In these cases, you're not really losing the present moment because you're not projecting yourself into the future and how it's going to turn out or imagining that when you do whatever it is you're planning that you're going to feel really fulfilled. There is a time limit for the planning. Further, sometimes you need to go back into your past and extract information, but again there is a time limit." Then there is **Useless Thinking**. Useless Thinking, Tolle says, "Leads to worry, anxiety, etc." You might say things like "how awful that was" or "how things went wrong." You can lose yourself in the past...or you can lose yourself in the future when thinking about what could go wrong.

This takes us to the next segment of Joseph Campbell's Hero's Journey: "Transformation" (you come through the challenge and you are transformed).

Google defines "transformation" as "a thorough or dramatic change in form or appearance." For example, a caterpillar transforms into a butterfly. There is also a spiritual transformation. Wikipedia defines this as "a fundamental change in a person's sacred or spiritual life." Usually, a transformation begins with the crumbling of the old. Be it a perspective, a way of thinking, beliefs, relationships, careers, or anything else that sustained our false belief in who we are and how we fit into society or the world at large. This phase can often be dark or scary, as we cannot see the outcome; just as the butterfly has no perception beyond its cocoon. The word to remember is "phase"...it will end.

At the start of my Hero's Journey, I didn't realize the intensity of the power that would fill me, nor the incredible transformation that would occur. Standing up for myself in the face of adversity rewired the way I see myself and my place in this world. When I walked out of that courtroom for the last time, I left behind any doubts of what I could achieve. Anything was possible! The new Paula had emerged. I went head to head with the False Healer's defense counsel and stood my ground. I helped bring the False Healer to justice and protected the integrity of *Heaven's Wait*. It was indeed a battle; one that dropped me into the deepest of despair and out again to the highest of highs. The way of the soul awaited me.

When I reflect back to the week before the trial, walking the way of the soul had not yet taken shape in my consciousness. I definitely understood my role in the trial and in this drama, but I was yet to realize how the trial would elevate me spiritually. I recall hoping and praying for a plea agreement because I thought that would be best for me emotionally. I understand now that a plea deal would have eased my emotional distress, but I would have missed out on the profound transformation that occurred with my testimony.

Stepping into the realization that a trial was going to happen, I reluctantly prepared myself for what lay ahead. The court had set aside 10 days for the trial. At this point, it was still unclear when I would testify. Victim Witness would keep me informed as to the schedule. The Crown prosecutor maintained close contact with Victim Witness and kept them up to date of all developments before and during the trial. Once the trial started, I was officially put on notice. My case worker kept in constant contact with me. I was to report to the Victim Witness office upon receiving a call from my case worker when I was scheduled to appear. It seemed that the days moved very slowly. I kept myself busy as best I could, but the waiting was painful.

I selected the outfits I would wear to trial. I knew neutral colours were best and that I should have very few accessories. The prosecutor said to wear whatever is comfortable. To me, informal business attire feels comfortable, so I chose outfits I would wear to a work-related meeting. As I looked in the mirror, I realized that my business jacket made it look a little too business-like. Then, I heard, "Dress like you can be their sister." Once again, Spirit weighed in, and I smiled. I switched the business jacket to a casual tan blazer and white shirt for the first day and a white sweater over a blue shirt the second day. The pants were simple and black. I was satisfied with the look.

The early days of the trial were dedicated to procedure. This included selection of the jury and the opening statements. I believe I was slated as the third witness on the trial schedule. Following day two of the trial, I received notice to report to Victim Witness the next day. This was sooner than I wanted, though not completely unexpected. I called my sister and friend to give them the news. I was to report to Victim Witness at 11 am. That evening, I went over my notes and reread parts of my book. I was not looking forward to the cross-examination. I didn't know how the False Healer's lawyer received the news of my amended statement. I wondered if it impacted his game plan.

The image of the courthouse played in my mind. I recalled the tour. It was an old building of just two floors. Offices and a security station were located on the first floor. A deep brown wooden staircase led to the second floor where the courtrooms were located. I believe there are two courtrooms on the second floor, though I had only viewed the one. At the top of the winding staircase are washrooms and a staircase landing with direct access to the courtroom. A little more to the right is a small waiting area that leads to a back staircase that acts as an exit for the building. This exit is used only by officers of the court. The staircase landing felt cramped and was not big enough to congregate in. Large wooden double doors open up to the courtroom. When I entered, I noticed that the layout was consistent with how they are portrayed in the movies. There were seats to the right and left, a judge's bench high and to the centre, a jury area to the side and prosecution and defense tables in front of the judge. I noticed immediately the solemnity it conveyed and felt intimidated by the burden that I knew lay ahead. It smelled of polished wood, like an old church. The ceilings were high, and light streamed in through the windows. It was bigger than the courtroom where the preliminary hearing was held. I knew here that there would be no interruptions or schedule delays. It just had that seriousness about it. My case worker showed me where all trial participants would sit. That included the judge, court reporter, prosecutor, defense counsel, the False Healer, security, bailiff, jury, spectators, and, of course, me. I decided to get a view of the courtroom from all angles. First, I sat in the witness stand and then in the jury seats, the prosecutor's seat, the defense counsel and False Healer's seat, the jury's seats, and finally the spectator galley. I asked if any media members would be in attendance. I was told that it's a possibility. This too unnerved me. What would they report? I was reassured that media members were legally required to adhere to the publication ban. As such, my name or anything that could identify me would not be released. The tour was helpful, but, ultimately, I would be alone on the witness stand, and alone I would go to battle.

I texted my friend to let her know that I had been requested to come to the Victim Witness office in the morning. I had asked her months before if she would attend the trial with me. She graciously accepted. She was on standby, waiting for an update. When she got the news, she rearranged her shifts to be there with me. I let her know that it could be two days. The preliminary hearing was difficult on me. I decided afterward that if my case proceeded to trial, I would ask my friend to be with me. She knew me well and could help me focus. We share a deep spiritual connection and have been through a lot together. Hugs and prayers come easy to us. This type of support is not something a case worker, detective, or prosecutor could give to me. My husband would not attend the trial, a choice we had made together early on in the judicial process. My large extended family live in another province, though had I asked, they would have been there.

The day was finally here. I did my usual routine, getting the boys' breakfast and packing their lunch for school. It was a momentous day, and they gave me a big hug before they left and wished me luck. My husband held me for a while and reassured me that I was going to be fine. I stood by the door and waved goodbye to them as they drove away. My eyes welled with tears. It was going to be an emotional day. Looking at the time, I knew I had to hurry to finish getting ready. I told my friend that I would pick her up at 9:30 am. I checked my outfit and double-checked to make sure it was appropriate. I had to feel 100% comfortable with what I was wearing. I could not be distracted. When it was time to leave, I said a prayer. I prayed for guidance, strength, and courage to tell my story. I asked my mom to watch over me and prayed for my angels to protect me. Though it didn't need to be said, I asked God to open my heart to love and compassion. I didn't want hatred to be the basis of my testimony. I walked out my door surrounded by love; it is a powerful feeling.

I arrived at my friend's place on time. She asked me how I was feeling. I told her I was nervous but ready. We drove downtown to the Victim Witness office. We had trouble finding a parking spot and had to park down the street from the courthouse. There was a lot of on-street parking that was closer, but there a two-hour time limit, and parking is regularly enforced in the area. As we walked over to Victim Witness, I noticed that it felt chillier than near my home. The wind blew through my blazer. My friend also wasn't dressed for cooler weather. We did a half-walk, half-run all the way to Victim Witness. We laughed a bit, and it lightened the seriousness of the mood. We arrived at the building and were buzzed into the office. (A buzzer system is a security feature common in this line of work for the protection of the workers and clients.) Upon entering the inner foyer, a case worker greeted us and introduced herself. She was not my regular case worker, and she explained that she would be helping out due to scheduling conflicts. My case worker had part-time hours. I would see her the next day. The new case worker was friendly, and we made small talk easily. She gave me an update on the trial proceedings and informed me that a witness was currently on the stand. When that witness was finished, the prosecutor would drop by to provide an update and that would indicate it was my turn to take the stand. At this time, I would walk over to the courthouse with both the prosecutor and the Victim Witness representative to provide my testimony to the court. For now, all I could do was wait.

The atmosphere at Victim Witness was far different than at the preliminary hearing. The seats were more comfortable, and there was tea, coffee and water available to us. At the preliminary hearing, there were no refreshment areas in the courthouse. If you didn't bring a snack with you, then you wouldn't have it. My friend and I passed the time chatting together and sometimes with the case worker. 11 am came and went. As it approached noon, we got word that the court was going to break for lunch. It was expected that I would begin around 2 pm. I was not happy. I knew this meant I would go into a second day of testimony like in the preliminary hearing. Even though the prosecutor informed us that it could be two days, I had hoped it would be just the one.

My friend and I prepared to leave for lunch. The case worker requested that I report back in an hour. We walked back to the car and drove to a nearby Tim Hortons for lunch. I ate because I knew I had to, but my lunch didn't taste the least bit appetizing. I was quiet and didn't know what to make of my mood. The realization that my testimony was going to carry over to a second day weighed heavily on me. If they needed two full days, it could possibly carry over to my birthday, which was in two days. That would really be disappointing. We got our things together and made our way back to the courthouse.

I remained in contact with my husband and sister via text messaging. It was as long a wait for them as it was for me. Not being there is also hard on the mind, and I know they worried about me. We returned to the Victim Witness office and again got buzzed back in by the case worker. She didn't have any updates, so we sat in the same seats we had occupied earlier. I excused myself to freshen up in the washroom. It was good to get a few moments of quiet. I returned to my seat, and about 45 minutes later the prosecutor appeared. He couldn't tell me anything about the trial other than that things were moving along well. He was there to walk us over to the courthouse.

It was a short walk to the courthouse, maybe two minutes. We talked of nothing in particular, perhaps the weather. The prosecutor led us through security, and we were escorted up the stairs by a uniformed police officer. The prosecutor peeked into the room to see what was happening. The court officer who manned the door directed us to have a seat in the waiting area, but the prosecutor went in. She said she would come get us when the session officially resumed. The three of us: my friend, the case worker and I, sat in a little waiting area. The False Healer's lawyer walked passed us on his way to the courtroom. He entered through the back stairway reserved for officers of the court. The case worker said it was also a back way to their offices and could be used to avoid media if the situation arose. I didn't see the False Healer or his supporters.

In those 10–15 minutes of waiting, my strength began to waver. All of a sudden, I grabbed my friend's hand and told her I needed her energy. We clasped our hands together, and I closed my eyes. I could feel the tears welling up in my eyes, and I was starting to get choked up. My friend talked to me until I calmed down, reassuring me that I was going to do great. "You got this!" she said. In those moments, I didn't feel like I did. I felt overwhelmed with stage fright. I didn't know what to expect with a jury. Would they like me? It took a few minutes, but I finally began to relax. We had a long hug, and I began to feel more like my confident self. It was just in time too, as the court officer returned to escort us into the courtroom.

The three of us walked behind the court officer into the courtroom. She showed my friend where she could sit; it was a front-row seat where she would have direct eye contact with me. The case worker sat next to her. I was escorted behind and around the jury and then up to my seat beside the judge. I glanced quickly at the jury and noticed they were all staring away from me. It felt strange to not make eye contact. I settled into my seat and prepared to be sworn in by another of the court officers. I'm not sure if the judge was in his seat at this time or if he came in afterward. I remember standing at different times throughout my testimony when either the judge or the jury entered or exited the room, but I can't recall that moment. I believe it was because the trial process and seeing the jury overwhelmed me, and I was more focused on remaining calm than on the procedure. I was sworn in, and the prosecutor began his questioning.

As with the preliminary hearing, I cannot provide any details about my testimony. However, there is one thing I would like to share that lifted my heart and cut through the seriousness of the moment. It was a question that lightened my mood. The prosecutor commenced questioning by asking my age. He joked that his mother taught him it was impolite to ask a woman her age, but he was required to ask for the record. Thinking about my own mom brought a smile to my face. I felt that she was with me in that moment. I smiled and said, "I'm 54; I'll be 55 in two days". The unknown suddenly became known, at least in that little moment – and it was enough.

Thereafter, I grew bolder and felt more in control. I knew I was not at the mercy of an unknown situation; I was an active participant. If I wanted my story told, I had to help it along. I had to convey to the jury what it was I wanted them to know. I felt freer to express myself than I did at the preliminary hearing. I knew there were important aspects about my story that only I could share, and I forgot I was nervous at all. Breaking down a long story takes time, and the people gathered in the courtroom were there to hear my telling of it.

I'm not sure what time I started that afternoon, perhaps it was 3 pm, but before I knew it the judge was calling the day to a close. To my dismay, I was not yet finished with the prosecutor's questioning. We were scheduled to resume the next morning. The judge informed me that I was not to discuss my testimony with anyone, and he asked if he could trust me not to do so. "Definitely," I agreed. He smiled. Court was adjourned, and we were free to leave for the day. I was escorted back to the Victim Witness office by the prosecutor and case worker. I had hoped to receive some feedback from the prosecutor regarding my testimony, but I was disappointed to learn that he could not talk to me about anything related to the trial. The same gag order applied to the case worker, though she mentioned to me that I did very well, and so did my friend. I chatted with the case worker for about five minutes before departing. My friend and I walked back to my car. We were not allowed to discuss my testimony. I did my best to focus our conversation on other things, but in my mind I had so many questions for her. A part of me wanted validation that I was doing a good job. I wanted feedback on my answers, much like when I did assignments in school. It felt too big to not talk about it. If ever there was a proverbial elephant in the room, then this was that time. I asked my friend if she planned on attending the next morning; she said she did.

When I got home, the normalness of it didn't fit in with my day. I did my best to let everything go, but then I would fall back into the intense energy of my testimony and get wound up again. It was challenging to keep quiet about the trial. I wanted badly to talk to my husband about my testimony, but there were rules, and, if anything, we follow the rules. So, everything about the day's events played around in my head with no outlet to release my anxiety. My mind strayed to the next day's questioning, especially that of the False Healer's defense counsel. Would he be harder on me this time around? I wondered if my amended statement would impact his defense or if it made any difference at all. I tried to predict his questions, which only led to more anxiety. I was used to prepping for matters that required my input, but in the trial it was all spontaneous. I read through *Heaven's Wait* again to ensure I was aware of potential areas for misinterpretation. In my mind, I wanted to protect my book because I thought the False Healer's lawyer was on track to discredit it and perhaps neutralize its impact. I highlighted areas I thought might require clarification, but the next day I forgot to bring it along.

I woke up early the next day and kept to my usual routine. I readied myself, did a quick meditation and left to pick up my friend. The day was warmer but overcast. I parked in the same spot as the day before. It started to rain on our walk over, and I hadn't brought an umbrella. I put my sweater over my head and made a dash for the door. Fortunately, I didn't get too wet. I was scheduled to resume questioning at 10 am. I think we arrived around 9:30 am. The case worker again walked us over to the courthouse. She wanted me to know that the prosecutor said I had done very well the day before. I laughed. *Now I get the feedback!* When we arrived, we went through security, were escorted upstairs by a uniformed police office and were directed by the court officer to have a seat in the waiting area. She would come get us when it was time. Just like the day before.

I was anxious to begin. I don't believe I saw the prosecutor that morning before seeing him in the courtroom. He resumed questioning close to 10:30 am. It was the same process as the day before, except this time the case worker didn't stay in the courtroom. She returned to the office and said she would check up on me periodically. I again walked to the stand, but this time I took a look at some of the jurors. I was surprised by the jury's diversity, which was reassuring in a way. I sat down and removed my sweater. It was very warm in the courtroom. I adjusted a pin I had attached to my shirt collar. The day before, I had received a surprise package from my sister. It was waiting for me when I got home. There was a note to open the box immediately but to save the card for my birthday, which was in two days. I opened the box, and inside were two items. One was a pin depicting Jesus with outstretched arms and the sacred heart glowing within him, and the other was a medal of Archangel Michael that I could hang on a chain. There was a prayer attached: *Saint Michael the Archangel, defend us in the day of Battle; be our safeguard against the wickedness and snares of the devil. May God rebuke him, we humbly pray, and do Thou, O Prince of the Heavenly Host, by the power of God, cast into hell, Satan and all the other evil spirits, who prowl through the world, seeking the ruin of souls. Amen.* My sister said she had an overwhelming feeling that she needed to send me protection, so she drove to a monastery and selected these two items and had them blessed. I teared up when I read the information card because "going into battle" was exactly what I felt I was doing. The next morning when I got dressed, I attached the pin to my shirt collar and attached the medal to a chain and placed it around my neck. I wore them that day, safe in the knowledge that my family was with me.

The prosecutor resumed his questioning where we had left off the day prior. About a half-hour into my testimony, he asked me a question that sparked deep emotions within me. Once the emotional response started, I couldn't contain it. I bowed my head, hoping my hair would hide the tears. I tried to calm down, but the tears continued to pour out like a dam had burst. The judge quickly called a 15-minute recess to give me time to pull myself together. I stepped away from the witness stand and hugged my friend. While we walked out of the courtroom, her arm was over my shoulder. That was the first time I had displayed such deep emotions throughout the entirety of the judicial process. I usually kept my emotions in check or was able to get myself under control quickly. These were deep tears, flowing out from the depths of my being. When I look back, I feel I had to cry. I had lost a lot through the interaction with the False Healer, and it took me a long time to recover and heal. Add on top of that, with the judicial process and all the stress of testifying not once but twice, it's no wonder I cried. My tears told my story because no words could.

When I returned from the break, my brain was a little foggy. I answered questions but felt a little strange; it was almost like the prosecutor was far away. It wasn't until the judge corrected me on my testimony that I emotionally came back to the room. I straightened in my seat and concentrated on the prosecutor. I forced myself to listen to his every word. I was so intently focused on my testimony that I was surprised when the prosecutor said he had no more questions. *That's it!* I thought. The judge called for a lunch break, and we were dismissed.

My friend and I returned to the Victim Witness office before heading off to lunch. We opted to go to a restaurant this time. It was a birthday lunch, as my birthday was the next day. My body still carried the emotions of that morning, so I was a little quiet. I recall thinking, *Paula, you're halfway through, just a little longer and it will be over.* How many times have we conveyed that very sentiment to ourselves, our children, or our friends? Just a little longer and it will be over. At this point, I still didn't know the power I would exude in my cross-examination. I was still ruminating on potential outcomes. However, deep down, I envisioned success. I had dreams and intuitive thoughts that indicated victory, but the doing still had to happen. Just a little longer and it will be over. There was nothing else I could do but finish what I had started. No one else was going to do it for me; it was my Hero's Journey. We returned for the final showdown. I went to the washroom to freshen up, and one of the False Healer's supporters was in there. At this point, I didn't care who I ran into. I wasn't the one on trial. I returned to my seat and waited to be escorted back into the courtroom.

The trial resumed, and the False Healer's lawyer stood up. For a moment, my stomach did a flip-flop. I can't begin to explain how discomforting a cross-examination is for a witness. Every word can be twisted and turned until you don't recognize your own answers anymore. It didn't help matters that the False Healer's lawyer seemed emotionless. But maybe this made him a good villain and not to be underestimated. Had he been more affable, I could have been lulled into a false sense of security and believed he was looking out for my best interests. I understand that the lawyer was hired to do his job. He was paid by his client to find a way to disprove the charges or discredit the evidence, including my testimony. As a victim, I had a job to do as well. I had taken the extraordinary measure of filing charges against the False Healer because I believed he sexually assaulted me. Within that action is my job to uphold the integrity of the investigation by assisting when I'm asked and maintaining confidential information about the ongoing judicial process. Providing my testimony is all part of that process.

The Defense Counsel's questioning went on for about an hour, and then a break was called. I think as a matter of protocol, the jury receives a 15-minute break in the morning and then again in the afternoon. During the break, I chatted with my friend, and she reassured me I was doing a good job. I mentioned to her that I couldn't quite read the prosecutor's face. I assumed I was doing okay since he didn't interrupt. There was only one time when he objected on my behalf and that was to provide context for one of my answers. After the break, things moved quickly. I really surprised myself. There were a few moments when I absolutely challenged the False Healer's lawyer head-on and would not back down. The judge even sided with me on one point. I knew I was aggravating the lawyer, not with flippant answers but by holding strong to my values and the integrity of my book. I had never known myself to act in that manner, especially in a setting that was so formal. Then again, I had never been put in a position before where I had to defend myself so valiantly. From the start, I felt I was in a battle and there was only one winner and that was going to be me. In the end, the lawyer's questioning ended in a whimper. I couldn't believe it was over! It was uncomfortable for sure but not as bad as I thought it would be. I felt exhilarated and exhausted all at the same time. It's kind of the same feeling you get when you write an exam you're worried about, but then you ace it. I knew I had done well, and it was a powerful feeling. The judge dismissed me, and I was free to go.

When I left the courtroom I was walking on clouds. I gave my friend a big hug and thanked her for her support. We walked together over to Victim Witness and talked about my testimony, as I was free to do so now that my part was finished. The case workers at Victim Witness were overjoyed for me. They had a lot of confidence in my ability, and I was glad I didn't disappoint them. Unfortunately, I didn't get to see the prosecutor before I left, but he left a message for me the next morning, saying that I had done wonderfully. He was still busy with the trial. There were six days remaining on the schedule.

The day was so full of drama that it was nice to be home and in my own comfort zone. I was more exhausted than I thought. Even though I felt the day had been a success, the jury still had to decide on the False Healer's fate. I was finally able to give my husband an update on what had happened throughout the two days of testimony. He was happy for me that it was over. When I woke the next morning, I felt lighter than I had in years. I was happy to celebrate my birthday, especially now that I didn't need to go to the courthouse. A couple weeks earlier, my case worker learned that the trial was scheduled around my birthday, so she made a point of telling the prosecutor to avoid scheduling me on that day. Not that he had control of the schedule or how long everything would take, but in the end it all worked out perfectly. I spent a beautiful and leisurely day shopping, went to a movie, and had dinner with my family. What a great way to end the week.

10

THE VERDICT

In the night, we lose sight
Though at dawn our eyes revel
I can see, I can see
For the cloak of the night
Is removed
And clarity
Is Ours

astly, we stand peering into the long night, the unknown of our journey just out of sight. We feel around for familiar holdings, but alas they exist no more. For the unknown journey formed new footings, new holdings, all the while we battled. Come with me, and I'll show you the myriad ways to the whole that is you.

In the days following my testimony, I awaited word that the trial was finished. The False Healer was the last to give testimony, though I chose not to attend. I didn't want any unnecessary contact with the False Healer. I had no interest in what he had to say because I knew he would not admit to any wrongdoing. I periodically called Victim Witness for updates on the trial schedule. It was all so slow. I was anxious to hear when the jury might be instructed by the judge regarding deliberations. That would mean the end was near.

It was a long process, but I didn't lose hope. Even though the judicial process was crawling at a snail's pace, it was still moving forward. We would have an answer soon. A few days following my testimony, I got the call I was waiting for – the presentation of evidence was finished. We were that much closer to a verdict. However, both sides still had closing arguments. This requires the prosecution and defense to sum up why each believes they should win. My case worker said closing arguments could take another day and then there would be the process of the judge reading instructions to the jury. The Canadian Judicial Council describes jury instructions as "…a script for judges to read when informing juries about the nature of the criminal charges and the issues that are specific to the case." This too would take more time, perhaps two or more hours. It was painful to wait.

Finally, nine days after the trial began, the jury commenced with their deliberations. I think they began after lunch. I'm sure it was as much of a tedious process for them as it was for me. I was instructed to stay in close proximity to the courthouse. I would have about 20 minutes to get to the courthouse when the jury returned with a verdict. I initially informed Victim Witness that I didn't want to attend the reading of the verdict, but I changed my mind after my testimony. I couldn't go through all I had experienced and not be there, especially when everyone had put in so much time and effort towards its end, including the jury. I picked up my boys from school and drove them home. I had intended to stay home, but I was too antsy. What if I couldn't get to the courthouse in time and missed everything! I packed some snacks and drove to the courthouse. I parked close by and waited. I watched a movie I had downloaded on my phone and waited for any information. I was close enough to see that it was quitting time for Victim Witness and the court staff. The vehicles cleared from around the courthouse. My case worker called to say she was heading home and would call me when she heard from the prosecutor. I remained nearby.

I'm glad I have tinted windows in my car so I didn't look suspicious sitting there for hours. I took one break and went to a nearby pharmacy to get some gum and use the restroom. When I returned, I parked even closer to the courthouse, though I couldn't see the main entrance, only the side staff entrance. At around 6:30 pm, I saw a lady enter the side door and wondered if it had anything to do with the verdict. At 7:05 pm, I received a call from my case worker directing me to immediately go to the courthouse. She had just received a call from the prosecutor that the verdict was in. She was on her way back from her home. Things were apparently moving very quickly behind the scenes. I jumped out of my car and ran over to the front entrance, but it was locked. I ran to the side entrance and that was locked as well. I didn't know what to do. I ran back to the front door and repeatedly knocked on the door. A lady finally let me in and told me to hurry upstairs, as the verdict was being read. I rushed up the stairs and lightly knocked on the courtroom door; it was opened by the court officer. "We've been looking for you," she said. I replied, "I've been right outside. The doors were locked." The jury was in the process of reading the charges and the verdicts out loud – Guilty, guilty again, guilty again, on and on. I started to cry. The court officer handed me a box of tissues. It was electric in the room. I didn't look over at the False Healer's supporters. I'm sure they were devastated for their own reasons, though that was not my concern. I could see the side view of the False Healer, and I knew he was stunned. The jurors were dismissed.

The next order of business was quickly rendered. The False Healer's defense counsel argued that he should be free on bail until his sentencing. The judge decided that due to the seriousness of his offences, he would be sent to remand until his sentencing. It was within seconds of this decision that the False Healer was placed into handcuffs in front of me by a uniformed court officer and escorted out of the room. His supporters could not even talk to him at this time. I watched in disbelief as he was escorted away. It all happened really fast. A date was set for a sentencing hearing, and the court was adjourned. The trial was over. The prosecutor came over to me to fill me in on the next steps. He was just so pleased with the verdict and my testimony. He gave me some highlights of the questions he had asked the False Healer during his cross-examination and the False Healer's responses, which the prosecutor easily countered. Still, I'm glad I didn't attend, though it would have been satisfying to see the False Healer on the hot seat.

When the hearing was finished, my case worker arrived. She was sorry she missed everything. Even the prosecutor said he was surprised by how fast the court was called into session. He said he made a plea to the judge that I was on my way, and the judge did pause for a few minutes, but the court officer couldn't locate me. The prosecutor was happy I had made it after all, and so was the judge. He thanked me for my testimony and being there to hear the verdict. We waited a while for the room to clear, but the False Healer's supporters were still milling about on the stairs and outside. They were hoping to talk to the False Healer, but the prosecutor told me the False Healer would not be allowed to speak to anyone until he was processed through the remand system. That could take a few days. The prosecutor and case worker walked me outside. They were being cautious in case any anger erupted from the False Healer's supporters. I thanked the prosecutor for all his hard work, and he humbly replied that he was doing his job. But it meant a lot to me, and I wanted him to know that his work had made a difference in my life. My case worker walked me back to my car. I gave her a big hug. I just couldn't hold back. Before I drove off, I sent a quick text to those waiting to hear – Guilty on all counts!!!

11

THE RECKONING

> Time knows no lies
> It stays in the heart
> What was once pure
> Weakens
> Only the truth
> Restores
> That which was lost

When all was said and done, I thought a giant wave of energy would enfold me, but that was not the case. I was tired from the battle. I finished my project and went into hibernation mode. A sense of soul healing embraced me as I warily gave in to my all my body's demands for rest. My mental, emotional, physical and etheric bodies needed restorative care. I was near the end of my Hero's Journey. I needed to lie down and rest a while before picking up my sword again.

During this time, I simply enjoyed being with my family and

friends. I went to the movies a lot and enjoyed a series on Netflix. I had no other ambition than to meditate, exercise and research new spiritual teachings. Of course, I did all the normal things that come with the love and keeping of a family, but I had no outside intrusions. It was just me figuring things out.

In Joseph Campbell's *The Hero with a Thousand Faces,* this part of the Hero's Journey is referred to as "Atonement" or looking backwards to who you used to be. It is the penultimate piece of the hero's return. In my case, I was readying myself to write my victim impact statement. But that was only one part of a process that combined atonement and transformation in preparing me for the way of the soul. The trial transformed who I thought I was and the strengths I carried. But the deeper, more profound transformation came a few months later.

First, I had to write the victim impact statement. I was not legally required to do so, but it would help provide the judge with insight into how the False Healer's actions impacted me physically, emotionally, financially, and any other way I wanted to express. It took me a couple of days to get in the mood to complete the questionnaire. I downloaded the Victim Impact Statement Form off the website and began writing my submission. Although the sentencing date was still three months away, I wanted to submit the victim impact statement early so it wouldn't be on my mind. As I expected, it came easily to me.

When put altogether, my answers fit into a page and a half. Each question had its own box in which to provide an answer. I believe the box increased in length if needed. I stayed within a reasonable word count and felt I could convey my meaning within the space provided. Not that it was easy, but it was necessary. It was also my chance to speak without censure. The False Healer was found guilty as charged, so he was no longer the alleged offender. In turn, I was no longer the alleged victim – I was the victim.

I sent the draft of the victim impact statement to my sister to review. I wanted to ensure I didn't come across as whiny or bitter. She said I had conveyed my feelings well. However, I did some minor tweaking before sending it to my case worker. I removed an end section that is usually set aside for poetry, drawings, etc. When I reflected further on the content I had removed, I thought it was judgemental. It is my belief that it is not my place to cast judgement upon another. We walk this life without knowledge of our purpose nor our true beauty and light. But when we do come into this knowledge, it is incumbent upon us to open the door for others.

When the victim impact statement was finished and submitted to my case worker, I felt so much relief. The sentencing was in three months. In between the time when I wrote the victim impact statement and when it was read aloud in court, I disconnected from the judicial process. I also chose not to attend the sentencing hearing. I was already scheduled at that time to travel with my family to my First Nation community for summer vacation. Plus, I didn't want the expense of rescheduling our flights. I informed my case worker of my wishes to disconnect. She understood my position and was happy that I had agreed to submit a victim impact statement to help the judge in his sentencing. She agreed to keep me posted on the day of sentencing.

I started looking at my life and thinking, *What's next?* The judicial process had preoccupied my mind for three years, and now that I was free of its entanglement, I didn't quite know what to do with myself. The only thing I knew for sure was that a new door was opening up for me. That was the ongoing message in meditation after meditation. But knowing that a door is opening up for me and knowing what it is are two totally different things. I had to trust that it was all in divine order, though sometimes a little peek would have been nice.

This is where "atonement", which I touched on earlier, came in. In a Wikipedia overview of Joseph Campbell's Hero's Journey, atonement is described in this way: "In this step the hero must confront and be initiated by whatever holds the ultimate power in his life. In many myths and stories this is the father, or a father figure who has life and death power." Another definition is described in an article written by

Tamara McCleary, The Hero's Journey: Atonement, November 16, 2014. She writes, "There are two great dictionary definitions that I believe are symbolic of this step: 1) satisfaction, reparation, or expiation given for an injury or wrong and, 2) the state in which the attributes of God are exemplified in man." It is the latter that is of interest to me.

To me, the state in which the attributes of God are exemplified in man is the way of the soul. What are these attributes of God? They are Joy, Oneness, Peace and Belonging. Through aligning with each of the Soul Virtues: altruism, right action, clarity, humility, love, happiness for others and temperance, we are able to express our divine truth. Joseph Campbell writes, "…The problem of the hero going to meet the father is to open his soul beyond terror to such a degree that he will be ripe to understand how the sickening and insane tragedies of the vast and ruthless cosmos are completely validated in the majesty of Being. The hero transcends life with its peculiar blind spot and for a moment rises to a glimpse of the source. He beholds the face of the father; understands – and the two are atoned."

The separation from God we experience when we walk the earth plane is thereby healed. As I mentioned earlier, without challenges and trauma, the element of fear is not triggered. And without fear, there can be no experience of separation. Separation is only a feeling. It is not that God has let us go; it is us who let God go. Why did we do this? In my soul reading, this was the answer I was provided with: "You came to experience separation so that you could eventually become a healing remedy to that very state of separation that you knew many would be engulfed in in these times…you immersed yourself in worlds where you would 'contract' feelings of separation from them. Like the chicken pox…you came to in a similar vein contact a kind of 'separation pox' so that eventually you could learn how to heal and remedy it."

There is important information I want to share. It is derived from a channel in a Kryon series by Leo Carroll. Carroll is an American channeller, speaker and author. He has written 13 books on channelling from an entity he calls "Kryon." His former profession is as an award-winning audio engineer. He started channelling more than 30 years ago. In this particular channel, "Kryon" provides information regarding the difference between the Higher self and the Soul. Kryon also describes the attributes of the soul: Joy, Oneness, Peace, and Belonging. This series can be found at www.kryon.com. It is titled "Live Kryon Channelling, Basel Switzerland, September 6, 2014." Due to copyright law, I will provide only a brief educational note on each description.

Higher self: "Is like the 'soup of God' that has your name on it. It is part of your Akash (record of your soul's journey). It is you, the part of God that is you, walking on the planet. Each time you incarnate it is the same Higher self that comes with you. It's been with you all your lifetimes. When you are NOT on planet Earth, the Higher self is not present."

Soul: "The soul is the spark of God. It is forever, and it doesn't have your Akash within it. Instead, it has the imprint of the Creator, and it is all that is. The soul is not that which communicates with you with words or thoughts or gives you intuition. It's more than that. It's not on the other side of the veil either. It's with you…it's the beauty of you; the magnificence of all things."

Kryon describes four attributes that he wants us to start practice feeling in meditation. Kryon says, "Every moment you spend in this kind of communication, changes you." We are meeting our soul.

Joy: "The Creator has a smiling face all the time…you do not need to suffer to get God's attention…do not apply the attributes of humanism to the Almighty…Your soul is the essence of God…Your soul is overflowing with joy."

Oneness: "Oneness in All Things…All creation has the source of God and you have the ability to become one with it all. It is a state of being…you can feel it. It helps you relate to God with the others like you."

Peace: "Complete peace…This is not partial peace, not peace just for you, or for now, but complete, eternal peace. It's the peace that surpasses all understanding, for there is no logical reason for it."

Belonging: "…You are not alone…This belonging is forever and absolute. You can't hide from it, and you always have it. Because you are a piece of the Creative source called God, that means you are never apart from it…"

These attributes are what I began tapping into during meditation. I knew something in my meditations had shifted, but it was just a feeling. And that is the most important element – feeling! I was beginning to sense in a new way the love and joy that was pulsating through my energy field. I wanted to stay there and not return. After one particularly powerful meditation, I felt like I could actually see my husband's heart beating, and I couldn't get close enough to the energy he was radiating. It is funny, but I said to him that I wanted to crawl inside his heart because I could so strongly feel the love of God radiating from him and connecting with mine. I was supercharged and wanted to live in that energy…I know that I do, just not at that intensity every moment. If I did, I would only want to go around and tell people how much I love them and feel them; surely they would get creeped out. All of this happened before I came across the Kryon channelling I shared with you; the channelling helped validate what I had experienced.

When this new meditation shift started happening to me, it was not long after that the vision for this book and the feeling of it appeared. I mentioned to my husband that I had a vision about my work and that I planned on starting a new book the next day. Spirit, however, was having none of that. I went out onto my deck to enjoy a cup of tea when a feeling that I had to 'start now' washed over me. It was 8 pm; I was planning on relaxing the rest of the evening. However, the feelings were too strong. I got out my laptop and started to write. The first thing I was given was the poem at the beginning of the book. I read it to my husband, and he asked, "Did you just write it". "Yes," I said, "it flowed right into me". "It's good," he said.

I'm getting ahead of myself here. Let's go back to the False Healer.

THE FALSE HEALER: A TRILOGY

From the time the False Healer was convicted and the sentencing occurred, three months had passed. I mentioned that I was in a time of quiet. I understood deeply that renewal was taking place. Every part of me rallied for my transformation, but I had one more hurdle: the sentencing.

I knew it was going to be a challenging day, so I made a plan. I asked my sister if she would have a party. I was going to arrive home in the early hours of the day when the sentencing was scheduled to occur. My flight into Halifax didn't arrive until 9 pm. By the time we got a rental car and drove to my First Nation community, it was 2:30 am. That day, my sister and I cooked and prepped for the party. My whole family was invited, and it was going to be a big gathering. They had no idea why I wanted the party, only that an announcement would be made. Fortunately, it was also a couple of days before my brother and sister-in-law's wedding anniversary, so we had a double reason for the gathering. Before that time, only a couple of family members were aware of the charges and the judicial process. I kept it very quiet. Doing so helped me focus on what needed to be done. It was my burden to carry, and it made no sense to me to lay my troubles on others who were also experiencing tremendous stress in their lives.

Throughout the day, I was in constant contact with my case worker at Victim Witness. I thought it would have been finished that morning, but it rolled into the afternoon hours. Plus, my First Nation community is in the Maritimes, which is an hour ahead of the Victim Witness office, so it felt even later. I remember being in the grocery store with my husband when I got the call. I quickly answered the phone, and the case worker said it was over. She told me all about the sentencing hearing and the judge's decision. I was elated. The False Healer was sentenced to a few years in a federal penitentiary (I don't believe I can report the exact amount of time here). To me, it was enough. It was my feeling that had the sentence been harsher, the False Healer may have been inclined to appeal the sentence and it would have dragged on even longer. I could now officially put everything behind me.

The detective called to congratulate me, just as he did when the trial ended. Our conversation was bittersweet. The sentencing marked the last of our official business. He had walked me through one of the most challenging times of my life and I was grateful for his kindness and professionalism. I wished him well and jokingly said, I'll write a book about the trial someday! He said, "Make me six feet tall and 200 pounds." We both laughed.

My family started to arrive. I was so happy to see everyone. I sometimes forget just how big my family is, but it was great. The food was delicious. Following the big and crazy dinner, my sister presented the family with a cake…it had our family name on it. But first she said, "We have a couple of announcements." The family gave a surprise gift to my brother and his wife for their wedding anniversary. They were overjoyed. Then, I made my announcement. I was holding my three-month-old great nephew at the time. As I recounted the details of the past three years, I knew it surprised everybody. At first, they were all a little sad because my family hurt for me. But after many hugs, the laughter and love flowed freely again. Though I don't eat many sugary treats, that cake tasted heavenly. We all took a family photo afterwards. The once-threatening day turned into a beautiful memory. Thank you, my family. I love you all.

12

THE FALSE HEALER

> Cowering in darkness
> The light cannot attend
> Release your soul
> To heavenly delights
> Free yourself of that
> Which darkness claims
> You are the light
> With the Almighty's sight

I will begin this chapter with an excerpt from the "Kryon" channel discussed in Chapter Nine, Live Kryon Channelling, Basel Switzerland, September 6, 2014 at www.kryon.com. In this channel, Kryon explains a healer in this way:

"Healers don't heal, they balance. No human being can force healing on another. However, most patients are asking for balance so they can heal themselves with the assistance of the balancing healer. True healing requires this cooperative process."

At no time was I given the opportunity to cooperate on my so called 'healing journey' with the False Healer. I was told what was going to happen, and if I didn't agree then bad things and even death could supposedly happen to me. That is why this person is called the False Healer.

Kryon also states that, "A healer can balance to help clear the way within your thinking process. This clearing may help you make a decision, enabling you to move to a different level of understanding. It is healing the mind." Unfortunately, this balancing didn't happen with me either. The False Healer's only objective was seemingly to keep me in a place of fear, where I would be subjected to his healing whims and rituals.

I know there are healers out there that do great work. They often work as part of an integrated health network because they understand that it takes all kinds of interventions and skills to bring a person to wholeness. I know of one healer who doesn't even meet with women alone. He feels that since he isn't a woman, he cannot possibly know what a woman is feeling, and his wife works with him in these cases. But the False Healer had no such code of ethics. His development was likely encumbered by his past, and if that is the case, he should never have put himself out there as a healer of anything or anyone.

It takes great strength to come to wholeness. The highest teaching of the Creator is *not to do harm unto others*. But the healer had it in his mind that I had to pay as a way to atone for my sins. Today, I know differently. We can heal ourselves in a loving and sacred manner. God helps us see ourselves as our true divine creation. In doing so, we mirror God's attributes, and we are atoned. Doesn't "atoned" sound a lot like "attuned"?

Through our souls, we are emitting God's frequency. As Kryon explains, our soul has the "imprint of the Creator", and it is "all that is." The soul is the conduit for Divine Intelligence. Our soul feels and helps us feel the attributes of the Creator: joy, oneness, peace and belonging. Through the soul, our higher self is activated to express

God's attributes in ways that are unique to your person. This expression could come in the form of writing, painting, drawing, architecture, speaking, or anything else in which creativity is activated. The higher self assists this well-spring of Divine Intelligence being brought in through the soul by activating skills from your previous lifetimes (Akash) to help you manifest that which is divinely guided. You step in to all this activity through your intuition. Your intuition should be sharpened by a steady meditation practice or spiritual practice of some manner. It all comes together with you taking the right action and manifesting, for example, by writing a book. So, to summarize, we must bring into our awareness the following: 1) Divine Intelligence, 2) Soul, 3) Higher self, 4) Akash, 5) Intuition, and 6) Manifestation (Right Action). If you didn't follow this, go back to the start of this paragraph and review again.

When this flow isn't working properly, it is because the process has been stymied in some way along its path. That is when self-reflection and examining your intention is necessary. It's like when your car is not running properly; sometimes a look under the hood can reveal an issue. So too is the case with self-reflection. Maybe it's the ego wanting to control the situation or resist stepping into the unknown. We get very comfortable in our own little spaces, so we often resist change or prompting from our higher self. So, be honest with yourself. What's stopping you from walking the way of the soul?

I'm not a psychologist, but I believe the False Healer was stuck in his ego. Instead of reading that which was of the soul, he got stuck on information of his own design. That information could have been taught to him by a supposed mentor, from books he read, or even by cultural practices he didn't fully understand or adhere to. It also could have come from his own desire to feel power over those he deemed less initiated in spiritual matters. Finally, we cannot take free will or choice out of consideration. He simply could have chose to disregard the soul for his own ends.

For whatever reason or reasons, the False Healer himself was not a balanced person, and thus he could not teach about balance. Our energy is always talking to the energy of another. When you yourself are balanced, someone could be speaking to you and saying all the right things, but your senses are telling you differently. In these instances, we may feel that caution is necessary or question their motives. In contrast, when we're out of balance, the energy is like muddy water and our senses are not able to filter the energy quickly enough to receive the messages. It's like trying to see, hear or feel through a muddy film. When this happens, our choices do not reflect our souls. We have, by choice, decided to walk alone.

This is when our journey or our path gets all crazy. If we could map it, we would see the many unnecessary excursions we take. Perhaps our journey loops around and goes in many different directions before it makes its way back to the path, only to do the same thing over again. After a time, if we don't begin to recognize the crazy patterns we're generating, a higher perspective may be necessary to get us back on track. It is different for each of us. It may require taking us to our lowest low to show us this isn't the way. Then, when we're placed back on our path, it is our duty to cleanse and rid ourselves of all that blocks our internal compass. Study, pray, meditate, and learn more about the ways of the soul. Finally, don't be lazy. There are no quick fixes or one method to use to fix everything. Our wholeness depends on us cleansing all our bodies: the physical, emotional, mental and ethereal (spiritual). This will look different for each of us. For me, my physical body aligned by eliminating many foods/drinks from my diet and physically pushing my body to become stronger and more flexible. I learned how to do things like the Lifted Lotus and Full Splits, something I had never thought possible at my age. The emotional body requires constant cleansing. For me, the trial and writing about my experiences helped facilitate great emotional release. However, each day requires the cutting of cords to emotional experiences. This I do every evening through visualization. Our emotions can hold us hostage when we allow them to fully gestate within our body. You know what I mean by gestate...fester and grow. By cutting the cords, we release the emotional energy of the day so we can greet the next day with a clean slate. The mental body likes control, so discipline is necessary. The mental body will tell you all kinds of things to maintain the status quo or keep things just as they are. Why does it do this? It does this because change is difficult, and it has worked in the past. I relayed to you earlier in this book about my temptation to drop the charges against the False Healer because I was afraid of the unknown. I didn't want to face a trial because I couldn't control the process or its outcome. I forced myself to take each step as it came, regardless of what my mind was telling me. I learned through meditation how to push aside the mental chatter that kept trying to tell me "it wasn't worth it" to go to trial or that I wasn't "worthy" of a 10-day trial. The etheric body comes into alignment when the three other bodies (physical, emotional, and mental) succumb to the spiritual call of the soul. The etheric body is constantly whispering its needs to you through intuition, dreams, visions, insights, etc. It is our spiritual soul song to answer this call to ascend. The etheric or spiritual body glows brighter with each soul missive to ascend. *Higher, higher,* the soul sings...*you are worthy.*

You might say that it sounds all too overwhelming, and it can be if you're only fixated on the work. It's the same as walking into a messy kitchen after a big party. It looks chaotic and you can't see your beautiful kitchen in all the mess. You might first start collecting garbage that was strewn about and left behind by the countless people in your kitchen. Then, you might look at what can be salvaged and used again for another time. Then, you might wash the dishes and put them away in the proper space. Then, you might wash all the counters and appliances until they sparkle. Then, you might sweep and then finally wash the floor. You see, you didn't immediately move from chaos into a sparkling clean kitchen – there were many steps in between. So too it is with healing.

My healing journey began in Divine right time. Through my

intention to know why, I was put on a path of discovery. In this discovery, I cleansed myself. It was a slow process, just like cleaning the kitchen. This is a simple truth I learned. Our discovery is one in which each new spiritual truth feels like you've reached the pinnacle and you are content; then, you are shown another, then another, then another and so on. But in each moment is a feeling of contentment that you have discovered the truth. This helps you stay in the game. I am still playing the game and will until the time I leave this planet. That is the beauty of illumination.

That is why I feel compassion for the False Healer. Passion is when you feel that which is of the Creator: joy, oneness, peace, and belonging. Compassion is when you share your passion with another who lacks it. It is the way of the soul to help others ascend.

It took a long time for me to embrace this teaching. I truly wanted to hate the False Healer, but every time I tried, I would picture God. I came to realize that by hating the False Healer, I was walking on dangerous ground. If I couldn't consciously separate the actions of the human from the God within, then hatred would fill my life and no God would exist for me. I would not only hate the False Healer; I would hate all of humankind because we are all the same energy of God. So, yes, I loathed the actions of the False Healer, but I couldn't hate the False Healer because he is and always will be the energy of God.

I wish I could give you some satisfaction by saying that it's okay to hate, but that is not the way of the soul. We must walk this life in the knowledge that many people live in muddied waters, some more so than others. We should not drink of this water nor swim in it. Often times, we are warned of "hazards" by our intuition, yet we sometimes fail to respond and enter at our own peril. But, like anything, the muddied waters can be filtered and cleansed with intent. If we send only negative energy to the person that harmed us, the chance of their ascension is reduced. Staying neutral is also not an option, for it doesn't help anyone but ourselves. So, we must trust our benevolent source and mirror attributes that help, not impede. This may entail humility on our part. "Humility" is one of the Seven Soul Virtues. Its meaning is a modest or low view of one's own importance – humbleness. It is right to send the False Healer prayers of healing. The ascension of mankind is greater than my feelings of hurt. To walk the way of the soul is to help others ascend.

13

THE TRUTH

We walk the path
Of Enlightenment
It twists, it turns
It forces our hand
Yee who know
Will understand
The beauty of its demand

*F*or a moment, stand still and sway with the trees. Plant your feet firmly and allow yourself to move in a gentle manner, back and forth. Close your eyes and feel the energy you share with the trees. The movement of Gaia's breath is felt by all. It is truly a magical force.

These little truths or revelations are what the hero shares on their "Return." Joseph Campbell writes that the "Return" is the last component of the Hero's Journey. Though I only list nine labels in this book, Campbell refers to a total of 17 in his work *The Hero with a Thousand*

Faces. He also accounts for when the hero refuses the "Call to Adventure" or the "Call to Return."

Joseph Campbell writes that, "Refusal of the summons converts the adventure into its negative. Walled in boredom, hard work, or 'culture,' the subject loses the power of significant affirmative action and becomes a victim to be saved...his life feels meaningless." For whatever reason, when a person refuses the call to adventure, their growth is stunted. Sometimes they fear the unknown, or they don't feel they have what it takes, or they even feel they have too much on their plate. Whatever the reason, some know what they're doing, and others don't. We must always be mindful of our intuitive promptings.

Campbell also notes that some heroes refuse the call to return. Wikipedia says, "Having found bliss and enlightenment in the other world, the hero may not want to return to the ordinary world to bestow the boon on his fellow man." The boon is "the ultimate achievement of the goal of the quest. It is what the hero went on the journey to get."

In regard to the "Return," Joseph Campbell writes that, "...the hero shall now begin the labor of bringing the runes of wisdom, the Golden Fleece, or his sleeping princess, back into the kingdom of humanity, where the boon may redound to the renewing of the community, the nation, the planet or the ten thousand worlds." Wikipedia sums up the return in this manner: "The trick in returning is to retain the wisdom gained on the quest, to integrate that wisdom in a human life, and then maybe figure how to share the wisdom with the rest of the world."

This book is my boon. It contains all the trials and tribulations of my nine-year entanglement with the False Healer. Though I wanted to close the chapter on this experience, the transformative nature of my experience needed to be shared so others who embark on their own journey will have a guidebook of sorts. Even if I had read Joseph Campbell's book prior to this experience, I would not have put two and two together. It wasn't in my mindset that I was being called to adventure; my only awareness was the intuitive prompting I received to move forward with the criminal charges. I would never have thought, *Oh wow, I'm starting my Hero's Journey!* However, it now helps to use that terminology.

For many, they don't put their experiences in this context. Perhaps if they did it would help with their healing process. They could see the points at which they made decisions and how these decisions impacted their journey. For those still in the struggle, perhaps they will be able to evaluate what the experience has brought to them, a why of sorts, that will allow them to harvest only the good fruit of the vine and leave the rest. In doing so, they will be able to help others recognize the difference between the good fruit and the bad fruit and when it is time to harvest. We are all in need of perspective. That is why the Hero's Journey is in all of us. Think about yours…what is your story?

1) Call to Adventure (there has to be a reason for the journey)
2) Supernatural Aid
3) Threshold (the threshold across to the unknown)
4) Gather Helpers (you don't do this alone)
5) Challenges and Temptations
6) Revelation (that which is going to change your life)
7) Transformation (you come through the challenge and you are transformed)
8) Atonement (looking backward to who you used to be)
9) The Return

The one thing I recognize and stick to is that I cannot change the past; nor do I linger in it any longer. It serves no purpose but to inflame negative emotions. The new now is happening with every breath I take. I don't want to miss a moment of it by looking back to a time…that had its time.

14

THE END

We all must go
It is the nature of things
When we anticipate
We participate
Not long from now
Your dreams will reveal
Freedom unsealed

Yes, this book is a very simplified version of the Hero's Journey described in Joseph Campbell's *The Hero with a Thousand Faces*, but my story is simple. There are no hidden truths, only the reality of the experience. Each one of us is capable of great things and even greater feats of strength. It is you who carries this magic; you were born with it embedded in your DNA. I represent only one journey among many. I walked my journey and express to you its transformative effects. I carry these with me now; I am emboldened by their presence. I yearn to learn more because truth is eternal and for as long as I am, truth will unfold.

The end of my journey marked the beginning of a new story, one that is yet to unfold. But for now, my recent story had to be told, inscribed. In doing so, I leave a legacy of wholeness. Wholeness is described in my Soul Reading as follows: "...the more you can weave and make room for the shadow <u>and</u> the light to be part of One and the Same Whole in YOU...the more you will help to weave and make room for the shadow and the light to be part of One and the Same Whole <u>in others</u>. Others will be able to attune to seeing that you have more successfully created a Home Space for the <u>All of it</u> inside you... so that they will began to glimpse the pathway ahead for themselves to do the same."

The Soul Reading continued, "This is a very powerful medicine... this is **Wholeness Medicine**. And you are divinely designed to be a living Teacher and Expression of this Soul Awareness in form."

Wholeness Medicine...that is the purpose of this book! By making a home for the good and not so good to live harmoniously, we create balance and wholeness in our lives.

I'm with you always in Joy, Oneness, Peace, and Belonging.

Thank you for walking this journey with me.
Paula
Light from Creator

II

HEAVEN'S WAIT (2014)

In November 2010, Paula Sevestre was approached by a traditional Aboriginal healer who said he had a message for her. This encounter would lead her down a path of fear, manipulation and warped spiritual guidance. It chronicles Paula's life journey as an Aboriginal growing up on a Canadian reserve mired in poverty and family violence while being deeply rooted in the Catholic Faith. It describes how she reconciled her guilt and shame for all she had done and how she overcame an introduction to spirituality based on fear and the punitive. Finally, it provides a narrative of Paula's own spiritual development, including the loving guidance and intuitive messages she received from Spirit and the ultimate triumph of healing, love and forgiveness.

"He (the healer) said he had a dream, a vision, and it wasn't good. It concerned our boys. He said he saw a white work van with dark windows and somebody grabbing and kidnapping my boys..."

PREFACE

I don't know when it started, but early in my life, I was able to project what other people saw in me. This would have both negative and positive implications. I didn't realize it at the time, but this would shape my entire life. It wasn't easy. If anything it was tiring always molding and shaping the person inside me. I was always told I got along well with others and that I communicated effectively; however, much of that communication was one way. I sensed what would make an individual responsive to me, and I became that person.

Manipulation is an art form. It can be used for both good and bad. If you are equally challenged to overcome this lesson in your lifetime, it is much more exaggerated. You will be presented lesson after lesson until you recognize that which you have come to this earth plane to learn. Only then will you be able to take the necessary steps to lessen the effects on your life. It becomes important to understand your life's purpose and seek ways in which to rein in the negative aspects of that life lesson—to begin to build upon only that which is positive to prevent further lessons from creating obstacles to your development.

INTRODUCTION

It was Tuesday, April 15, 2014, and I was standing at the kitchen sink washing up the breakfast dishes. My mind was lost in thought with the upcoming long-awaited family vacation, which included my friend and her two girls. It was three weeks away. What made the wait even more difficult was the snow that developed during the night. Spring was put on the back burner for this day. I could sense the energy around me, guiding through my hair. I was trying to shake it off until I finished my housework, but they were insistent. Finally there was a thunderous boom in the house, almost like a summer's rainstorm. I opened the kitchen door and asked my husband, who was changing his tire, if he heard the sound too. He didn't—not a thing. I closed the door and pondered whether the noise could have been something else. In my heart I knew it wasn't ... I thought, *I had better meditate.*

My name is Paula Sevestre. I was born on a small First Nation community in Cape Breton, Nova Scotia. For those unfamiliar with the term *First Nation*, it is reserve land that has been set aside by the federal government of Canada for the exclusive use of registered Indians in Canada. There are 634 First Nations in Canada consisting

INTRODUCTION

of many different nations and tribes. I am Mi'kmaq. I have been married to my husband, Mark, for twenty years, and have twin boys Nathaniel and Bradley. We currently reside in southern Ontario. My husband is Mohawk.

I would be turning fifty soon, and that was the reason for our upcoming family vacation. My spiritual journey began three years earlier, and we had not traveled for leisure in that three-year time period. I had traveled to Cape Breton to assist with my ailing mother's care but not travel that would be considered vacation travel. All this was set aside as I made my way through an often-challenging spiritual journey. I am currently a consultant, and I have completed contract work of varying degrees over the past fifteen years. I work hard and enjoy research. I credit this love of research for saving my life, my very existence, from something that could have destroyed my life, my marriage, and my belief in God.

1

OUR FIRST MEETING

I was raised Catholic but floated in and out of regular practice. I was continually struck by the notion of time. I would see others around me checking the time; is it time to leave, time to get on with my day, time to have a drink, time to eat, time to get out! Unfortunately, I understood this because I was that way too. I wanted to believe I was spiritual, I was one with God, but it had a time limit. I didn't want it to interrupt my life; I had important things to do!

Then, seemingly out of the blue, on November 22, 2010, time seemed to stand still. There was no big accident, no big, life-altering event, just manipulation coming back to take a great big chunk out of my backside. When they say, "What goes around comes around," you better believe it!

I went to work like any other Monday morning. We had a few beers the day before, so I was feeling tired, but I had a full schedule that day and got straight to work. I was planning to host some workshops later that month, and I still had a lot of tasks to complete. I really didn't feel like socializing and stayed in my office to eat my lunch. However, I was called to join someone else; reluctantly I went.

That was the day I encountered an individual who called himself a traditional healer. He had a message for me.

Aboriginal traditional healers were not common in the community in which I was raised; the only thing I knew about traditional healers is what I may have read in books. I may have been aware of some medicine people in our nation, but we were firmly entrenched in Western medicine and the Christian faith. So I was definitely unnerved when this person said that he had a message for me—especially from someone I thought had supernatural powers!

My own family members have experienced spiritual happenings, so I was not unfamiliar with the concept of the spiritual realm, including visions, apparitions, and communications with spirit, but that was them, not me!

This healer was my age. His message was that if I went home to see my mother in December, my family would not let me leave because they did not want the responsibility of looking after her. He said my siblings would abandon me and I would be forced to stay there and would eventually be driven to a mental breakdown from which I would never recover.

This sounds crazy, right? Because it is crazy!

My family is very loving, and there was no reason whatsoever to believe any of this, but I did! I asked him what I could do to prevent this from happening. He said I would need to come for a reading at his place. We scheduled one for 5:00 p.m. that evening. He said it was urgent. I remember the day like it was just happening.

I arrived at his little place behind his homestead. It was raining. I was feeling a little nervous, but I made sure to let my husband know where I was going. The one twelve-by-twelve room was small and smoky, with the smell of white sage. There was one window open, but it was still very dense with smoke. I went in and sat down. There were only two chairs at the small table. He asked me if I was there out of my own free will. I said yes. He asked me to put my hand in some tobacco and hold it for a few seconds. He then touched the tobacco where I had held it and began to communicate with someone he said was my spirit guide.

He said my spirit guide was very upset with me and that it had been trying to get my attention for a long time but that I would not listen. I began to shake at this time. He said that I had a lot to make up for and that I would need to change my life—that I would not even look like the same person when I was finished with this work. He said that I looked like a clown with the makeup I wore and that my hair should not have the blond highlights that it currently had. He said the spirit guide showed him an image of when I was a child, and I looked nothing like I should look as a native person. (I am considered attractive and I wore the proper amount of makeup and highlighted my hair, but in no way did I think this would be a concern to my guide.)

He then said I had lived my life for myself long enough and that my boys, who were seven at the time, needed to learn their path in the traditional way. They would need to learn how to survive without modern conveniences and understand plants and medicines. I too would need to learn plants and traditional medicine and ceremonies. I was to reinvent myself into a person people could easily connect with and not have my image getting in the way. I would walk this earth in moccasins, close to Mother Earth.

He said if I didn't change my ways that he saw my death; I would be full of cancer. It would be in places around my body that he said I used to manipulate people but first I would be viciously gang raped by people who were watching me. It would be so savage that they would leave my face beaten to a point that I would be unrecognizable.

In this time too, I was directed to quit drinking. It had to be my free will to do so. I had to make a promise to the Creator that I would quit drinking. I was told to go home and empty any remaining alcohol into the earth at the end of my property. I was not to have any alcohol cross my doorway again. At this time I lived in the city of Brantford, Ontario. He also suggested that negative spirits were around me and my family and that we would need to protect ourselves. This scared me in ways one can only imagine. Images from movies like *The Exor-*

cist, *The Shining*, and *The Amityville Horror* filled my head. By the time I got home, I was beginning to feel afraid of the dark.

The first reading went on for over an hour. It rained hard the entire time. I got home and emptied all the alcohol that was in the house. I told my husband what had happened and that I was going to quit drinking. My husband was not so sure of the whole thing and did not want me to make any snap decisions. He didn't feel we drank in an out-of-control manner or that we neglected our sons in any way. We were quite happy and lived our lives quietly. We were both in our forties and had children late in our lives, so we were both very content with being homebodies. We were both busy and enjoyed our work.

I think, too, that things would have remained the same was it not for another message I had to see the healer; it was urgent, and it involved my husband. My husband had just left for a trip to Ottawa that day. I was still thinking about the reading, but it didn't have as much impact on me, and I was not as frightened as when I first met with the healer. I was willing to let it go—to continue on with my life.

I went to see the healer again after work; I was frightened beyond belief. I sat down, and he asked for my wedding ring. I gave it to him, and he held it while he did the reading.

He said that he was shown a vision of how Mark, my husband, would die. He said that if Mark prevented me from taking the steps necessary for my healing, that spirit would not allow him to stand in my way. He could not interfere with my path. He would be in a car crash with some friends, and he would not be found for a long period of time. In that time, he would suffer terribly before he died. He said that something sharp would pierce Mark's chest during the car accident, and it would be a while before he died. He would be calling out to the Creator for help, and he would be made to see the error in his ways. I started crying. How could I stop this? I didn't care about my own damnation, but Mark didn't harm anyone!

I was told that I would need to commit to a year's healing and that it involved a tremendous amount of work from both me and my husband. It was my responsibility to bring my husband on board with the healing process. We had to walk this journey together but could not interfere with the other's path. It would be easier for us if we were both committed to the healing process. Mark could not drink any alcohol, especially in our home. We had to sacrifice to save our own lives and the future of our children. The healing process had to start immediately. I left the small cabin and drove home in tears.

I called Mark and asked him to come home; he would need to leave his meeting early. He said he would be home as soon as possible and promised not to have any alcohol at the event in Ottawa. When he arrived home, I was prepared with my argument. I was ready to convince him to start the healing journey with me. We lay in bed together as I walked him through the reading. He was shocked. You have to understand that Mark is very pragmatic. This did not make sense to him, and it was a lot to absorb. However, I was insistent that we not put our kids in any jeopardy and that he had to know I would move forward on this healing journey alone if it meant that the he and the boys would be safe. I couldn't allow him or the boys to suffer any punishment because of my sins. He reluctantly agreed to a reading with the healer.

I basically forced his hand. If Mark didn't go to the healer, our marriage would be over. I was willing to destroy our family because of fear. Everything I put trust in was turned upside down. I didn't have a strong foothold on any one spiritual path, so I was easily influenced. I was so frightened at this time that I was scared to even take the garbage out to the bins in the laneway. I was scared of the dark, of negative spirits and entities that could invade our home. I was told that demons were everywhere and that I had to be prepared to encounter them when the time was right. If there was any fear in me, they would take advantage of this fact. I was told of all the people who used bad medicine in the community to win at gambling, sports, and competitions, to get lovers, for vindication, and the list goes on. But he was good. His duty was to help people afflicted by bad medicine and negative spirits. Everything the healer directed me to do, I did.

That first week was surreal. I tried to do my work and not think about everything. I didn't have my usual support because the healer warned me against talking to anyone about the healing process. I had Mark, but I couldn't express any doubts with him as it would weaken his reluctant acceptance to move forward with the healing. I began to feel awkward with the way I looked. I dyed my hair to its normal color of brown. I didn't want to dress in my usual business manner. I slowly started eliminating makeup from my morning routine. I didn't trust anyone at work because I was told by the healer that a few people at work used bad medicine and to watch out for them. I was also to buy a dream book and start recording my dreams to share with the healer who had the same dream book. (In hindsight, this was not a good idea as all of the dreams I reported were shaped by his interpretation. I did not trust my own.)

My best friend didn't know what hit her. All of a sudden she had these friends who were changing before her eyes. She didn't know if we could still be friends with her and if that was acceptable in our new traditional life. She was not an Aboriginal; I actually asked the healer if that should be a consideration. I note this because the healer had some very biased views about non-natives. On one hand he would say that we are all equal, but then he would say that he couldn't wait to see white people suffer when events unfolded in the future—events that would mark the end of the world as we know it.

Fortunately, we remained best friends. I could not have made a recovery without her.

We were directed to drink protection medicine that the healer prepared. Our entire family drank this each morning for the first month. In addition, I was asked to drink herbal tea that was meant to cleanse my body. It tasted like dandelions. I was asked to smudge our house to protect it from negative spirits. Mark was given another protection medicine that he was to sprinkle throughout the base of our entire house.

This was just the beginning of the payments to the healer for various protection medicines or teas that he prepared for me, Mark, or our family. Each time this cost could be anywhere from $40 to $120, depending on the stated need. In addition, each reading was another payment. The healer would determine when a reading was needed. This could be once or twice a week for each of us depending on the messages he got from his spirit guides. He required our cell numbers so he could text us instructions. We both grew to hate the sound of our cell phones' text message indicator.

That first week also marked the beginning of the release sessions. This was overnight work that came with a hefty price tag. It was $900 for my first release session. It was $1,100 for my husband's. This was startling. I remember getting the amount texted to me, and I didn't know how I would tell Mark. The healer's response was that we had to pay because of our arrogance and our way of life. He said our spirit guides said we were going to have to pay big time! I truly believe the healer thought we had more money than we actually did.

In preparation for my release work, the healer scheduled a three-day body cleanse session using red whip tea to induce vomiting. This was done for three consecutive mornings prior to the release session. It would usually last an hour and start at sunrise.

According to the healer, release work is examining every aspect of your life and letting it go to the Creator for healing. Situations that may have created fear, anger, resentment, jealousy, vindictiveness, or any type of negative feelings were to be remembered, examined, and let go in the morning with a pipe ceremony. The healer said these sessions were between me and the Creator. He said he had the ability to go elsewhere in spirit while I was doing the release work. (I thought to myself at this time, *Well then why do I need him!*) The memories were not to be brought up again once released. It had to start at my very earliest memory.

2

THE EARLY YEARS

I arrived at my first release session at 9:30 p.m. When I arrived the healer left the cabin so I could wash with a protection medicine that would protect me from negative spirits. The release work was to be done at night. The healer said this was the time when spirits would be most active; the spirit world is backward, and when we are asleep, they are awake. The spirit world would guide the sessions. A reading was then done to direct the healer on what was to be discussed in that first session. During this time the healer said the spirit guides said I was a very bad person and that it would take a long time for me to complete all the release sessions. I was immediately on edge.

I wanted to please the spirit guides by doing all the work and not feel tired throughout the night. I would only get a few short breaks from talking about my childhood for bathroom breaks. I had to drink three large jars of protection medicine throughout the night, so bathroom breaks were a necessity. There was only an outdoor toilet. The healer would warn of negative spirits outside the cabin, and he would stand guard while I went to the toilet. This scared me even more. I didn't like being in the dark outhouse. I couldn't wait to get back to the safety of the cabin, where at least I was not alone.

The healer opened the session with a pipe ceremony, and I was directed to go to my earliest childhood memory. The healer said he would go into a trance state while I spoke throughout the night. It took me a while to remember events in an age sequence like I was directed. They were jumbled, skipping all over my childhood, ten years old to six to eight. I was getting confused and nervous. I felt like I had to say something, anything!

I started. Our house was small and old. It had a wood stove and was heated by a coal furnace. There was a big heating vent in the middle of the hallway, and it had three bedrooms. There were nine children in total, five girls and four boys. I remember sleeping in a room with my sisters. There were two beds, one a double and the other a cot. I sucked my thumb. I remember my sister trying to pull my finger out of my mouth. I got earaches that were very painful. My mother used to heat an iron, unplug it, and place it near my face with a towel over it to help ease the pain of the earache. It seemed to work most times, and I was able to sleep.

We were a typical family that lived on the reserve. A few families were in better shape than ours, and some lived in worse conditions. We were definitely poor, but our door was always open and my parents welcomed many friends and relatives who traveled from other communities. Like many families on the reserve, alcohol and spousal abuse were common and had a significant impact on our entire family to one degree or another. However, there were many fun times that our family experienced. But I was not to remember those times, only times that created negative feelings or bad memories.

I was climbing around our kitchen sideboard. I always liked to look in the cupboards. My mother had just placed a pot of boiling water in the sink. Our water was heated in that manner as we didn't have hot water. I tried to step across the sink to the other side of the counter, but I slipped. I fell into the boiling water. My backside landed in the water. I don't remember crying, but I remember the ride to the hospital. A man who had a taxi service on the reserve drove us to the hospital, which was only a short distance from our home. I was just scalded. It was expected to heal, and the redness would go away in a short while. I don't think that stopped me from looking around in the cupboards. I always thought I might find money.

Usually when my father, who was a barber, got paid, we would get some pizza and pop on Saturday night. Sometimes we would also get an extra treat. I loved flakes. They were turnovers with jelly and cream inside and cost ten cents. My father was going to the store one Sunday, and I wanted a flake. I begged for one, but my parents couldn't afford it. Angry, I walked out the back door and down our steps. The kitchen window was located near the back steps, and as I descended the steps, I bust my hand though the window and cut my hand on the side of my palm. What possessed me to take that action, I don't know; it was just an impulse. I don't think I intended to break the window, but I did; it was covered in cardboard for quite some time.

We used to walk to the main road, Alexander Street, to catch the city bus to school. It was only a fifteen- or twenty-minute walk, but it seemed really far. It was just off the reserve. There was a little store called Leslie's where we would get off the bus. One day my brother had crossed the road in front of the bus, and a driver did not see him. He was struck, and his rubber boots flew off his feet. I remember seeing his boots and taking off home. I ran all the way home and told my mother that my brother had been hit; I'm sure my older siblings were with him. My mother didn't believe me right away; I had to convince her it was truth. I lied a lot when I was a kid. He was in the hospital for quite some time and got presents from the driver who hit him; I'm sure the driver felt terrible for what had happened. My brother made a full recovery.

We lived in this house up until I was five or six. I remember the day we had to move out. I was playing in the back bedroom, the boys' bedroom. They had two old army bunk beds in the room and a home-made clothes-storage unit. It was leaning against the back wall. It had been raining all day. Our house had always leaked, and there were buckets and pots all over to catch the rain leaking through the roof. I was playing in the boys' room and could see the ceiling drooping near the back wall above the storage unit. It had been leaking all day, but now it was raining so hard that the water was gathering in the ceiling. It was getting heavier and heavier. I remember looking at the sagging ceiling; it was starting to bulge. The whole back corner was starting to bulge. The water that accumulated in the ceiling crashed through and left half the ceiling hanging down. It was a disaster. I don't know the exact sequence of events that happened, but we had to move out of the house. We were going to move temporarily to a house where an older man had just passed away and the house was vacant.

We moved to the house using whatever means available to move our furniture, including toboggans and wagons. I'm sure my brothers were very busy going back and forth to collect our things and move them to the temporary house. I didn't mind moving, but when we got to the house, my mother pointed to the room in which the girls would sleep. I didn't want to sleep in that room. I remember attending the recent wake of the man who had just died, and our bed was being placed in the exact spot where his coffin was positioned. I had the spot against the wall. It was creepy! I don't know if I slept that entire first night.

It was and still is very common to host a wake for the recently deceased in our homes. The wakes are usually packed and are open to visitors around the clock for two nights and three days. The family, with the assistance of other community members, provides food and beverages to all visitors. Alcohol is not served at any of our wakes or post funeral dinners. A salite or auction is hosted as part of the post-funeral dinner. Items that are auctioned are donated by community members and may be offered as individual items or items that have been grouped together such as bedding, dishes, etc. Many items are brand new and are purchased by community members to donate to the salite. In most cases the funds raised during the salite are enough to cover the entire funeral expense for the deceased.

137

I guess I got used to the room and the creepy walk-up stairway to the attic that was located in the bedroom. I know we had rats. They were from the stream that was located near the end of the road. We had cats to help with the situation, but they could always be heard in the house. Our old house was being rebuilt using funds provided to our reserve for housing from the federal government. It took almost three years to build depending on funding availability.

We didn't have a telephone, so we relied on a neighbor across the street to assist in emergencies, and we had a lot. It was usually to call the police because my father was drinking and would beat up my mother. It wasn't that he just drank—they both did, and the situation easily got out of control. My father was usually so kind and gentle when sober but was the biggest asshole when drunk. One of us would usually run over to the neighbor's house in tears screaming to call the police. My brothers would do their best to get my father out of the house, but he would often try to get back inside. On one particular night, we were running from room to room trying to close the windows, but he caught my mother by the hair in the boys' bedroom as she leaned down to shut the window, and he dragged her right out the window. It was terrifying as he hit and kicked her outside.

I don't know what happened later that night, but usually the police showed up. They could not take my father to jail in those days because it wasn't illegal for my father to be in his own house. The police would have had to witness the fight to make an arrest. They would usually just talk to him and tell him to calm down; but he was always allowed back inside.

We moved back to our house when I was in grade four. I must have been eight or nine years old. The house was not completely finished. The stairs leading to the second floor were only partially built, and you could see through to the basement. Also, the floors were just plywood, and we didn't have any kitchen cupboards. Again, we didn't have hot water, so water had to be heated on the stove and carried upstairs to the bathroom. One night my eldest brother was very badly scalded carrying hot water up for his bath. We all felt so bad for him; he was only a young guy.

The house was much bigger, and we felt good about it. My mother did all the washing in a ringer washer that she moved to the kitchen sink. We took turns helping hang all the laundry on four different clotheslines. Usually it was our clothesline, our neighbor's next door, my uncle's beside the neighbor, and then our other uncle across the street. We had a lot of laundry, and good weather had to be taken advantage of to get the laundry done in one day.

We had a television set that we would rent from a local businessman. He would come collect his payments each week; he was always on schedule. I don't know how often he was actually paid because we had that television repossessed more times than I care to remember. But he would always bring it back when we paid our bill. I remember one day my mother saw him, and she told me to say that she wasn't home. I went up to the wooden storm door when he knocked and said to him through a tiny crack, "My mother said she's not home. Come back later." I could see my mother roll her eyes. I shut the door.

I woke up. I could hear screaming; it was really loud. When I went to bed, my parents and their friends were playing cards at the kitchen table. They were drinking throughout the day and evening. I used to get up in the middle of the night to check that no lit cigarettes were put in the trash or anyplace that could start a fire. On this night, I was awoken by my mother's loud screams. She was really mad and shouting swear words with that voice that is between anger and tears. My stomach instantly became upset; that bad feeling that overwhelmed me when another fight was starting. All had seemed fine when I went to bed, but now my mother had a big knife in her hand trying to get at my father. I don't know who was holding them apart, probably my brothers. But I saw that knife in her hand, and I ran for it. I yanked it out of my mother's hand by the blade. It was probably not that sharp because I didn't do too much damage to my hands. I can still see the light scars on my hands where I yanked it from my mother.

It's weird to think that after all the crazy traumas we witnessed, sometimes during the week, that it was normal to go about our usual business the next day. Whether it was to school or hanging with friends, life just went on. I couldn't imagine how the scenario would have played out if we had a school psychologist or counselor at the time to inquire after our home life. I suppose child protection would have been made aware of our situation. However, for many of us on the reserve, it was just normal. To this day, in any situation that requires quick action or indicates trouble in some manner, my stomach reacts in the same way every time.

All night I talked about hurts, slights, violence, poverty, wants, needs, and rejection, both real and imagined. Every memory every year recalled and examined. I was exhausted. By the time I reached my brother's death when I was fifteen, it was morning.

3

A CREATIVE PATH

As I meditated that morning after hearing the thunderous bang in the house, I was a little nervous on the message that I would receive. I had been receiving guided messages for the past nine months in one form or another. It could be two words or a stream of thoughts that I would need to quickly write down following the meditation. As a vibrational feeling encircled my forehead, I awaited the message. I could feel and sense energy all around me—through my hair, down my back, arms, and legs. These feelings could last anywhere from ten minutes up to an hour, depending on the comfort level of my seating. At times two hours could easily pass before I would release the connection.

A few days before, I was guided in meditation to attend a psychic tea church fundraiser in the local area. The meditation session was particularly strong that evening. I could feel the energies trying to get my attention while I watched television with my family. I said to them, "Sorry, guys, if I don't meditate now, the angels are not going to stop." As I grounded myself, the message was immediate. I was directed specifically by name to one of the mediums who was scheduled to give readings at the psychic tea fundraising event. I had to check the church website to see when the event was scheduled; it was the next morning. However, when I arrived that morning at the church, I was informed that particular medium did readings by appointment only and she was pre-booked for the day. Disappointed, I asked if there was another time when I could see the medium. I spoke to a couple who scheduled her readings and was surprisingly given an appointment at the end of the day. Generally the medium started at 8:00 a.m. and gave readings until 4:00 p.m. Today they would add another appointment at 4:00 p.m., which meant I could see her that day after all, but I would need to come back later. When I returned, the psychic tea had ended a couple of hours earlier, and I was the last one to get a reading.

 I previously attended lectures at a spiritualist church, and readings from spirit are common. Over the last couple of years, my spiritual growth was aided by a vast array of books on spiritualism and psychic phenomenon, many of which I had been guided to as I worked through different concepts and issues involved in the healing process. At the time I didn't realize I was going through a healing process. I just thought I was reading because I enjoyed the books. But anytime I had a question, off to the library I would go, and I would return with three or four books that would expand my knowledge on the topic. I would often finish a book in a day, sometimes two. The list of books went on and on. I started organizing my thoughts on poster boards, figuring out what different authors were saying about the afterlife, about our life purpose, about God. What could I say to a person that would make most sense to them? Where could I start the conversation if it presented itself? I knew this was going to happen. Something in me told me to learn how to communicate clearly, with a knowing that would invite the other person to perhaps ask questions but not frighten the person or impinge on his or her sense of reality.

 I sat down, and the medium began. The reading was for a half hour. Names were put forward, more as validation that she was connecting with spirits connected to me. All were confirmed. "You know you are very much guided with spirit in many ways," she said.

"Do you make people aware of spirit?" she asked. I do, but it is mainly family and only the ones I know are open to messages from spirit. Even then, I'm not sure how the messages are received.

I imagine it's somewhat challenging for my family to engage with me in one manner our entire life and then have our relationship altered by my recent spiritual awakening.

The medium continued, "I see that you get thoughts, you get impressions. I'm going to say why don't you start carrying around a tape recorder or book to record these thoughts because you are going to have the opportunity to put a lot of things together that are going to help people?" She asked, "Who are the men in soldiers' uniforms who were connected to you; I have one that is taller than the other?" I replied that they were my uncles. She said, "They are bringing a beautiful vibration. I feel like I want to say to you that he says nothing is too big, too small, or too awkward for her to handle. She will get through it all! He says if you told her the water was too deep to swim across, she would do it just to prove a point!" We both laughed.

The medium said, "Have you talked about writing a book on your experiences?" I did at one point, but I didn't really want to expose myself. "Well, I think you are going to do a lot of writing and I don't know what's that all about, but I feel good about it. There are a lot of things that you are going to set straight; people are going to finally listen. You are not beating the drums for nothing! Have you been talking about getting a group together to meditate?" she asked. No, I replied. "Well something is going to happen and you are going to draw people to you. There is going to be meditation groups, and you will be surprised what is going to come out of that for you."

She asked, "Did you go home recently and come back with a lot of memories?" I went home for my mother's funeral last September and did come back with a CD of pictures of my mother and father that was played at the funeral reception. "I see a fancy teapot. Who loved their tea?" No, that was a teapot I bought my mother when I traveled to Saudi Arabia in my twenties. I brought it back home with me. I brought home letters my mother had saved that I wrote to her during that time as well. "Well, your mother is just validating that she is here, and she wants everyone to know that everything is all right and that she is at peace. She wants you to know that it was a celebration when she arrived. I feel like I want to say to you that I don't know who did all the dancing, but I feel like I danced all night, if that means anything to you!"

In reference to this last comment by the medium, prior to my mother's passing after a long, often challenging three years in which her health deteriorated, my father, who had passed fifteen years prior, had managed to send a message to my brother through a local medium in our community. A little part of the message indicated that when my mother passed, he would be there to greet her and would dance my mother away.

I had also received a message from a cousin who had passed and wanted to get a message to his mother. He wanted his mother to know that he would be persistent in trying to get her attention until she recognized that life continued after this life. I asked for validation that I could share with her, as I was a little wary of delivering the message to his mom. I didn't know how she would receive it, if she would believe it, or perhaps if she would think I was flaky. The medium said, "Your cousin is saying that he moves things. She thinks she is going crazy, losing her mind, but it is him!" When I passed on the message to his mother, she in turn validated his message by confirming that a statue she had on her dresser drawer in her bedroom was constantly being moved. One moment it was facing one way and the next it was facing another way. After much angst over delivering the message to his mother, it was received in the manner in which it was sent—in much love and laughter that was part of their family bond.

I left the session feeling that perhaps I was guided there by my cousin to deliver the message to his mother. Then a couple days later a new development occurred.

My meditation was deepening. I began to focus; the vibrational circling on my forehead was now pulsating. I was being drawn away, aware of the energies surrounding me. Information was starting to come through. All I heard was, "Write your book."

"About what?" I asked.

"Your life," I heard.

"How long do I have to write it?"

"April 28."

But that was only two weeks away! My mind was reeling. How on earth would I be able to write a book in two weeks?

I started to receive lines that opened with, "I don't know when it all started, but at an early age I was able to ..." It continued. Images flashed in my mind of events, sequences. It was like an outline was starting to take form. I was intrigued. I was getting anxious to start. I walked out of my bedroom and informed my husband that I was going to write a book. He was surprised, not with the concept of writing a book but with the timeframe. He asked, "Do you really think you can do that amount of writing in two weeks? An actual book!"

I was positive that whatever I was guided to do would be a success. I could write a chapter a day. It would get done. I had just come off a very intense project that had a very tight deadline, so I felt confident that it was just a warm-up to what I had to do to write the book. I got out my computer and started to write. That first day I wrote two chapters.

A couple mornings later, I woke up, uncertain of what my dreams were telling me. I didn't feel myself; I felt like I didn't want people to know about my life. The dreams were showing me people who would laugh at me, doubt my story, doubt my validity. I put it aside and started to get ready for the Easter long weekend. It's just my insecurity, I surmised, and went on with my weekend activities. The dreams persisted.

I thought to myself, *I worked through all of these feelings. Why am I now feeling insecure?* I meditated again and asked about the timeframe. Maybe I was wrong. Then I heard, "It's like a Band-Aid. Rip it off quickly!" I knew instinctively what the guidance meant. The book was to be written quickly, so as not to drag out the feelings that I was experiencing in writing the book. My dreams were my own ego, unwilling to let my guard down, to reveal the side of myself that I had kept hidden. I thought about the people who might read this book; what would they think? Was I going to allow my ego to dream up some possible scenario in which I would be humiliated, pointed at, thought of as less of a person because of the life I have led? No way, that already happened, and I wasn't going to let it happen again. Definitely not by me!

I was led back to a little affirmation that I was guided to remember during a meditative healing session. "I am the sum total of all my experiences; to love from one heart … not to be diminished in any manner." In this healing, the two halves of me were recognized, loved, and forgiven. I reached down to bring up and demonstrate love and forgiveness to my other half. She was very small. I cried for her. She was the one who experienced all the lessons. She was the one who was broken, ashamed, embarrassed, burdened, and frightened. I took her hand, and she rose up and joined with me, our blood vessels fusing together to form one heart, beating as one. I loved her.

4

BOUND BY FEAR

The days following my first release session were filled with learning what I could about my husband's traditional culture. These were the traditions in which the healer said we would raise our children. I also spent time reading books that he suggested which would help with understanding the traditional path. I read all these books with fervor. I wanted to do a good job, be a good student. I encouraged my husband to read the books as well. He didn't care to read beyond what was required for business, but he read a couple that I pushed him to read.

The books the healer recommended were mainly on traditional hunting and gathering, tracking, preparation of game meat, traditional code of ethics and morals, and so on. The healer was convinced that an apocalyptic event within the next couple of decades was going to decimate much of the population and that only a few pockets of society would survive; and in anticipation of that event, we had to teach our kids how to survive in the wilderness. The kids needed to be trained to help lead people to caves in areas that were predetermined as locations for the First Nation people to gather. He also directed me to authors of a spiritual nature who supported this theory.

I was excited to read all the books that were suggested by the healer. I thought it would help me accept what was being taught to me. I wanted to learn even more than what the healer had already revealed. I felt it was my duty to understand the traditional ways of my husband's nation. I included additional books into my review, books on traditional ethics and morals that he referenced occasionally. However, I started to notice contradictions from what the healer was teaching to what was stated in the traditional books on ethics and morals and the eternal punishments that would damn all those who did not show observance. He laughed when I brought these up to him, like he had insider knowledge. He was quick to dismiss the literature as uninformed. He said they were written by people without knowledge of the traditional language. The healer was not fluent in his traditional language, so his insistence that these books were uniformed didn't make much sense to me as some parts of the books on morals and ethics he quoted exactly.

At this same time, my dreams were changing; they felt different, more real. They came not every night, but frequently. I got into discussing my dreams with the healer during our sessions together. I would try to interpret the dreams myself using the dream book that I purchased—one that the healer recommended. I would give the healer my interpretation, but he seemed to always have a different meaning. I was confused. I was using the same dream book. Then one night, I had a dream that involved traditional healers. They were seated around a table when I entered the room. One was preparing traditional medicine near the kitchen sink. I sat down, and the healer came up from in back of me and started forcing the medicine down my throat. I was choking. I woke up gasping for air.

When I revealed the dream to the healer, I said that I couldn't find anything in the dream book to help with the interpretation. The healer said anything with traditional medicine could not be interpreted through that manner. He said that in my life, there were going to be four men who would try to use bad medicine on me and that I had to protect myself; they wanted to have me for themselves, and they would attempt in various ways to draw me to them. The healer revealed that certain medicines were used to seduce an individual who otherwise would not show any interest in them. I was not to leave my jacket any place unattended as medicine could be put around the collar; this included my office as well. I also had to watch that no one touched the back of my neck or put anything in my drinks. I could not take anything from anyone such as coffee, tea, water, etc., as it could be tainted with bad medicine.

This freaked me out to say the least. I was heading out of town on business, and he said there would be someone at the workshop who was interested in me and would attempt to seduce me in this manner. Talk about paranoid. I don't think I had my back to anyone the entire trip. I was exhausted keeping an ever-watchful eye for anyone around me. The workshop was packed and I was hosting it, so it was quite a challenge to stay away from anyone who could be seen as suspect. Generally, this was any person of the male gender, and it was a construction trades workshop.

Unfortunately, had I been confident in myself to interpret the dream, I would have understood the message that was being shared with me by my higher self to not trust this healer who was filling me with negative influences. Had I been strong, I could have at this time moved forward on my own spiritual journey, in my own way; however, I did not trust enough in my own abilities to communicate directly with God. As often misinterpreted by the faithful, I felt as though I needed an intervener to help absolve me of my sins. My guilt and fear were continuing to steer the ship, and the healer continued to manipulate this weakness.

I never really showed this guilt and fear to the outside world. It was internal, festering, primed for any illness that could take root. I appeared to those who didn't know me well as confident, outgoing, and perhaps a little conceited. I dressed well to help create an illusion of sophistication. I absolutely did not feel that way as I struggled with my own personal demons. I didn't have my own identity; I was too busy creating one from those around me. I went through life feeling like I was owed something, what, how much, I don't know. Just something!

Driving around town, I started taking note of certain license plates with the same four letters that appeared over and over again. I would stop at the traffic lights, and there they would be! This continued steadily and has not stopped to this day. The license letters were BEVJ. One night I again had a dream that was unforgettable and sent me back to the healer for interpretation.

In the dream I slid into home base as though I was playing baseball, but I was on a toboggan. It stood up, and there were three older native women standing around me. I stood up and asked them if they knew what BEVJ 368 meant! (That was the last license plate I seen that day.) They indicated that they did, and I seemed to be moved forward, but they didn't tell me the meaning. I was then pushed from behind toward a childhood friend. My friend said to me, "Paula, the hawk is coming to help you, and you must be ready!" I moved forward again toward a voice that was speaking to me and I listened intently, but when I woke from the dream, I couldn't recall the message.

The healer interpreted this dream as one in which I was being given direction to participate in a traditional ceremony of his clan that involved the hawk. I thought at the time; this made sense! I felt honored to participate. (Later I would learn from my sister that our own family is from the hawk clan. Since that time, I have had many dreams that involve the hawk; it flies into my window and whispers into my ear.)

When I was finally given the go-ahead from the healer to visit my family, it was five weeks since the healing process began. I was not the same person. I could go home for two days, but that was all. My mother's health was still stable at this time, even though she had a near-fatal bout with flesh-eating disease in which her arm and partial shoulder were amputated. Fortunately, she was able to still live independently and had readjusted to life as an amputee through rehabilitation and support from the community health services unit on our First Nation. It was two weeks before Christmas.

The healer told me that there were many negative spirits around my community because we didn't follow proper burial rites for the deceased. He said some negative spirits were around my mother's home, and they were making her ill by touching her food because she took too long to eat it. He recommended that she cover her food with a white tea towel when she was not eating; this also applied to any food left out on the counter. The earthbound spirits were hungry and would touch her food; they had not lost the appetite for earthly things, such as food, liquor, drugs, or sex. He said some spirits around there were going to want me; they could watch what I was doing and become physical if they so desired. I had to be especially careful when I was asleep as my defenses would be down. I was given protection medicine before my trip.

To say the least, I was scared to be at my mother's home. It no longer felt like my childhood home. The healer had convinced me that the house would require a cleansing, and protection medicine would need to be sprinkled throughout the base of the home. However, he made it clear once again that protection medicine would not work if any person using drugs or alcohol entered the home. My mother would need to request it; I never asked.

Even in our own home, we would not allow people into the house. We would talk to them outside because we didn't know if they did the things that the healer said was forbidden.

That first evening, my mom and I talked into the night. We drank tea and ate sweets that she was so fond of; she had such a sweet tooth. I was very grateful that she allowed me to talk about the traditional path that I had accepted as part of the healing process. She listened to all the traditional concepts that I was sharing with her and simply acknowledged that she was unfamiliar with traditional ways as that was not part of the community in which she or our family were raised. She did not judge. She had been a drug and alcohol counselor for the past thirty years and helped many in our community. I understood at this time that she wanted me to be happy. She knew I was struggling with the past. She knew I needed healing.

Actually, I was afraid to go to bed. The healer said I was to receive from spirit three medicines that I would need to bring home with me; this was a test. I tried to sleep, but I was too unnerved. I could hear my mother slightly snoring down the hall. I wanted to wake her, to tell her what I was really going through, but I thought she would think I was crazy. I wanted to tell her of all my fears—to let her know that I was afraid to sleep alone. It was 2:00 a.m., and I was restless. I needed to sleep to receive the messages, but I couldn't because I was scared of the spirits. It was getting close to morning, and I was panicking. *Oh no, I can't go home without those messages!* I had just the one night in which they would be revealed to me. I texted the healer, who told me to sleep when it got light; he laughed, said I was weak and the spirits kicked my ass.

I slept a couple of hours in the morning but then got out of bed because I had little time to visit everyone. Some family members dropped by to visit throughout the day. It was good to see everyone. I reviewed the traditional path I was journeying and some of the books I had read. As I mentioned earlier, many of these books were focused on apocalyptic and negative spirit activity. I'm happy I was not successful in encouraging my family to read any of them; it is not a positive means by which to begin a spiritual journey.

I know now that fear will only lead you to make temporary or casual changes—changes that will crumble or collapse at the slightest provocation or opposition from family, friends, or even your spouse. All it will take is one suggestion, one invitation, one more time, and you are back to where you first started.

That second night I slept with my mother; I was exhausted. She didn't ask any questions.

I returned home to Ontario and immediately experienced again the guidance dreams. I was in the living room at my mother's home, and I was floating up the stairs. I knew I didn't want to walk down the hall to the bedroom where I had slept. I was standing at the landing at the top of the stairs. I heard a voice behind me say, "*Go.*" I was being pushed from behind but still floating. I reached the doors to the two back bedrooms, but they were closed. I faced forward but pushed open the right door with my hand. I was scared to look inside. There was a young boy standing beside the bed. He was bald, dark skinned, like a monk. I saw my father sitting on the bed; he was holding someone who was ill. He was comforting them; it was compassion. The young boy moved me to the other room. I opened the door. There were babies under the covers—babies who had recently passed but needed to be cared for and loved. This represented a doorway—a doorway to heaven.

5

AN ADOLESCENT VIEW

It was 1977, and my mother had quit drinking. I was starting my second release session from where I left off at the first session. It was summer, I continued, and I was visiting relatives in Ontario. I couldn't return home yet because my mother was in a treatment center. I was surprised because I never, ever saw my mother as an alcoholic. I thought alcoholics were people who were drunks. My mother drank, but she still looked after us.

It was her decision to do the twenty-eight-day program. I would have to wait to return home. I had been away for three weeks already and missed my family.

When my mother quit drinking, our life was changed. She became a regular at Alcoholics Anonymous (AA) meetings and later started work as a Native Alcohol and Drug Addictions Counselor. My father still drank, and this created hardships on the family as he would often binge drink. Every few months, my father would go on a three- or four-week bender. He would leave work and just not come home. Each time he would need to enter a detox treatment center because of the effects the alcohol would have on his body. He could not just quit without assistance. He would have DTs (delirium tremens). He would spend anywhere from one week to three weeks in detox depending on the severity of his bender. Sometimes I would see him when I got off the school bus, and I wouldn't even recognize him. He looked like a homeless person. He was usually clean shaven with his hair nicely styled and well dressed; this man was a stranger.

My father's binge drinking would continue for several more years. In this time, we still had a couple of incidences where my father became violent, but they were controlled quickly. We were all older; we could get my father out of the house faster. The police were also more willing to take my father to jail where he would be detained for night. However, my mother was exhausted from the ups and downs and the stress his binge drinking created within the family. Eventually she took matters into her own hands, got a court order, and he was not allowed to return home after yet another binging episode and requisite treatment to regain his health.

My parents' separation lasted six months. It was a relief not to have my father at the house, but we missed him too. We would visit him at his brother's home; he genuinely missed all of us. He wanted to come home, and after some time we would plead with my mother to let him move home. After the separation my father's binge drinking became less intense. He drank, but illness would overtake him sooner. He developed diabetes. He would need to take better care of himself; eventually the drinking stopped.

My brother's illness began with a sore knee. Bradley complained throughout 1978 that his knee hurt. He was a year older than me. My mother would take him to the doctor, but they always advised it was just water in the knee; a needle would be inserted to drain the fluid. My brother played hockey and other sports, so this procedure was not unusual. He lost weight, but that we attributed to his age. He was fifteen and getting much taller. Nothing seemed amiss.

Bradley celebrated his sixteenth birthday in late 1978; he was in grade ten. Early the following year, he got a cold he couldn't shake. His chest was congested, and he was bedridden for a few weeks. He lost a lot of weight at this time. I'm not certain what the doctor attributed the illness to, but it was most likely pneumonia. For a little while, he got better. I remember the night he went to see *Saturday Night Fever*; we all met afterward at a local teen dance club, and he told us about the movie. I was impressed that he got into a restricted movie; he looked so grown up.

I stop writing here. My heart is heavy, and I am struggling with words to capture a personality that was so incredibly vibrant with life that in only writing about his death seems to do him a great injustice. I pray. Dear God, please give me the strength and courage to share our family's darkest moment of grief, loss, and powerlessness in such heartbreak; but also to share the love that was Bradley, his humor, his ingenuity, his drive, his beautiful spirit. Help me, holy Father, write this with integrity, truthfulness, and love. Amen.

Brad worked from an early age. He delivered newspapers but sometimes asked for my mother's assistance when he had difficulty collecting from some customers. Not that she was about to break any knees, just a word or two with the customer. All of his customers were from our small community, so my mother grew up with most everyone on the reserve and felt comfortable seeking them out. He always seemed to have a little cash. He would babysit for friends and help out where he could, but his biggest money maker was his regular after-school job working at a convenience store. It was locally owned, small, and had gaming machines. Not gambling, but a pool table, pinball machines, and a jukebox. We would all hang out there. I used to constantly ask Brad to loan me a dime or quarter to play the pinball machines or a game of pool. He would usually oblige, but I don't know how I ever thought I could pay him back! He worked at the store for three years.

Oh my brother wasn't perfect, that's for sure. He had this way of joking that could strike at your most vulnerable perceived weakness, whether it was a secret, your appearance, or anything you may have felt the least bit insecure about. For me, that was any number of things; he could embarrass me with just a look, but he never humiliated. He knew the fine line between what was considered humor and that which was outright mean. His friends spanned all age groups. He had a special way of connecting with people; they felt immediately they could trust him. He was just a kid in physical years, but his soul was very old. To this day, I am reminded by community members how much Brad meant to them personally, what he did for them, how he helped. He made a difference in our life and in the lives of those in the community.

Bradley's knee started to hurt again. It was April, just before Easter. My mother brought him to the hospital to see our regular doctor, who was working the emergency room. As it so happened, a surgeon was in the emergency department who took a look at Brad's knee and immediately informed my mother that he would like to schedule a biopsy. My mother informed us when she returned home that the surgeon wanted to do a biopsy and she would need to take Brad to Halifax. I didn't understand at the time what this all meant. It isn't like today when a quick search on the computer can tell you everything you need to know in seconds. As a matter of fact, I didn't even really understand cancer. I knew older people often got cancer, but I didn't know anyone our age who had cancer.

My mother traveled to Halifax with my brother for the biopsy. It was a five-hour trip. I'm not sure if they took a bus or the train. It is a blur. My mother stayed with my eldest brother, who lived with his wife in Halifax. Bradley was admitted to the hospital for the biopsy. A few days later, my mother called with the results. It was cancer. Brad would need to have his leg amputated. He had a type of bone cancer called osteosarcoma. My father delivered the news. We were all in shock. We called my sister who lived in Boston to come home. We were barely able to function that day. The surgery was to be scheduled within the week.

A very close friend of the family managed to raise money from community members so we could travel to Halifax to see Brad before surgery. The following weekend, we arrived at the hospital. A few days had passed since we received the news. Nothing had prepared me for seeing Brad so incapacitated. I didn't know his health was starting to decline so drastically. He needed to wear an oxygen mask to help clear out his now-congested lungs. His leg was propped up on a pillow. It was difficult to understand what he was saying. He would occasionally take off the mask to talk, to joke a little, but he was tired. Our family dropped in to see him throughout the weekend. It was difficult to have us all there at the same time; the hospital room was small, and we have a big family. We stayed at a hotel not too far from the hospital. Before we knew it, the weekend was over and it was time to go. We said our good-byes to Bradley and Mom and returned home. We waited for the surgery to be scheduled.

The surgery was delayed a couple of times. It was now into May. Bradley's lungs were still too congested to undergo anesthesia. My mother stayed by his side the entire time. Finally, we were informed that the surgery was going ahead on May 10. It just happened that it was my birthday; it was a Thursday. My mother called that day to say the surgery went well. Bradley was in recovery, and the surgeon was optimistic that they were able to get all the cancer. It was bittersweet news; I had trouble imagining what my brother's life was going to be like for him with only one leg.

My father was with my mother in Halifax following the surgery. A couple days later, on May 12, my sister was sitting outside on the front step with her friend. His parents were there, standing talking to my sister. She came into the house crying, screaming that Brad had died. It was chaos; I didn't know what to do. We were all caught off guard. I ran into the woods. It was too much to handle. The pain was palpable; we didn't have our usual support system. My parents were with my brother, and our closest aunt and uncle traveled to Halifax that morning with my younger sister to visit my brother. After getting the initial news, I have no memory of what transpired until the day of my brother's wake.

Apparently my brother had suffered a heart attack. A blood clot had formed and traveled to his heart. He died quickly. He was waked at the house, and his funeral was a beautiful memorial to his life.

As usually happens in families that experience a tragic loss, a gap was left in our family, and we each tried to fill that gap in our own way. For me, it was new friends, going to parties, and hanging out. My cousin introduced me to her friends from school who were my brother's age. They knew Brad and they understood the loss; there was no need to fill them in on what had happened. They were there at his wake; I just didn't know them at the time.

The night when we all met, my cousin invited me to a house party. It was the third floor of a house that had been converted to apartments. There were quite a few people from school; almost everyone was drinking. I had a Canadian Club Whiskey. I didn't drink up to that point, so I didn't really know what to select when asked. I sat quietly on a barstool in the hallway. I was chatting with people around me but then noticed my cousin wasn't there; I asked a few people where she went, but nobody knew. This upset me because the house was downtown, and it was my first time at a non-native party.

The whiskey started to hit me. I said to a couple people that I couldn't believe that my cousin left me at a white person's party! I was about to stand up and see if my cousin was outside, but my foot got stuck on the stool, and I hit the floor. People checked to see that I was okay, and I went to sit on a chair in the kitchen. By now I had two or three drinks and was getting very animated. I was telling a story and knocked an iron off the counter that landed on my head. I started to cry; it was all so dramatic. Apparently my cousin went out to get mix for the whiskey; she hadn't even been gone long. We all remained close for many years.

I started high school the next semester. I was grateful to have friends who were already attending the school. It was easier to fit in with everyone. I started dating, and life seemed to move forward. I hung out with my friends most weekends, so they are the memories that I have of that time period. I asked my mother a few years ago what she went through following Brad's death. She said it was a very difficult period in her life and that she struggled a lot. She said she was happy we had our friends; that we didn't dwell, that we were all able to move forward. I wish today that I could have been there for her; to have shown her more compassion, understanding, empathy.

But she had her friends too, and my father, and for that I am grateful.

I worked most summer breaks and got my first job away from my community when I was in grade eleven. I was very excited. A new roller rink was opening in our town, and a lot of people had applied for jobs. I had to go through three interviews, plus a polygraph test, to get the job. I enjoyed working there on the weekends; it was a lot of fun. I even worked a couple of shifts during the week sometimes if they needed extra help. I was able to meet people from all around the area. Normally, I just knew the kids from school. The staff all got along, and we had a great time working together. I was there for three months and fully expected to stay as long as possible. Then one evening I was talking to the manager. He was not from around the area. We were joking around, and I said something like, "Well then why did you hire me?" He said, "Quota!" I didn't know what he was talking about at first. Then he said they were required to hire from minority groups to fulfill a quota. I thought about this for a while but didn't say anything to him. I was upset. Why did I go through the entire hiring process if they were just going to hire me on a quota basis!

I felt angry. I didn't quite enjoy the work anymore. I had never been confronted with that blatant admission before in my life. We had certainly been accustomed to positions that were set-aside for native-only applicants, but we were aware of the program from the outset. It was not long before I left my job at the roller rink. I knew that I would not be given the opportunity to move up to any position in the office, which I had fully anticipated would happen prior to our conversation. I looked around. Other than a couple of minorities, it was mainly Caucasians who staffed the roller rink, and it was mainly Caucasians who did all the hiring. This was something new to me. I never before felt that there could be any barriers to what I set out to do in life.

I then thought about the year before when I started dating. My boyfriend had confided in me that his mother didn't want him coming to the reserve to pick me up for our date. His mother told him that she grew up near the reserve, and she thought it was dangerous; she was afraid he would get hurt. I had spent my entire life playing around the entire reserve. No area left me feeling unsafe; creepy maybe, but never unsafe. I was embarrassed and resented his mother for her ignorance. How dare she judge us! I didn't quite get over that embarrassment. After a time, I began to notice just how poor everyone was, including us. I didn't want to be there; I didn't want to be an Indian.

I graduated high school in the usual three years. However, my last year was scheduled with eight classes, including a night class in grade twelve biology. I had failed to attain the number of credits necessary to graduate in the previous two years. I received special permission from the principal to undertake extra credits. I didn't have any distractions; all my friends had already graduated. The classes were easy when I put my mind to studying. I had applied to university and received admission to the only one I had on my list. It was a small university located in Halifax.

That same year, my mother became ill. Her back was so painful it could be days before she would feel stable enough to come downstairs. She had to be assisted most days and required hot compresses on her back; they were so hot at times that her skin would scald. She didn't care, but we were the ones applying the hot compresses, especially my older sister, who scalded her hands frequently. During this time, my mother was also on medications to help with pain and depression. She was unpredictable most days. I didn't know what to expect when I got home from school. She could be angry, crying, or out cold. This went on for a very long time. I'm positive it lasted at least a year. My older sister bore the brunt of it, but it had an effect on the entire family.

As quickly as the pain afflicted my mother, it was gone. Again, I asked her about this time, and she told me the pain had been related to stress and all the changes that were happening at work. The Native Alcohol and Drug Addictions Program in which she was employed underwent transformational change, and education requirements were applied to all positions. This required my mother to return to school for upgrading at a specialized NADAP Program hosted by a university in Halifax. She did not adjust well to the program, and the stress affected her, mostly in her lower back. Later her job position was changed and she was not required to complete an educational component. She continued in her position for the next ten years.

My parents threw me a big surprise party for my high school graduation. I remember the absolute shock I felt when I walked into the house. I didn't see it coming at all and was actually taken aback and wondered why my friends were in the house. It was a wonderful night that I will remember forever. My high school days were over; I made it through. I started university in the fall of '82.

6

A SPIRIT CONNECTION

While writing the book, I set aside meditating for a few days. However, on this day I was feeling blocked; my writing had no direction. It was all over the place. I sensed the need to meditate, to relax. Reliving past events and finding the right words to share my memories and feelings had been emotionally draining. I closed my eyes.

I felt the energies quickly form around me. I asked for clarification on whose energy I was feeling most strongly near my arm. I was quickly shown an image of a woman slicing apples for an apple pie. The apples were falling into the pie crust that was already laid out. I immediately recognized my mother. I recognized the apples and the way she sliced them, always leaving a little on the core that we would eat. The energy moved around me but mainly focused on my right arm. It moved up and down my arm; I was being gently caressed. I relaxed for a long while as the energy stayed near; I didn't want to break the connection. I could hear my husband preparing for dinner. It was time to let go. This was a new development.

The first time I connected with my mother was a month after she died in September 2013. I felt like I needed some direction. I had just worked through my grief as well as some lingering issues from my childhood. I sensed that it was time to seek out someone who could help validate the intuitive connections I was experiencing. I definitely was not ready to seek out another healer or seer in the traditional sense. Fortunately, I was able to learn a lot on my own, and I focused my own healing; but now I was looking for help to understand where my emerging intuitive gifts were directing me.

I picked up a book at the library that provided resource material on psychics and mediums, and it included a directory of practitioners in Ontario. I was able to locate a few practitioners in our area and decided on one in nearby Hamilton. I sent an e-mail to the medium, but after a couple of days, she still had not returned my call.

As I meditated the following day, I saw an image. It was an image of a woman being knocked off a stool. Then I sensed someone there and asked for a name. "Sylvia," I heard. Sylvia, I questioned? "Yes, she says as in the song; Sylvia's mother says, Sylvia's crying …" And then she was gone.

I recalled that in the book there was a medium who was profiled who fell off a stool. I thought I would send her an e-mail. I figured she wouldn't get back to me or was probably booked, but I took a chance anyway. I didn't hear from her for a few days. When she did finally call, she apologized for the delay; she had been out west visiting friends. We scheduled a date for a reading.

The medium was a two-hour drive from where I live. My friend Dawn traveled with me. It had been some time since we had ventured out together without the kids. We had a blast. We talked, reminisced, and just enjoyed each other's company. When we arrived at her house, I wanted to be brave, but I admit that I got a little nervous. I thought, *Here I go again sticking my nose where it doesn't belong. Didn't I learn my lesson the last time!* I convinced myself I was there for career direction; I thought this would be easier for my husband to accept as well.

The medium had a warm welcome. I immediately felt at ease as we sat down opposite each other on comfortable wingback chairs. The room was bright and sunny. I had booked an hour-long session. She began, "I immediately see two people who are around you. They would have been very close. I'm not sure if they were parents or loved ones, but they are extremely close to you and I feel that because you are on your spiritual journey, these people are going to be around a lot more than they would normally be because I don't think these people felt that there was a life after this one when they passed. I feel that their belief system was that they were praying that they would go to a good place, but their belief system was when you passed you passed. I feel that they are around you because they are very pleased that you are not just hanging on to the old religion. You are looking for more—searching for more."

She continued, "One of them to me would have been a very religious person in their own way, very religious but at the same time when I say very religious I don't think they were completely tunnel vision. I think that they would have listened to what other people had to say, but not necessarily that that was okay; they would respect where you were coming from, but they still had their own belief system. Now that they are on the other side, they're recognizing that all the religions, there is only one God, and that all religions everybody takes a little piece from here, there, all over … This person wants to say that they are doing everything they couldn't do while here, and that they are in a good place.

"I also want to say to you that they are very proud of you that you made a lot of changes in the last year, year and a half; you don't dwell so much on the negativity anymore. It's like okay, that happened, but I'll move on from here. I need to keep growing. I can't keep always looking at the dark things; I need to always look at the positive things. I want to say to you that it hasn't always been easy because people haven't always accepted that you're not falling into the same category as they are—that you are always looking for more.

"I want to say to you that you just don't take what people have to say and think, *Oh that's so right.* You have to find out for yourself whether it is right or it is wrong. I would say to you that that is really a great thing that you are doing that because I feel like I want to say to you not only do you not take someone's word for it, but you need to pay attention to your gut feelings about what this person has to say or what this person is teaching because if it doesn't sit right with you, nine times out of ten it's wrong. So whoever's around me is very, very adamant about this. Not only do you observe, you listen, and then you decide if this is for you or not. I feel like this person is saying you will meet many along the way, all right, who are going to appear to be so sincere, appear to know it all, appear to want to have you part of who they are; but what I sense is that you need to be aware of that because you have a special gift, and they're concerned because many will say they can help you, but it is not so much for you as it is for them because they want your energy to help them do these things. You need to be very aware and always put a bubble around yourself so that you keep the energy around yourself so it is not taken by others.

"I am feeling a woman grabbing my hand. She is a grandmother or great-grandmother. She is a worrier, and she is wringing her hands. This woman would have had many spiritual gifts but because of the times and the life, it was always kept very close to her heart, but she knew when people were coming. She knew when things were going to happen; and in her own way try to steer things around to give people warning or try to change things, just a very loving and caring person.

"You will start to write before long. The information you are going to receive you're not really going to want to share with anybody because you're not going to believe what you are writing, all right. But I want to say, just keep the writing because I feel like I could be reading a book and my hand would be writing over here. This is going to come to you down the road. First you are going to be writing what you are hearing, but something tells me that down the road, it could be that either you are going to be reading and you think you are reading a book but your hand will be writing. Or that you can be in deep meditation and when you come back, you found that you had written something. I always want you to have around you a pen and paper.

"Your journey is going to be a very powerful one, all right. Because I feel in another lifetime you were a very gifted person and you had a lot of wisdom and a lot of knowledge, but you were before your time. So therefore, your life was cut short, and in this lifetime you have to complete all the things you didn't complete in the other one. It is only coming to you now because you had to have all those years before in order for you to come into where you are now. I would say to you that the next years are going to be very busy years for you. I feel at times you are going to be sitting there rubbing your head and saying, 'Okay, where do I go from here?' I want to say to you that when the time is right, you will be drawn to either go to this church or that church or this group, and when you do, you will either feel very comfortable or you will think, *Hmm, there's something not right here, but I need to be here,* because you maybe need to be there to see what not to do! Spirit is going to work with you to draw you to where you need to be. They're going to open your eyes to what is good but at the same time may show you what is not good because you need to have both.

"I will say to you, down the road in four to five years, you will be teaching. You will have a group of people who will be coming to you. You will be probably having a home circle or you will be having something.

"Your mother was a feisty lady. She wasn't going until she was good and ready, and even then she was not ready to go; she fought to the very, very end. She was a loving, caring person in her own way but also a very stubborn person ... Did your mom do a lot of things with her hands? Was she a baker? The reason I'm saying that is I can smell things, and around Christmas is when she would have excelled. I hear your mom saying that she has few regrets, few regrets; but one of them was she didn't take the opportunities that came her way, but to let you know that when opportunities knock you need to take them, okay! I think your mom was one of these people who always put the family first, always making sure there was enough money for everybody so everybody had what they needed; I believe she would have scrimped and saved and done without herself in order to make sure that the family had things.

"The family home—is the family home where somebody is still living?" I replied that we all have a say on who will live in the house. "Your mother had a sense of humor; she is saying that for everybody to agree is like pulling teeth. She is rubbing her face in her hands; I think that she is happy that she is not there to have to make the final decision.

"Do you have a chief or was there a native chief in your family? At some point was there a native chief in your family! Because you will be drawn to some ceremony here, and when you are drawn to this ceremony here, you are going to meet somebody who's going to have some connection to you. It's like when you meet someone for the first time you know you know them, but you don't know where you know them from because you never met them before, all right. I want to say in another lifetime, you two were very connected, okay, whether you were sisters, brother or sister, or I don't even know if it is male or female; I just know that you are meeting this person, and you are going to know. But I feel it has to do with some reserve here. I just feel that you're going to have a strange handshake, and your mother is saying it will be good.

"I just feel that in the coming months, you will be more peaceful than you have been in a very long time, and that is because your mom is around you and she is trying to steer you in the right direction. " The session came to a close.

As I was getting ready to leave, I casually mentioned to the medium the meditation regarding *Sylvia* and how I came to select her to book a session. She was surprised; her friend's mother had recently died, and her name was Sylvia. Her friend was looking for a sign about whether to take her mother's remains to England for burial with her father.

I drove home that day with mixed feelings. I was familiar with all the concepts discussed in the session, and I also knew the commitment to spiritual practice that was needed to fulfill that journey. Everything started to make sense; the direction I was seeking was provided. All the way home, two hawks remained in our sight. I was certain it was my parents.

7

THE HEALER'S INFLUENCE

"I have to see you immediately," the healer had texted. "It's very important!" I was at work but agreed to drop by at the end of the day. I was on pins and needles the whole day. I made sure to have forty dollars for the reading and went to his house. It was nearing the Christmas holiday. He said he had a dream, a vision, and it wasn't good. It concerned our boys. He said he saw a white work van with dark windows and somebody grabbing and kidnapping my boys. They would not be able to survive the kidnapping. This would happen in our neighborhood, and it was imperative that we move! We had to move to a community where my mother-in-law had land; there the boys would be safe. I was paralyzed. He said some other stuff after that, but I can't recall what. I had to get home. Oh my God, this was too much handle. How was I going to convince Mark to sell the house!

My husband understood my terror, and he too felt like things were out of control. We questioned everything and went through different scenarios all night. Could this be true! But by the end of the night, we didn't want to take any chances. We decided to put the house on the market immediately. There were no ifs, ands, or buts about it. We were not going to risk putting our boys in harm's way if there was any way we could avoid it.

It just so happened that I had been in touch with a Realtor regarding a house I had been interested in viewing in a nearby neighborhood. I made an appointment with him, and he came over the next day. The house was all ready for sale and didn't require any work. So he took some pictures and drew up a contract, and in a few days our house was on the market. The viewings started immediately. I didn't let the kids out of my sight. If they played outside, we were always with them. I couldn't wait to move out of the house.

It took us six weeks to find a buyer. We signed the deal, and our move-out date was set for April. But where would we live?! The healer was adamant that it had to be in the community where my mother-in-law lived. Rentals units are very sparse in that area; we had to think of something else.

In the time our house was on the market, the healer was providing us direction on where we could build. My mother-in-law had twenty-six acres of land, but there was a problem with the parcel of land we had selected. The healer said we could run into problems if we built there because there was a curse on the land. We had other restrictions too; we could only use the cash from the house sale to build the new house. In addition, the house would need to be very modest and built only big enough to meet our basic needs. We would have to build most of the house ourselves. It could not go any deeper than four feet into the ground. It had to be built before Christmas of that same year. We could not get a mortgage.

We were floored. How could we do this and pay for all the release sessions, the ceremonies, the readings! It seemed an impossible task to complete. On top of all this, the healer also told me to return to school in the fall. I felt like we were both going to lose it—like our marriage was going to crack under all the stress. Could this really be happening?

(I already planned to return to school; I even had the program selected. This information was generally known by people who were close to me.)

Of course, in the weeks leading up to our closing date for the sale of our home, the curse on the land was resolved by a very expensive ceremony. We could build on the land after all. But still, the question of where we would live while we built our house remained an outstanding concern. My mother-in-law's house is built in a loft style and has only one bedroom, so her home was out of the question. We could rent a trailer, but it would cost $1,500 a month, plus we would need to pay fees to set up a septic and cistern for the trailer. We could not afford all these extra costs and build the house at the same time. Our budget was very limited.

I thought I could get around the money shortfall by taking on extra contracts, but the healer told me this could not be done as it would take time away from the boys during weeknights and weekends. Plus additional work by my husband was out of the question; he had to build the house plus do his regular job.

I was in a meeting one day and happened to mention to a lady sitting next to me about our need to rent a house. By this time it was March and getting very close to our deadline to move out of our home. She mentioned that her brother had a house that was empty, and he sometimes rented it out to family. She could ask him if he would consider renting it to us. I was so excited to hear this; at this point, I was willing to rent any home that wasn't rat infested.

She gave me the address and said to have a look before she called her brother. The house was beautiful. It was thirty-five hundred square feet and sat back in hickory trees on about fifty acres of land. There was a veranda that surrounded the home; it looked stately. I hurried back to the office and told her we were interested in renting the house. Could she contact her brother right away! I hoped the rent wouldn't be too high.

We heard back in a couple of days. Her brother was happy to rent it to us, and we could have a look that day. I was happy for the first time in a long while. We arranged a time to look at the house, and we all went to the viewing together. It was larger than I had even first imagined. The kids loved it on sight. It had hardwood flooring and was huge inside. A chandelier hung down from the front entry with a window to showcase the light; it looked majestic. The upstairs section hadn't yet been floored, but temporary carpeting could be put in place. The bedrooms were all painted, and blinds were on all the windows. It had five bedrooms in total. The kitchen and living room comprised most of the main floor, with a den in the back area. I was in love.

My husband handled the rent. He spoke with the owner directly, who offered it at $700 per month. That was exactly our budget. I was ecstatic!

We all thought we would feel miserable to move away from the home we had lived in for nine years, but we didn't—not exactly. We would miss the conveniences of living in the city, but we had to move on. We had to do this; there was work to be done. Prior to moving into the house, my husband needed to go through the cleansing and protection activities that we were directed to do at our old house. Some of it had to be done at night, right at dusk, so he was kind of nervous going around the perimeter of the new home and not being seen by neighbors.

We moved into the rental house the third week in April. The kids slid across the hardwood floors as we placed the first of our items in the vast kitchen of the new home. I had always wanted a big home, and I would get to live in one—at least for a little while. I felt like a child. It was exciting. We all felt the excitement. My husband was anxious to move in as well. We couldn't look back. I handled retrieving the final items from our house in the city. I said my goodbyes and looked at the boys' bedrooms one last time. A brief sadness overwhelmed me; this is where they grew up, and this is where we shared so many memories of when they were babies. I quietly walked downstairs and retrieved our hamsters. They were the last to go; I packed their cages in the car and took one last glance at the house. Good-bye, my home; be good to the next owners.

When we were settled into the rental house, we started our search for a builder. A lady at work mentioned that her niece's husband was a builder. He built her house, and she was very satisfied with his work. We arranged to meet with him the following weekend. We explained our situation to him and let him know that we had a limited budget and he could only take the build to a certain point before we had to take over. I shared some designs that I found online for smaller homes. The house would be no bigger than a thousand square feet. However, the build I selected had vaulted ceilings and a walk-out basement, so it was still like a two-story build. We agreed to work together and prepared our contract.

His only stipulation was that the outside of the home would need to be complete. It could not be left in an unfinished state due to his building standards for his business. His signage advertising his business was on the property. He agreed he would take the home to a finished state on the exterior but only build to a framed state on the interior, with electrical and plumbing roughed in and the shower installed. My husband and I would do the rest. He brought us the architectural design of the house based on the initial design I had provided. They reshaped the design to add some extra square footage and maximize the space. It was beautiful. It would be built into the hill next to my mother-in-law's home overlooking the river.

Prior to the contractor being hired, the healer was constantly bringing up doing the job as a contractor himself. He worked construction for many years and could easily do the job. His wife even suggested that we should consider him as our building contractor. I brought this up with my husband but asked the healer to speak directly with my husband about anything related to the construction bids. The healer always seemed to filter everything through me; he would never ask my husband directly.

My husband said no. There was no way he would entertain having him as a building contractor. What if we didn't like his work? What if he didn't do the work in the time we needed! It was an outright conflict. How could he even suggest such an arrangement? It was unethical. What if we had to fire him? No, definitely not. I was not disappointed. I delivered the message; we were going with the building contractor we had already selected.

Later the healer brought up the bid during a session with my husband; again he reiterated his concerns. The healer said he was a professional; he could separate the healing work from the construction project. It would not create any problems. Again, Mark said no.

8

JOURNEY TO ADULTHOOD

As the release sessions continued, they were interspersed with different types of ceremonies. The traditional ceremonies were primarily to assist us in our life journey and the obstacles we would encounter and offer us protection. I had two ceremonies, and my husband had three. Each of these ceremonies cost anywhere from $500 to $1,100, depending on the type. They were usually paid a week in advance.

I didn't mind the ceremonies; they seemed legitimate enough and involved other people who were truly dedicated to carrying out the ceremonies that were requested and needed by community members. However, I struggle with the fact that I received these ceremonies and wonder if perhaps they were even meant for me. I don't distrust the people who helped with the ceremonies because I believe their intent was genuine; but I question the integrity of the healer and wonder if he was engaging us in the ceremonies as a way to manipulate us further. I will never know, but I respect the gifts nonetheless.

The ceremonies in a way created a tiny crack in the healer's assertions that all information was coming from my spirit guide. One evening prior to a release session, the healer did his usual reading and indicated to me that now that I had three ceremonies, I could move forward to learn medicine, but I had only two. Shouldn't he have known this information!

We started that night's release session where we ended at the last session; I was about to start university. I attended a small university in Halifax. I was unprepared for the transition. My parents didn't travel with me to Halifax. I carted my luggage and trunk into a taxi when I arrived in Halifax and made my way to the university. I didn't really know what to do with my things when I arrived; the taxi driver just left them near the door. After searching around the residences, I finally located security and asked if there was space available to keep my luggage until I finished the registration process. It was midafternoon, and I was tired.

I walked toward the residence registration, approached a girl I thought was friendly, and asked her if she could direct me to the line to register for the apartment style dorms. She indicated that this was the line and that she had just arrived as well. We chatted while we waited. The apartment dorms were a high-rise unit with over twenty floors. The line took a long time, but we didn't mind; we chatted the whole time. When we reached the front of the line, we split into different directions. When we met up again later, it turned out that she was my roommate. She was a few years older and enrolled in an advanced program, but we got along great.

I made a few friends in the first couple of months and did well enough in my courses, and everything was going well. But then things changed. A relationship in which I was involved the previous year ended when he graduated college and moved away, but then I received a call; he had relocated to Halifax. We picked up where we left off. It seemed to be going well until it wasn't. Abruptly he ended the relationship, which seemed to turn my life upside down. I didn't want to stay; it was difficult to be there. The worst thing was that when I ran into his friend at home during the holidays, he informed me that my ex-boyfriend had eloped over the Christmas holidays. I didn't return to school.

I didn't tell anyone what had happened. I just moved home. My parents didn't really mind because they didn't want me to move away in the first place. I returned to university the following two and a half years, but I didn't make enough credits to graduate in the three-year program in which I was enrolled. I had some problems during this time and could not seem to focus my life. It seemed I just moved from one problem to another.

I fit in, but I didn't. Not in my head. I felt too insecure to connect with anyone I could consider a friend to confide in and seek support. Don't get me wrong—I knew a lot of people and would often hang out in groups, but I didn't have friends. I dated one person most of my years in university, but that too was doomed to failure. Deep down, I always felt he was better than me. His family was close knit, with none of the family violence or financial stressors that I had experienced throughout my life. They were educated and socially confident. I came to resent what he represented—a social class system that I didn't belong to and couldn't quite get!

After a couple of years, I began to manipulate every relationship and every situation to ensure I got from it what I needed. I took what I wanted and didn't care who got hurt. It was a dog-eat-dog world, and I was hungry.

As my mind-set changed and I fully embraced this new and more aggressive personality, I moved to Toronto. It was easy not to feel. I wandered in and out of people's lives like a plague. I was in it for myself, and if you happened to come across my path, you would most likely remember me.

I was fun to be with and would not appear in any way to be a menace, but I did have a dark side. I didn't care about you, only what you could do for me in that moment. In my mind, I was going to hurt you before you ever had a chance to hurt me. I couldn't even begin to remember the lies I told or who I told them to; I just let people talk until I knew what they were about. Everybody seemed to want to talk about themselves and impress; I usually knew fairly quickly what they desired and who they wanted me to be! By this time I was twenty-four, and life was one big party. I didn't have friends, but I had a lot of acquaintances I would hang out with at clubs.

My family saw the change in me, but I didn't care. I felt I was living the life and they were just jealous. I was living the life all right but not how I told it! I had nothing. I moved from place to place, never really settling. I was often destitute. I had little by way of material things and always rented furnished rooms until I couldn't pay the rent and would need to move again. I worked, but I also partied. It was more important for me to go out clubbing than it was to pay the rent. I just thought I was owed something in life; I swear if someone offered me their soul, I would have taken it!

Then I hit what I thought was the big time; I was going to Saudi Arabia to work as a flight attendant in Jeddah. It was exactly what I wanted to do. I had always wanted to be a flight attendant, and when this opportunity presented itself, I was not going to turn it down. My parents were very concerned; they thought I was going into some type of white slavery situation that I didn't know enough to avoid. For me, I just wanted to get as far away as possible. I wanted to see the world. After all, I deserved it!

I arrived in Jeddah, and everything was as I imagined. On the way from the airport, I admired the huge homes that peaked out from behind the secured compounds. The walls were eight feet high. We were housed at a female-only section of an American compound. I shared an apartment with four girls. The accommodations were very nice, and the grounds were well maintained. There was a swimming pool and recreation area located in our section; I think the female compound had three to four sections. Many of the girls were quick to find out where the parties were located from other girls who had already completed a contract with the airline in previous years.

Even though the country is considered dry, there are many places in which liquor is available. However, if you are caught, it could lead to your deportation. Many of the girls had hooked up with groups of people, often from the male American compound. Others got to know some of the locals and would head to their homes where parties were held. I fell in this latter group. It was safer and a lot more discreet. I didn't think I would have any booze during my stay in Saudi Arabia. I truly thought it was dry and was quite prepared not to drink for the length of my contract.

I did have a lot of fun and seriously wanted to get to know the country. I enjoyed the visits to the lavish homes with all their high-tech gadgets, vehicles, and servants. It was like nothing I had ever seen. I wanted to see more of the country; I wanted to go out to restaurants and really experience the country. Unfortunately, I was limited, but I managed to integrate to some extent. I learned the local ways and could easily move around assisted by a hijab and a few of my friends. I went to restaurants along the beach, each a little gazebo separated by curtains. It was beautiful. I went swimming in the Red Sea and drove around the countryside. I wanted to stay.

I traveled to countries near Saudi Arabia situated along east Africa, United Arab Emirates, and India. I often stayed overnight in Cairo and was lucky to be booked on these trips regularly. The hotel where we stayed had a night club, and it was a big party every time. I would always think to myself that it couldn't be real. I couldn't be in Egypt; it was like a dream. I received good reports on my employment records, and it wasn't long before I was seriously considering staying longer in Saudi Arabia. It was a good fit.

My first layover in Cairo was memorable. We had been in Saudi Arabia just two or three weeks and had just finished the remainder of our training. The first part of the training took place in Toronto. A lot of the girls were heading out to party that night, but I had been booked on my first layover in Cairo. I was scheduled to be away for three days. The evening I left for airport; word reached us that there was a big arrest, and over twenty Canadian girls were arrested. They were in jail.

I didn't give it much thought; I believed they would be out in no time at all. However, they were jailed for several days. Word broke in Canada, and my family thought for sure I was among those arrested. They couldn't reach me or get clarification from anyone at the compound on my whereabouts. Their worry escalated, and they made contact with the Canadian embassy, but there was still no news on my whereabouts.

It was a long few days for the girls who were arrested. They were released before I returned, but they were all immediately deported.

There was a message to call my mother. I thought something happened at home and had no idea the news of the arrest made it to Canada. I finally connected with my mother and explained the situation to her. I was sorry to have worried her. I didn't have a clue the story was so big. But I was still not deterred. I was excited to be there, and I wanted to take advantage of every opportunity to continue my contract beyond the completion date.

I was there for three months before I slipped up. I was getting comfortable in making the transition from the bus that dropped us at various locations for shopping and into a waiting car with my friends. It was all so easy. The car had curtains, so I only had to make it to the car. Then this one day they were late. I waited near the mall doors. The religious police and others approached me to ask if I needed a taxi; I said I no. I didn't even realize they were watching.

After waiting about forty-five minutes, I saw my friend get out of the car and walk toward me and turn abruptly. I too stopped and walked back toward the mall. It was too late. I was quickly apprehended and taken into a location in the mall. The police were searching my bag. They took my passport. They were very upset. I was then taken to a police vehicle that was parked outside and put inside. I was in there for over twenty minutes in the extreme heat.

I continued to say I didn't know the person who walked toward me and that it was all a mistake. I was taken to a police station. I remember being led to an older area that was sort of like an interrogation room. As I sat in the room, I kept getting hit in the head with a long bamboo pole. It was more annoying than painful. They continued their questioning; I still denied that I was waiting for anyone. Finally I was taken to another building; it had offices.

I was seated in front of a lieutenant colonel. He wanted to know what happened. I was pissed off by this time; I was tired of all the contradictions. Yes, I was going out on the boat, and yes, I was being picked up by my friends. "I'm tired of this," I said. "I see other girls getting off that bus and getting into cars every time I go out. What was the difference today?"

"You should have got right back on the bus when your ride wasn't there to meet you immediately," he replied. "You made it obvious that you were waiting for someone. They couldn't avoid it; too many other people noticed you waiting."

I was screwed. The airline was finally called to notify them of my detention. I think it was three or four hours since I was taken into custody at the mall.

The officer asked why I didn't cry throughout the ordeal. He informed me that most girls would cry and get extremely agitated during their detention. "It's not so bad," I said. "I've been through worse and been in far less desirable accommodations than what you had available."

We had some time. It would be a few hours yet until the airline officials could arrange my release. I started to relax a little more; he seemed like a nice guy. He asked me about Canada; where was I was from? I said, "I grew up on a reserve. I'm not sure if you are familiar with the Indian reservations in the United States; our reserve system is somewhat similar." He did, and he wanted to hear more.

"Are you hungry?" he asked. He called in an elder to sit with us. We would have some tea.

He went to school in the United States. One of his favorite things to do on his time off was travel to various Indian reservations around the country. He thought the culture was fascinating. We chatted for a few hours, and he told me about the places he had visited; it was after 10:00 p.m. when everything was finalized for my release.

It was around 11:00 p.m. by the time I arrived back to the compound. The Canadian team that recruited and organized flight attendants for Saudi Air were waiting. They asked, "Are you okay! Did they hurt you?" They couldn't believe that it was me who was taken into custody.

To them I was quiet, worked hard, and did as I was directed. They suspected I went out, but I kept it low key and made all my curfews. I didn't give them any cause for concern. My flights were cancelled. I fully expected to be sent home the next day, but I wasn't. I was informed that I would be grounded for the next few days and they would keep me updated.

The next day I got a phone call from my friends. They wanted to know if I was okay and said they were working with the authorities to get everything sorted. Later that week I was called to the airline's administration office at the airport. My passport was returned to me, and I was put back on the flight schedule. I was scheduled to work a flight the next day.

"You were very lucky," the manager said. "I don't know what happened, but everything has been cleared up, and there will no further actions in regard to this matter. I will expect that you will be more discreet in the future," he said.

"Definitely," I replied.

I stayed to finish up my contract, but I was no longer interested in a full-time position. I was looking forward to returning home. The rose-colored glasses had been removed. The reality of the situation and the manner in which religious infractions were dealt with was something I didn't want to mess around with. I was in their country and had to follow their laws; I realized that I had no control. I went out a few more times, but I was content to leave any partying to when I was out of the country on layovers. This was far safer, and I didn't need to constantly look over my shoulder.

I returned to Toronto and picked up where my life had left off. I immediately found a job, and for the next year or so everything was on track. I still went out two or three times a week, but it was different. I didn't feel like I needed anything from anyone; I was just enjoying being me. For this brief time, it seemed I was going to make a go of it. I was becoming confident in my ability to look after myself.

Then I had an injury that took me out of work; it was long enough to send me spiraling again. My life shifted back to the old ways. Back to the dog-eat-dog world of my earlier years. There were gaps in time, sometimes months, in which I wouldn't contact my family. They worried that I had fallen victim to some murderous individual. I didn't care; I was too lost to care.

Finally, as I approached my twenty-seventh birthday, I realized my life was truly falling apart and going nowhere. I needed stability. I decided to move back home with my family; it had been ten years since I left.

The first year was definitely an adjustment to all concerned. I was still in that fight-or-flight frame of mind and returned to Toronto a couple more times. The third time I returned home to Cape Breton, I stayed. I realized I really wanted to be home. I was getting to know everyone again, and my family helped with the transition. I still didn't have any thought as to what I was going to do with my life, but I was finally stable. I could finally relax, and I felt a little more at ease. I started to do contract work for my aunt. It was office support, but I enjoyed it.

The transition away from my old life was gradual. I reconnected with my siblings and all my childhood friends. I was finally losing the sense that I needed to impress all the time; I was good enough. For two years I was supported, cared for, and loved by my family, relatives, and friends. It was all unconditional; no one was looking for anything in return. The community I despised when I left was now my refuge.

9

HIGHER UNDERSTANDING

Two days before the deadline to finish the book, I was getting ready for bed and brushing my teeth. I could feel a sensation on my left calf. I swiped at it a couple of times, but nothing seemed to be there; it continued until I finished. I was very tired and knew I would fall asleep quickly; I felt myself relaxing, almost like I was floating. Then I felt a thud on my pillow right next to my face. I opened my eyes; I stared, hoping that whatever was there would manifest. I could feel the heaviness on my pillow next to me. After a half hour, I finally decided whomever was there was not going to manifest. I went to sleep.

The next day I attended services at the spiritualist church. It was a beautiful, uplifting service. Near the end, a woman who often officiated at the church shared a message with me from spirit. I am paraphrasing here as I didn't take notes. She said, "I see a big dog sitting next to you. It appears to rest his head near you." She demonstrated this with her hands resting under her chin. "It's like a dog who has put his head on your lap. He represents unconditional love. The angels are going to share with you much unconditional love. It is a gift. You, in return, will share and demonstrate unconditional love in your life. Open your heart."

This past February, after I had been attending the spiritualist church for several weeks, I felt particularly tearful while attending a Sunday church service. I felt as though I would burst into sobs at any moment. I knew my life was better than it had been for a long while, and I was very busy working on a project I loved. But obviously something was up. Usually I felt light—unburdened. People would often comment that I had a wonderful energy around me, so why the tears!

Following the church service, I sat with the same woman during the fellowship tea. I casually asked if she did any counseling. Well, it wasn't really casual; I was still feeling quite tearful, and it was obvious. I asked if she could meet with me sometime soon; she was a spiritual counselor. She happily obliged, and we arranged to meet in the next couple of weeks. We met in the church. Beautiful meditation music played in the background. She asked me what was on my mind. It all came pouring out, the guilt, resentment, and recriminations for not being smart enough to see how I had been manipulated, duped, exploited by a healer. "I worked through all of this!" I exclaimed after my outburst. "Why am I still feeling such negativity about that time in my life?" I truly felt I had forgiven–that I had let go of what happened and was moving forward with important lessons learned from the experience.

"There is something else that you are not seeing," she said.

We talked about forgiveness, love, and what we unknowingly attract into our lives because we think we deserve it for whatever reasons we conjure up to keep ourselves from growing to maintain the status quo. At this time, she recommended a book titled *You Can Heal Your Life* by Louise Hay, but I didn't remember. I was too caught up in that moment's angst to write it down.

We arranged to meet again the next week. She asked how my week went. I explained to her the revelation I had on the drive over to see her.

I didn't forgive myself! I went through a process of forgiving everyone else, but I didn't forgive myself. I didn't even consider that I needed to forgive myself. I couldn't truly love others because I didn't love myself. I was just going through the motions. I understood all the spiritual concepts, but I wasn't applying them, most especially to myself. My world opened up that day.

"Forgive yourself," she said. "You made the decisions you did with the knowledge you had at the time. We would all love to have twenty/twenty hindsight, but that is not available to us. We are on this earth plane to learn our lessons, to experience life, both good and bad. It is what we take away from those experiences that help us grow to help us fulfill our life purpose in this lifetime.

"By the way," she asked, "did you read the book I recommended?"

"No," I replied. I wrote down the information and purchased it a few days later. I read it in one sitting. Then I went back through the book to complete some of the self-healing exercises that were recommended and started on that too. But something stirred; I had done a lot of this work already!

During the church service the following evening, a message from spirit was given to me. *I was not to look back. Look ahead; good things are going to happen.* I knew this part of my healing journey was complete. The exercises were not necessary. However, as clarified in the book *You Can Heal Your Life*, we never stop the healing process. Healing is part of our life journey.

I believe as we awaken to our spiritual knowledge, it becomes essential to incorporate daily healing into our lives to ensure we're not creating imbalances in our minds, bodies, and spiritual connectedness. Energies cannot access an overloaded vessel or busy mind. Even then we may need to call upon others for assistance when the challenges are too great and we are at risk of overwhelming ourselves, for it is in these moments of weakness when we are at greatest risk of stepping off our paths.

That night I danced around the kitchen, I sang, and I laughed; my life was changing. I goofed around with my family, and my happiness was contagious. I was referred to as Happy Feet! I loved it, and I loved my family. The joy I was experiencing was real. I saw beauty in everything and gave my thanks to the universal energies that whispered their guidance to me, that whispered in the ears of those who helped me, that whispered into the ears of those who supported me, and for all the guidance yet to come.

A couple of weeks after my sessions ended with the spiritual counselor, I was meditating, and I kept hearing the name Louise Hay. I recognized it as the author of the book I had just finished. I thought, *E-mail her!* I thought this was crazy. Why would I have any reason to e-mail Louise Hay? It persisted all morning and through the day. Finally I said to myself, "Okay, just look up her name and see what comes up." I typed in her name, and the first thing that popped up was a Hay House conference, I Can Do It 2014: A Conference to Help Energize Your Mind, Body, and Spirit. It was scheduled for the following weekend in Toronto. I booked it immediately. I was so excited; the authors on the speakers' list were ones with which I was familiar. I was also surprised to learn that most of the books I read were published by Hay House. I didn't even notice that fact until that point.

I set out the next weekend to attend the conference. I brought some of my books along just in case there was an opportunity to have them signed by the author. I went alone but soon connected with three other women seated near me. We were all meeting for the first time. We had a great time chatting about what brought us to the conference, our work, and what we were hoping to get out of the workshops. For me, I knew guidance had led me to this conference, so I was curious to see why!

It was brilliant. The speakers were vibrant, and their energy radiated the stage. I laughed, cried, and rejoiced at the amazing fortitude and resilience of the speakers and at their continued awe and gratitude for the beautiful gifts of spirit that provided them with guidance. The venue was packed, but it was like each speaker spoke directly to me alone. Their messages resonated with love. I leaned over to one of the ladies I was sitting with and said out of the blue, "One day I'm going to be on that stage too!" She looked back at me and without even blinking an eye replied, "I believe you!"

At one of the book signings, I received a beautiful angel message to, "*Follow my guidance.*"

I returned home inspired and reenergized. I had a busy week ahead of me. A big project report was due on the Friday, and I was still trying to get as many people as possible to complete the survey that was part of the project. It was a targeted survey, so only certain health professionals could participate. I would attend one more conference, but it was close to my deadline. I was really pushing it; if I didn't get any surveys, it would have been a big waste of time. I knew for a while the exact number of surveys I would collect. It was revealed to me during meditation.

It was the second day of the conference, and we still hadn't got the surveys I needed. The conference would last only another few hours, and my survey would be closed that evening. My best friend was there with me as she assisted me in promoting the surveys. I needed six more. My friend is very open and also believes in the power of prayer. I took her hand and said a short prayer to our angels. I said to her to repeat after me, "One and one and one!" She did. Two minutes later the first of the six targeted participants approached the table to complete the survey. I thanked the angels again for their assistance. We talked about it all the way home.

10

THE DREAM CONNECTION

The build on our new house was right on schedule. It went up quickly. The contractor was finished with his part of the build in just six weeks. From the outside, it looked complete. The daunting task of finishing the interior was now on my husband, as well as making the budget work for the remainder of the build. There would also be additional costs to install the cistern and the septic units, which were estimated at $11,000. At the same time, the healer was pushing for him to do additional release work. My husband had already finished. He said there was honestly no more to talk about! The healer pressured me. "There are things he needs to talk about. He's going to cheat on you," he said. I couldn't tell my husband any of this but only ask him again to consider the release sessions. This was in July.

The pressure was mounting. Our budget was tight, and I was still being asked to do release work. It seemed there was always more that I had to review; the healer would tell me my guides were saying I was not telling him everything. I finally reached a point where I didn't have any more to tell. I racked my brain trying to remember things he said I had overlooked. The extra costs were creating more stress on our marriage. My husband postponed additional release work, and boy did I hear it from the healer. "Your husband is hiding things!" However, the healer still did nothing to communicate directly with my husband. It was all on me.

At this point, I had been married to my husband for seventeen years. I knew a lot about him, and he is pretty much an open book. The things the healer was saying about him and what I knew about him didn't make sense. Then the healer told me my husband's guides were getting angry and that they would soon teach him a lesson due to the delays. I wanted to scream; I was tired of this crap! The ironic thing is that the healer would delay many of our sessions because his schedule was busy or something last minute would need to be handled. Our guides didn't seem to be angry when he postponed!

July moved into August, and I was trying to work through my feelings about the healer. He shared a lot with me about other clients he had and would often tell me who they were and what some of their issues were. This put me on edge because if he was talking about them then he could be sharing information about us! He seemed to enjoy the secrets. He would tell me things my husband said in release sessions and what another person close to us said. It didn't seem right.

In a dream, I was walking with a young man. He had knocked on my door. I didn't know whether to speak to him, so I joined him outside. My house was covered in an embroidered purple fabric. It was beautiful. We walked for a while, chatting as we moved along; he was pushing a bike. He gave me his name, but I didn't recognize it. He was wearing a cream or white cable knit sweater, but it was all wet. The sleeves were all stretched. He had red hair, and I remember thinking that he was very tall for his weight because he was quite skinny. *Could anyone be that skinny?* I thought. We walked toward the river, and then we parted ways. As I returned home, there was a text on my BlackBerry from my husband to not open the door to the stranger. I walked in the house and woke from the dream.

I wrote down his name and some of the details of the dream immediately. It was a Thursday in August 2011. The next week I was reading the paper online when I came across an article about a missing person. It was the same guy who appeared in my dream. I ran to check the date of my dream and the name I had written. It was the same. I became ill. It was all too much; I got sick and started to vomit. After I calmed down, I reviewed the details of the dream with my husband. I had already discussed the dream with him on the morning it happened; the name was a little unusual, and I asked if he knew anyone by that name.

I didn't know what to do. I went for a drive and looked along the river banks close to the area I thought had appeared in my dream. Then, feeling upset, I went to the healer to try to get some clarification on the dream. He immediately said the person was dead and that he would be found in the river. I shouldn't look for him. He would be discovered in a short while. Further, he said he was being shown that I would help people find loved ones in the future. He had to help me with this gift, and I needed to use medicine to help with my development. He was very proud of himself and said he had never before helped anyone get so far in developing their psychic abilities.

The boy was found the next day—alive and well. I was relieved, but it opened my eyes. The healer was wrong. I saw this as a sign. I had been seeing the healer for nine months; my trust in him had weakened significantly, and this was another nail in the coffin. I had later learned that the boy had suffered a head concussion and became disoriented and ended up in another city six hours away.

Fortunately, at this same time I was led to a different kind of spiritual guidance in books I found at the library. They were focused on love, forgiveness, spiritual healing, angels, mediums, near-death experiences, and the other side. They were beautifully written and inspiring—nothing like the books I was asked to read by the healer. These new books opened a door; I was captivated. I read all night and sometimes would read passages to my husband. These books made sense; I read as many as I could that August.

I went to the healer only a couple more times after I read about the missing boy. My husband and I were both approaching the end of our yearlong healing process, and the healer told me we needed to focus on meditation and preparation for the final release session. The final healing sessions would be performed individually, and both were expensive. The sessions would include an overnight stay in the woods to eliminate any fear we had and would mark the end of the healing process. A final element of the ceremony would include silver coins that we needed to purchase.

I was scheduled for the meditation sessions which again were very expensive; my husband was too busy to attend any more of the sessions. I tried to meditate and open my third eye, but it was not working. I was finally asked to sit on a bench under a tree. I sat there for an hour, and a bunch of nuts hit my head. The healer said he was getting me used to the woods for the overnight sessions. He cleaned his yard.

A second session was scheduled, but that too didn't work. I could not relax. His talking irritated me. This was the last time I would see the healer.

11

PAST RECOLLECTIONS

The release work turned in a different direction; I was finding it difficult to completely focus on the negative. I was reaching a point in my life where I had started creating more balance; it was a period of positive change. I still had negative emotions to talk about, but they were not all hate filled like in my earlier sessions. I began my review of this period.

I enjoyed being back in Cape Breton; the year was 1993. Life was so different at home. Things that seemed such a big deal in Toronto didn't even register here. I enjoyed doing little things like mowing the lawn. People often stopped by to visit; it was no big deal arranging dates and times. I knew everyone, and they knew me.

My cousin drove past one day as I was mowing the lawn. "Hey," he said. "Are you interested in a job working for a development program?"

"Sure," I replied.

"Sounds good," he said. "Send over your resume." The next week I started a new job.

The office was located downtown; I worked alone. There was an occasional board meeting, but I usually scheduled my own hours. A couple of other native organizations had offices in the building, and I would often drop in to chat. I was twenty-nine years old and finally had my life on track. It would soon be time to get my own apartment. My sister mentioned that my parents were missing their privacy and were now getting a little annoyed by my schedule. I still went out a lot, especially on weekends, and bars were open until 4:00 a.m. I often arrived home on the weekends at 4:30 or 5:00 a.m. This wasn't working for my aging parents any longer; change was needed.

I gave some thought to where I might want to live, but options were limited. I didn't own a car. Plus some of the apartments I was familiar with downtown didn't really appeal to me. I wanted some place quiet. It was my thought that if all went well and I focused my search, I could possibly move into my own apartment sometime early in the New Year. It was December 1993. Then I met the man I would marry that first week in December.

I was out with friends the night before we met; I arrived in the office around 10:00 a.m. The ladies down the hall dropped in to ask me if I was interested in meeting a good-looking Mohawk; Mark assisted their clients once a month with economic development projects. He lived in Halifax. The ladies invited him to lunch, but he was going to work through and head back to Halifax early that afternoon.

I followed them to their office, and they introduced me to Mark. They were right; he was good looking. The women quickly left for their lunch break. I usually led discussions, and this was no different. We talked about our jobs and a little bit about school. He was from Ontario and was three years younger. He had attended a university in New Brunswick. The universities we both attended happened to be football rivals; he had been a tight end. I knew a little about football, so we eased into talking about the school rivalry. I was getting hungry and asked if he wanted to go out for some lunch. "Sure," he said.

We were comfortable with each other right from the start. We had an enjoyable lunch, and I invited him to contact me when he returned the next time for his scheduled visit. It was a month before I saw him next. He went home to Ontario for the holidays, and I had traveled to visit friends. We went out on our first date in January and married nine months later. I moved to Halifax full time in June, and we got our own apartment. We married in October. My family loved him from the start.

Not long after our wedding, my mother was diagnosed with breast cancer. She had a lumpectomy and went through radiation treatment. She made a full recovery but had some long-term effects to her eyes from the radiation treatment. She required drops for dry eyes and would often need more aggressive treatment due to infections caused by extreme dryness. She also had problems with dry mouth.

My husband and I moved to London, Ontario, the following year. He accepted a management position in banking, and we looked forward to the move. I worked at a nearby First Nation. It was not long after our move that I received a call from my mother saying that my father had lost his hearing and was completely deaf. My father's hearing loss was quick. It was difficult for him to deal with, and he was suffering from depression. He was sent to see specialist in Halifax, but the diagnosis was grim. The hearing loss was permanent. He was sixty-three years old.

The family was at a loss at what to do; it was so unexpected. My father started to lose weight, and his moods were unpredictable. It was by chance that he met a young man who changed his life.

I'm not certain of the events that led to my parents meeting this young man, but somehow they connected, and he stopped by the house to share his story; he too was deaf. My mother wrote notes for my father as he spoke. The young man had said he had a successful cochlear implant. He had been permanently deaf and underwent experimental treatment in London, Ontario, that restored his ability to hear. He thought our family should check out the procedure for my father; maybe he too was a candidate for treatment! My father was hopeful for the first time in months.

My family immediately went into research mode to have my father tested to see if he qualified for the treatment. A cochlear implant is a small, complex electronic device that can help provide a sense of sound to a person who is profoundly deaf or severely hard of hearing. An implant does not restore normal hearing. Instead, it can give a deaf person a useful representation of sounds in the environment and help him or her understand speech. Hearing through a cochlear implant is different from normal hearing and takes time to learn or relearn. The literature on treatment was encouraging.

The first audiologist my father visited for a recommendation refused to refer my father for treatment; his comment was that my father was too old to benefit from the implant. My family persisted. They traveled to Halifax to meet with another audiologist to review my father's case. This audiologist offered to recommend my father for treatment but doubted that the procedure would be covered by the Provincial Medical Care Insurer. It was not. The provincial insurer required more information on the procedure, and my father would need to meet with the cochlear implant team in London, Ontario, and return with a referral and treatment plan.

It was now a little over a year since my father had gone deaf. He was still dealing with bouts of depression. It was fortuitous that our recent move to London meant my parents would not need to spend additional financial resources on hotels. My parents spent a week in London; throughout that time my father was scheduled for a battery of tests that assisted the cochlear implant team in determining his suitability for the implant. At the final meeting, we were given the positive news. The team was going to recommend my father for the procedure; they were very optimistic in their belief that he would benefit from the implant. My parents returned home with the wonderful news.

It took another few months before all the details were worked out for the cochlear implant procedure. The Provincial Insurer wavered on their decision to pay for the implant and requested additional support from other specialist. It was frustrating for my father to wait;

he continued to lose weight and would still have severe bouts with depression. Finally everything was approved, and the surgical procedure was scheduled. My parents would need to spend two months in London. This marked the longest period my parents were away from the community and the family. They arrived in the spring.

The surgery was a success, and my father recovered without any problems. The implant could not be tested until he completely healed. This would take six weeks. My father was nervous on the day we returned to the hospital to test the device. It was not simply turning the device on. He was required to go through a series of vocal tests that were then input into a computer. This took most of the morning. The doctor arrived, and he underwent another examination. Finally, it was time.

The device was turned on; my father heard immediately. He started to pound his hands on the armrests on the chair; his excitement could not be contained. It was the happiest I had ever seen him!

We couldn't leave right away and waited in the cafeteria while my father adjusted to the device. The noise was a little too much for him, and the volume had to be adjusted. When we arrived back to my place, my father flushed the toilet over and over. He loved the sound. We called the family with the news, and they all eagerly anticipated their return. A week later my father was allowed to go home. By this time they were both desperately homesick.

We stayed in London another couple of years and then moved to Toronto. At this time, I worked as a national coordinator for a not-for-profit. It was my first management role, and I desperately wanted to impress.

My first business dinner with my boss was going well. We were in Vancouver to meet with the regional management team. A gentleman who was a director of a major funder for our organization stopped by our table, and my boss introduced me. I was reviewing the menu and tried my best not to appear nervous. I was asked a question by the gentleman about a project I was overseeing and was in the process of answering when he casually said to me, "You know your menu's on fire!" I freaked out; it was one of those long menus, and it got caught in the candle. I was mortified, but it was an unforgettable moment!

It seemed I was prone to crazy things that seemingly happened out of the blue. I attended a conference in Ottawa and accidently dropped my car keys as I entered the elevator; they somehow fell through a crack and landed at the bottom of the elevator shaft. It took two days to retrieve them; the elevator shaft is off limits and could only be accessed by a certified elevator repairman. Another time I was heading away on business and arrived at the airport and jumped out to get my luggage; I left the car running and accidently locked the doors. I was traveling with my boss, who was already in the airport and waiting for me at the gate. It took over an hour for my roadside assistance technician to arrive and unlock the car. Our flights had to be changed for later that evening, and his luggage was pulled off the flight.

These incidences seemed to occur on a regular basis. I always had a story to tell. It certainly kept my family entertained. I loved making people laugh; it seemed in recounting my most embarrassing moments, I was able to finally share a little bit of myself that didn't hurt so much.

We lived in Toronto for a year, and I got my feet wet in understanding management principles and project coordination. I realized I enjoyed research and could easily engage with other departments and the projects they championed. People often came to me for advice, and I was selected to lead a couple of major events for the organization. It was after one of these major events that another milestone was etched in my life path.

I had been away for over a week tending to the organization's twenty-fifth anniversary celebrations in Saskatchewan. Our organization was international in scope; however, we had a national Aboriginal development program that was celebrating twenty-five years of service in Canada. The three-day celebrations went off without a hitch, and I returned home to Toronto. Exhausted, I planned to take one day off then get back to the office to oversee projects I was responsible for managing. The phone rang at around 4:00 a.m. It was my mother. My father had died; he had a major heart attack.

I was shaken but not completely surprised. My father's health had been deteriorating over the past few months, and he had already been through one close call in which his prognosis was critical. My father had diabetes, and he had been experiencing organ deterioration over the past few years. His eyesight was failing, he was deaf, and he had a strange addiction to acetaminophen. He would often go through several bottles a week, usually containing one hundred pills each. I didn't know the extent of his addiction until after his near death a few months earlier.

The doctors couldn't figure out what was ailing my father. He was experiencing serious organ failure, and various treatments they were applying didn't seem to work. They met with my mother again to review my father's medical history. It just wasn't making sense to them; he should be getting better. Usually it was a simple case of adjusting his insulin and spending a few days in the hospital to recover. But this time he was near death. The doctors probed further, "Is he taking anything?" My mother indicated it was all in his chart. The only thing she could add was the acetaminophen. They asked, "How many?" She wasn't completely sure how many he took in a day, but she knew it was a lot. This was news!

The doctors immediately changed my father's course of treatment to adjust for the amount of acetaminophen in his system; it was having a dire effect on his health. He recovered but remained in the hospital for a couple weeks. His acetaminophen addiction did not end; as soon as he was able, he returned to taking his daily doses of the over-the-counter pain pills. My father was sixty-seven years old when he died from heart failure.

His life was not an easy one. My father grew up in extreme poverty on the reserve in which he spent his entire life. His home was nothing more than a shanty. It would barely be considered habitable by today's standards, if not outright condemned. His mother died when he was a young boy, and he helped his father raise his four younger siblings. His father eventually remarried, and his stepmother bore an additional four siblings.

My father contracted tuberculosis when he was a teenager and spent three years in a rehabilitation center ten miles from the reserve. He had a big scar on one side of his back where his lung had been partially removed. He married my mother when he was around twenty-one. They had grown up together, though my mother's upbringing was considerably more fortunate. My parents had children in quick succession; by the time he was in his early thirties, he had nine children. Although my father would become an alcoholic, he didn't start drinking until his mid-thirties.

He picked up barbering while hospitalized in the tuberculosis rehabilitation center. He also became an orderly, helping out the staff as much as he could. When he was released from the hospital, it wasn't unusual for the coroner at the local hospital to call upon my father to assist in post-mortem preparations for community members who had recently passed. He often worked three jobs to meet the needs of the family and to put food on the table. Social welfare had not yet been introduced to our communities; it was imperative to work to survive. We went through many long periods when transportation was not available, and my father would often walk to and from work. One night he almost froze walking home in a snowstorm. It was a very dramatic scene when he finally burst through the door. At that time his only protection against the extreme weather was galoshes and a lightweight overcoat; they didn't provide much warmth.

He was a good man. He was good to our family, to his brothers and sisters, and helped everyone in the community in any way he could. This is the way his friends remember him, and this is the way I choose to remember him now. I remember his laughter and his wild stories of when he was young and all the dramas that played out in his life. His friends and relatives traveled from all over Nova Scotia to pay their respects to him. He made an impact on those who sought treatment at the Native Detox Center where he worked for ten years and the many people who sought him out as a barber for over thirty years. My father was just one soul trying to figure out his way, and he had a lot to learn in this lifetime!

12

ANGERS' HOLD

The number nine seems to play into many aspects of my life. It often appears to represent a conclusion. Even though it has played out numerous times in my adulthood, I mostly remained unaware of its influences until recently. My husband and I started reviewing events in our life and realized that nine factored in most times. Whether it was nine days, nine weeks, nine months, or nine years, it repeated itself continually. We actually did this for two days, texting each other whenever we put together another nine association. We were amazed.

Most recently when I had finished a contract, we decided we could finally afford to book a family vacation. My friend and her two children would join us as well. Both our families had struggled financially over the past three years, so it was a relief to finally put aside our strict budgets and book a holiday. As I studied the itinerary, I noted that our holiday was booked exactly nine months after I had decided to make significant changes in my life; that was in August 2013. A part of this change included eliminating alcohol from my life.

I had stopped drinking before when I went through the healing process and didn't drink for another fifteen months. However, I felt I had sacrificed enough; it was okay to drink again. We had survived the worst.

I told myself it was okay because I drank only the lightest beer available, and I hardly ever went overboard. However, I quickly relied on beer in situations of stress. I was not in a good place mentally, and the beer helped me forget that my life was in such turmoil. I would note the number of beer cans each week. Should I be concerned? Was it too many?

After a year, I knew it wasn't good. I needed to change.

I hadn't worked in three years and felt like I was at the end of my rope. In those three years, I had finished school, but I should have had a job by now. My husband was trying to be supportive, but it bothered him that I was still not working. He knew I had a range of skills and knowledge that were transferrable to many positions that were available.

However, I was still caught up in the anger and resentment of the healing process—the process I felt I was forced to endure. I hated my new house; it represented the fear that the healer exploited. I hated being in a community I didn't have any connection to; they were not of my nation. But what I hated most was the feeling that I didn't have a choice of where we lived, and we were stuck here because we couldn't afford to move.

I had never stopped reading, but by May of 2013 the reading shifted. The urgency was greater. I was reading book after book, honing my knowledge on all matters spiritual. I started making poster boards detailing spiritual concepts. I was learning at a rate that most people would have difficulty keeping up with. The concepts were easy for me to understand; I easily recognized how they related to my life and those around me. I was beginning to ease up on myself. I was being shown a way out!

Then in August, I picked up a book by James Van Praagh titled *Unfinished Business: What the Dead Can Teach Us about Life*. On the day I finished reading the book, I closed it and made the decision to quit drinking right then and there.

I was well aware of our familial addiction challenges and group tendencies. That day I made the choice to live my life in another way —one where I didn't need to count the beer cans to determine if my drinking was out of control. I was committed to move toward a life based on self-love and the knowledge that my sacrifice to quit drinking was a necessary part of my spiritual growth.

I continued to read but at the same time taught myself a little about numerology and studied the tarot. They both involved detailed study; I now feel that I have a deeper appreciation of our life lessons and the many tools we have available to help us along our journey.

I studied the tarot exactly as it was presented. I didn't skip ahead and do readings immediately. I studied each card as it was intended and learned all seventy-eight cards in the deck, both their meaning and their application. I studied like it was going to be presented in an examination. I felt it was important to eliminate any fear associated with the tarot. When I finished studying each card of the tarot, I came to the realization that my life experience had touched on each and every one of the twenty-two major arcana and the fifty-six minor ones.

In my life, and as in the deck, I had come to the end … I had come full circle.

It was only after this study that I dared do a reading on myself. It was simple and telling. I saw clearly what the cards indicated. I would only use the cards a few more times. I knew the cards were a gift to understand my life's challenges, and every scenario that presented itself was a valuable lesson from which experience and wisdom was attained. I felt strongly that I needed to develop my own intuitive gifts without relying on the tarot to guide me.

Numerology, on the other hand, remains a constant friend. I practice by doing pyramids on random birth dates and usually carry a book with me for reference. I enjoy reviewing the lives of famous people who have crossed over and chart their lives according to their birth date pyramid. Also, if time allows, I will chart their names, especially those who had legally changed their names from their names at birth or changed their name to that of a partner. It's a satisfying hobby that I can do anywhere and is a constant reminder to myself to be mindful in all that I do.

At this time, I was moved to figure out the license plate BEVJ 368. It stayed in my mind over the three years since I had seen it and knew it was a message. I researched all meaning of the first three letters that formed the name BEV; this would lead to a website on biblical names. The name BEV was broken down in this way: Gracious Oath of God —*Peace and Harmony*; Promise—*Enlightenment*. Another interpretation is Hebrew—*Light Bringer, Radiating God's Light*.

I interpreted the meaning of the J to represent *Jesus*.

The letters BEVJ in numerology break down to the number 3. The number 3 is interpreted different ways in numerology depending on the author. It could represent the ascended masters, such as Christ Jesus, or that of the Holy Trinity *Father, Son, and the Holy Spirit*, or a triangle representing our connection between the mind, body, and spirit.

The numbers 368 add up to 8. In numerology, the number 8 is both my ruling number and my complete name number; I was born the eighth child. Finally, the number 6 represents my soul urge number derived from my name, *Paula*.

Yes, this could all be a coincidence, but I choose to see it as a message from my angels that they are watching over me and their messages will appear as they are needed.

As soon as I started to make changes in my life, my connection to intuitive messages began to expand. Before I intuitively knew I should go someplace or see someone, but I didn't hear or sense the guidance as I do now.

For example, last summer I had a dream of a young boy in the river. He had drowned. I could see him in the water; the river was flooded over its banks. I woke up feeling a little upset. Later that day, I was home relaxing and for no reason said to the kids, "Let's go to the park!" We packed up immediately, and we were at the park in about twenty minutes. I don't usually engage with people at the park and sit quietly reading while the kids play. But on this day, as I walked toward the play area near the river, I started waving my hands and calling out to a woman who was there with her young son. He was about four. The lady came over to me thinking we knew each other, but I said to her, "I just wanted to say hello."

We chatted anyway. Her son didn't have kids to play with near his home, and he was happy my sons had arrived. As we talked, the conversation got personal very quickly. The lady was very lonely. Her husband worked night shifts, and he often had to sleep during the day. Raising her young son fell on her, and she was often tired. She mentioned that she had severe kidney issues and was overcome with fear that she was going to need a kidney transplant in the next while; the doctor had recently informed her that her kidneys were operating at 20 percent. What would happen to her son if something went wrong with her!

For a moment I didn't say anything. I just let her get it all out. "You know," I said, "my mother is seventy-eight years old, and she has been functioning with 20 percent of her kidneys most of her life. She was born with a defect that she didn't even know about until well into her sixties. She follows a renal diet and lives her life pretty much normal in that regard. But up until she found out about the lack of kidney function, she ate whatever she felt like eating."

The woman was excited. "You mean she doesn't have any serious issues!"

"No, other than the odd infection, her health was never directly impacted by her lack of kidney function."

She thanked me for sharing my mother's story with her. She smiled and got up to leave; her husband would be awake soon.

The new, expanded guidance was more engaging. I was expecting that I would return to work soon, but I didn't know in what capacity. I kept going back to an advertisement for a "Request for Proposals" that I had seen on a Native Newswire. I just couldn't get it out of my head. I read it again. It seemed complicated. I didn't know if I could carry it myself, and it had a tight deadline. It was directed to "agencies" and "businesses." Finally I thought I would go for it.

I started on the Response for Proposal or RFP. It was a detailed proposal and required a significant amount of work to satisfy the deliverable schedule. I researched for three days and then began my RFP. It wasn't long before I felt overwhelmed. There was no way I could do all this work. I thought to myself, *I'm not even that knowledgeable in this field of study!* I stopped writing. *Maybe not,* I thought.

I decided to meditate. I realized that my fear was my only obstacle and that I needed to get past it. As I went into meditation, the sensations began, and so did the messages. Ideas were being given to me. I asked questions and received the answers. Even the budget amount was provided. I went back to the RFP and started again. I researched the new ideas and realized that with some work, they could be easily integrated into the RFP. They were new so I had to make it up as I went along. I also needed to itemize the budget in such a manner that would ensure the amount that was given to me in meditation was attained.

I was not surprised to win the RFP selection; I was amazed!

13

THE HEALING BEGINS

My husband and I were working on the house. I received a text from the healer to ask if I had talked to my husband yet about the additional release sessions. The healer was still insisting that my husband needed them and that he was still thinking of cheating on me. He said Mark would not be allowed to move into the new house if his mind was not right. He again said, "They will stop him!" I was scheduled to continue with my mediation sessions.

I called my husband outside to talk because we were told never to discuss any concerns in the house since it would weaken the protection medicine. If we did, we had to smudge right away.

By this time I had already read quite a number of spiritual-related books that gave me some confidence that evil didn't exist around every corner. Growing up Catholic, it was easier for the healer to manipulate me because I grew up with the constant thought of eternal damnation and a fiery hell. His assertions that we would be punished for every sin and providing the detailed description of that punishment didn't exactly help in assuaging my deep-rooted fears of the devil, hell, and damnation.

My husband, however, didn't have such fears. He didn't attend church as a child and wasn't influenced one way or the other. However, his shame and guilt lay in his lack of connection to his nation and the cultural traditions associated with his clan. Although my husband studied business in university, he also completed courses on indigenous studies and was well informed on his nation's history. Unfortunately, there was no interaction with the traditional peoples of his nation who maintained the cultural heritage and traditions. His mother's family discouraged learning the traditional ways and were part of the Anglican Church. Although his mother was Native, his father is Dutch. This too seemed to create self-imposed barriers to connecting in any meaningful way with the traditional community. He was ashamed of his Dutch lineage.

I was ready to talk. I'd had enough. I told Mark that I wasn't planning on returning to the healer; I was ending the healing process that day. I reviewed all the healer had said to me in our sessions regarding my husband's intentions to cheat and that if he didn't do release work, the guides would not allow him to move into the house. He was shocked. Everything came pouring out: the manipulation, the threats, the fear, the coercion, and the betrayal. I couldn't handle it anymore.

My husband sent the healer a simple text indicating that we were done, but the healer replied to my cell phone: "You are so close to finishing. Why stop now?" I didn't reply; there was no need.

Fortunately, I had started school in September, and we were busy working on the house. We also had our boys to look after and ensure all of their needs were being met. I didn't have time to think of all that had happened with the healer. Every day was scheduled to maximize the number of hours we could spend on finishing the house. On the weekends, we packed lunches and stayed at the house all day. The boys spent a lot of time next door with their grandmother.

We did everything in the interior. Initially my husband was to work on the house himself, but when we started, it was just too much for one person. I had to help. I didn't mind the work; it kept me from thinking too much. We managed to move along quickly. The entire house had been insulated, dry-walled, plastered, and painted by mid-December. In addition to the labor, I managed all the selections for the flooring, cabinets, appliances, lighting, doors, knobs, and anything else that went into the home. The cistern and septic were installed, as was the furnace. The electrical and plumbing were completed in December.

Although we were directed by the healer to move into our house in December, we felt confident that one month was not going to make much of a difference. We probably could have done it if we really pushed it, but I did not want to pressure my husband. We had enough of that over the past year.

Exams for school came and went. I managed to achieve academic honors in my program. I was booked to travel home for the Christmas holidays to help relieve my siblings, who were now providing twenty-four-hour care to my ailing mother. I drove two days each way and brought the kids with me. It was an intense week with my mother. Her needs were very extensive. I was appreciative of all the work my siblings put into her care; it was nonstop.

While I was away, my husband managed to finish the flooring throughout the house; he finished the trim soon after. The cabinets were installed, and we were ready. On January 27 we moved into our new home. We had completed our task.

I graduated from my program with honors in May 2012; I no longer felt like an academic failure. But all of these achievements could not hold back my self-loathing.

I would not accept the house as my own. I felt like a stranger in a strange land. I felt trapped. The house was beautiful, but it represented something I didn't want to remember. My thoughts were constantly focused on getting a job so I could get away from the community. It seemed every attempt to find a job was blocked. I had never experienced this before. I was always able to find something, meet somebody, or get some recommendation. Not this time.

Every day was another day I didn't have a job. My anxiety was increasing, and so was my resentment. I would sit outside and have a beer and look at everything with such disdain. I absolutely hated it! A few times I thought of moving home to Cape Breton. I tried to convince my husband that the move would be great. The kids could spend a lot more time with all their cousins, I implored! He didn't want to leave his job.

The only person who knew about my hatred of the house was my husband. However, he was also dealing with his own family issues. This seemed to irritate us even more, and the resentment grew deeper. Fortunately, we were never down at the same time, and we didn't make any rash decisions. When he was feeling low, I would help him manage, and when I was feeling low, he would do the same. This was how our relationship survived. We knew how to balance each other.

When I look back on that time, it was similar to what may be classified as post-traumatic stress syndrome. I managed to survive the event, but I was just holding on. With the boys being out of school that first summer, at least my focus was on their care, and I managed to set aside my anxieties. But as soon as they returned to school, the feelings returned. My husband was trying to give me space to heal, but he wanted me to work too. It was a never-ending circle. I wanted to move, but I needed a job to move. I couldn't find a job, and we were still there!

This went on into the following summer, when I finally decided I was going to change my life. I knew the change needed to come from within. No one could help me with this step. I had to do it myself.

Once the change started, it just kept rolling. My husband was still pressuring me to get a job, but I didn't worry about it as much anymore. I knew good things were coming, but it would be in divine right time. I was becoming stronger; my faith was moving me forward. My energy shifted, and people noticed the lightness around me; I appeared more youthful. I was constantly given healing strength by the energies that surrounded me.

I now danced around my home, full of joy and gratitude to be provided with such a beautiful shelter!

14

A LAST LOOK BACK

The release sessions continued to chronicle my life. Events were intertwined as I reached my thirties and forties. My life was more settled. There was not the angst of my childhood, teen years, and young adult years. I didn't leave as much debris as I worked my way through life. However, I was still guilt ridden about all those I had hurt and unsettled in that I would be found out!

The year after my father died, my husband and I moved to a smaller town an hour from Toronto. I had accepted an office manager position at another organization that was located back in London, Ontario. My husband accepted a consultant position near where we live today. We chose to live in a small community located halfway between our jobs. Fortunately for my husband, he was able to work from home most days.

Our lives were busy. We traveled a lot for both pleasure and business. We thought about having children, but I knew for quite some time that I would face challenges with conceiving a child. I had an ectopic pregnancy, and the prognosis was not very good. We were content with our lives. We celebrated in the new millennium quietly with my mother-in-law.

My mother would visit on occasion, and we would travel around southern Ontario visiting her sisters, nieces, and nephews. It was always a good time. I enjoyed all the stories from their childhood and of the people who lived on our reserve when they were growing up. It was wonderful to hear my mother speak with her sisters in our beautiful Mi'kmaq language.

In 2001 I had turned thirty-seven. I was shaken by the events of September 11 and the attacks on the World Trade Center and the Pentagon. It was so senseless. My view on life and children changed.

By this time, I was fairly certain I wouldn't have children. My husband and I didn't use contraception for a long time, so we knew intervention would be necessary. We were fine with remaining childless, though I thought my husband would make a wonderful father. He had a wonderful way with children; they adored him.

My sister had a baby in August of that year, and I went to visit her soon after the events of September 11. The first moment I held my nephew in my arms, I fell in love. I knew then that I would do whatever it would take to have a baby.

When I returned home, I started my research. I didn't want to go the usual route of referrals through my family doctor to a fertility specialist. I was getting older and felt I needed to look after this right away. I e-mailed a fertility doctor at a highly respected clinic in Ottawa. I didn't really expect to hear back since I didn't have a referral. I gave him a little information about my case and noted my worry due to my age.

In a couple days, his assistant sent me an e-mail asking for more information. I sent the information the doctor required immediately. She called to notify me that the doctor had agreed to see me, but they were not booking any appointments until the New Year; they would let me know in a few months when an appointment became available.

My husband and I went away on vacation in February of the following year. I was still waiting to hear from the clinic. I was lying on the beach when my cell phone rang. It was the doctor's assistant;

they had an appointment for the following month. From here everything moved quickly. Tests were completed, assessments were done, and decisions were made. We were going to start in vitro fertilization in June of that same year.

I love to mountain bike and would often go out for long jaunts through the TransCanada bike trails that run through our area. I cycled hard; I had a lot on my mind. Was I doing the right thing in moving forward with IVF! Would it work! I prayed to God to give me some sign, any sign, to let me know I was on the right path.

I was breathing hard, moving faster. I knew there was a bend in the path and I needed to be careful of other traffic that was coming from the opposite direction. It was a blind spot that often was overlooked until it was too late. I slowed and took the corner; there on the path were two fawns. I slowly came to a stop and got off my bike. I walked toward the baby deer; I was careful as the mother could be near. They didn't move. I was close enough to touch them now. I put my hand out, and one moved toward it; the other stayed behind, too timid to move forward. It was like time stopped; I didn't want to ruin the moment, but I knew I should leave. I said good-bye to the fawns and got back on my bike. I had my sign. I wept all the way home.

I finished my contract at the end of May and chose not to extend it until the IVF treatment was finished. For the moment we would focus on the treatment procedures. The whole process worked wonderfully. My pregnancy was confirmed in August, and we knew immediately, through an ultrasound that I was pregnant with twins.

I loved being pregnant and got very big. My sister said I looked like Humpty Dumpty. I carried to full term, and the boys were born in February 2003. They were named Nathaniel and Bradley. We celebrated their baptismal with my family in Cape Breton. I stayed home with the boys for the next two and a half years.

I finally went back to work when a friend asked if I would help him open a store. My husband and I had flexible hours, so we continued to care for the boys ourselves. I didn't know much about the retail business, but I quickly learned. I opened the store in six weeks. I was busy with the store and looking after the boys. My mother-in-law helped us out as well. We made plans to go home to Cape Breton for a family celebration that summer.

Prior to our departure home, I was having some feelings of unease. I would see flashes of light as I ran up the stairway to our bedroom. My mind was continually making plans to stay at a hotel the night of the wedding anniversary celebration, but we were scheduled to stay at my mother's. The night of the celebration, I went out with my sisters; my husband stayed with the boys. I arrived home late and couldn't get into the house. My husband opened the door and went back to bed.

I was eating pizza in the kitchen, and my mother came in and we started arguing. She was sure I was too drunk to open the door; she had left the key in the mailbox after all. I said it didn't work; I still couldn't open the door. I insisted the door handle was locked. The key was only for the deadbolt. It went on, and the fight escalated very quickly. My years of pent-up anger at my mother came pouring out; there was no going back.

My husband and sister came downstairs to intervene, but it was already too late. The situation was out of control; I was out of control. I left that night and went to my brother's house. I didn't see my mother again for two years.

I was in the store. We had since moved to a new location, which was situated on the owner's property. There was a small apartment above the store that the owner stayed when he was in town. It was Sunday, and the earlier rush had already dispersed. I heard banging coming from the apartment. At first I thought an animal somehow got in and went to check. There was nothing there. The banging continued. I called my husband to come have a look. I was getting nervous. He would be about a half hour.

As I waited, I stood outside. I was feeling unnerved. A neighbor who lived across the street came by, and I told him what had happened. He went upstairs to have a look around. There was nothing, he said. Then he heard the sounds too. He looked again. He said he would go speak to an elder in the community. My husband finally came by as well. He heard the bangs but couldn't find anything either. The neighbor returned. The elder said there was a matter that I needed to look after.

I closed the store and went home. The following day, I got a call at work from my sister-in-law. She said my mother was in the hospital and she had necrotizing fasciitis—flesh-eating disease. I had to call my brother right away.

My brother answered his phone on the first ring. "Paula, you need to come home immediately. The doctors are taking Mom into surgery in a few minutes to amputate her arm. They don't think she will make it through the night."

I was in a daze. My husband made arrangements for me to fly out on the next available flight. When I arrived at the hospital, my mother was in the intensive care unit. Her arm had been amputated to the shoulder, and she had some bacteria spread to her chest. They could not put her on penicillin; she was allergic. It would need to be high doses of other types of antibiotics. She was in a drug-induced coma.

It was a few days before Easter. Her situation was assessed on an hour-to-hour basis. She had made it through the night; the doctors were surprised. Relatives, friends, and community members brought food to the hospital for the family. The first couple of days we were there around the clock. Her condition remained the same. We began taking shifts. I did the overnight shift. A couple of my nephews and a young man who was close to my mother kept me company.

It was Good Friday, and I was settling in for my overnight shift. Most of the family who were there during the day had already left. My nephew and I were sitting in one of the family suites. My cousin walked in, and she had a cross that was very old. It was only taken out of the box on Good Friday. The wooden cross would be taken to those who needed healing. It was nearly reaching the time that the cross would be put away for another year. She had to rush in from another community located twenty-five kilometers away.

Someone within the family would need to pray for my mother; I was the only one. My nephew didn't feel comfortable with prayer. She asked me if I believed in God. If I didn't then someone else would need to do the pray. I timidly said, "Yes, I believe in God."

We said a prayer, and I held the cross in my hands. It was quite big, one that would have hung on a wall. I start to pray for my mother and her healing. As I did this, I sensed white light pulsating through my body. My eyes closed, and everything started flashing white. It was like it was spinning throughout my body. I began to shake. After a couple of minutes, I gave the cross to my cousin. I was deeply affected. I hugged my cousin and began to cry; it was as though every emotion in me had been exposed, and I sobbed uncontrollably.

My mother was brought out of her coma a couple of days later. She was beginning to stabilize. In her confusion it took a while for everything to fully register; my sister had to explain a few times what had happened to her. I returned home to Ontario; it had been a week since my mother's surgery.

I was home for a couple of days when I noticed spots on my body. Soon after, I broke out into a painful, blistering rash that lasted nearly a month. This had never happened to me before.

The following month, I decided to return to Cape Breton but this time with my family. I had planned to spend a month helping out with my mother's care at the hospital. My husband stayed two weeks. It was a time of reconciliation. My mother and I talked for a long time. We both regretted what had happened, and I apologized for my actions that led to our estrangement. Our healing was a slow process; we both needed to trust again.

She spent six weeks in the hospital and an additional two months in a rehabilitation center. When she arrived home, she needed assistance for the first couple months; however, it wasn't long before she was again living on her own. My mother's faith in God did not waver; it sustained her throughout her painful recovery. The source of the necrotizing fasciitis was never determined.

The boys are now getting older. They are four years old and starting junior kindergarten. It's their second year of school. I closed my friend's store following my mother's surgery. I was no longer interested in managing the business. It was time to move on.

I went back to contract work, doing small projects for various Aboriginal organizations. The projects were a lot more stimulating than managing the store, and I was again utilizing my research skills. I completed several small contracts for an organization in which I would later accept a longer-term contract. I was drawn to promotional work but didn't enjoy the spotlight. I felt more secure behind the scenes, executing every detail and coordinating the activities. I was able to come up with ideas quickly and knew exactly how to position them.

At one time I participated in a career assessment to determine a line of work that would best match my skills and interests. I was asked to answer all questions truthfully and to the best of my knowledge. The assessment took the whole morning and included various components. I tested well on the knowledge-based component, but there seemed to be some difficulty in assessing my interests. When it came time to provide final results for a possible career match, nothing registered. The instructor thought it was a mistake; that had never happened before. There were on average three to four career matches provided to each candidate. He ran the test again; still nothing. I had hoped the assessment would finally provide me with some insight into possible career options I could seriously consider for the future. I was disappointed.

I later joked about the assessment. "I guess it means I'm meant to make it up as I move along. No shortcuts here!"

Work that others found tedious didn't bother me; I loved bringing ideas to life. My focus was sharp, and I honed my skills. I enjoyed working alone and didn't mind the long hours involved in projects that required in-depth research. I often attended conferences promoting one project or another. It was at one of these conferences that I received a call from my sister. My mother was in the hospital; she had fallen and broken her femur.

Apparently my mother lost her balance and fell on the side on which her arm had been amputated. There was nothing to break her fall. She was not wearing her medical alert necklace; it had been irritating her neck, and she had taken it off a little earlier. It was on a table across the room. My mother knew she had to get to the necklace. The pain was excruciating, but she knew she had to drag herself across the room. She passed out a couple times from the pain. When she recounted the story, she said she now knew what injured war veterans went through to get themselves through a battlefield.

She slowly moved herself inch by inch across the living room floor. It took her over an hour to reach the other side of the room. When she got to the table, she had to turn herself to be able to reach up and grab the tablecloth that was hanging down. Once she did this, she was able to pull on it, and the necklace dropped to the floor. She notified the medical alert administers, who in turn called an ambulance. They also attempted to call the emergency contacts that included two of my sisters and a brother. They were all away at meetings. The ambulance crew couldn't get in the house; the doors were locked. They could see my mother on the floor; they tried all the windows and doors. A neighbor came by and was going to break down the door, but then he ran over to another sister's home to let her know what was happening. She had the key; she made her way over to the house, terrified she would find Mom dead. It was all very dramatic!

The pain was excruciating for my mother. The paramedics had to provide her with morphine to move her onto the stretcher. There was another hospital stay, and once again my mother entered the rehabilitation center. She fought through the therapy until she was able to walk again. She used a cane for a while but soon didn't need that either. She was seventy-five at this time and enjoyed her independence.

In 2010 I started on a full-time contract. I loved the work promoting a new program. I felt confident in my work and truly enjoyed engaging with all the staff. I thought this could be it. Maybe this time I had fallen into a field of work in which I would eventually settle. I worked hard, diligently. For ten months everything was wonderful. Then I met the healer.

15

A MOTHER'S LEGACY

My life had taken a precarious path. I believe on a couple occasions, I had one foot over the cliff, and one more step or misstep would have resulted in grievous injury or even death. I am thankful each and every day that I was shown a way out—that I was guided out of the darkness!

I'm sure for some this seems a bit of an exaggeration, but I knew the darkness that had taken up residence in the heart. I knew the guilt and shame intimately because we had shared many moments reliving and chastising ourselves for all the pain and suffering we had caused. We were merciless in our attempts to punish ourselves—to never forget one single act of evil we inflicted on others. We examined ourselves under the brightest light so all flaws were exposed!

This darkness primed me; I was a walking billboard with fear, guilt, and shame written all over it in gigantic neon letters. I made myself an easy target.

Then I came to love myself—not in a conceited way but a knowing that I am part of God. I wouldn't knowingly hurt God, so why would I hurt myself!

Today I am proud to be a new walking billboard—a billboard that flashes big letters that are bathed in white light and radiate love, forgiveness, and healing. This light connects me to all the universal energies that aid and support me. My connection to my mother remains strong.

Three years earlier, my mother had fallen for a second time, which resulted in a broken hip; she would not fully recover from this fall. Her health was starting to deteriorate, and her bones took longer to heal due to osteoporosis. During these three years, her every medical need was met, and any construction on the home that was required to accommodate her declining mobility was made. My siblings reorganized their lives to ensure my mother had twenty-four-hour care. They were there for every doctor's consultation, appointment, or hospitalization. Her every need was met.

I went home to visit my mother a couple months before she passed away. Every part of her body was pained at the slightest touch. She was completely bedridden. Sleep was intermittent.

I spent a week with my mom; in this time she would occasional give me a smile, a little laugh, or a gentle look. They passed quickly; the pain was too intense.

Back home in Ontario, I woke from a dream feeling a little bit uncertain of its meaning. It was my mother; she had walked down the stairs and was standing near me in a housecoat. She seemed a little bewildered. She appeared as she would have been in her late forties or early fifties. I asked her how she got down the stairs, but she just stared at me. The dream ended before she could reply.

I called her that day, but she could only say a few words before she was overcome by pain. A week later she was admitted into the palliative unit. She was aware of her surroundings until she was taken to her room, and then she became unconscious. Friends and relatives streamed in to pay their respects; her room was never empty. She didn't regain consciousness and died three days later. As we said our good-byes, flashes danced around the ceiling in her room. "Do you see them!" I kept asking. No one else did.

Mom was brought home one last time for her wake. Our family

gathered around her—not in grief but admiration and respect. We knew she was with her loved ones—with my father. Her heaven's wait was over. The love she shared would remain her legacy, as would her final teachings to her family—teachings that in experiencing her last earthly lessons would help teach us patience, compassion for the elderly, and unconditional love.

These teachings, shared in her greatest time of need, brought with them grace to all those who provided her love, comfort, nourishment, and prayer. Her love lives on in each of us.

When my mother passed away last September, I had just started my journey. It is now nine months later, and she is participating in my birth yet again! She helped bring me peace, and in that peace I am the light.

AFTERWORD

The journey to healing starts in many different ways. For some unknown reason, we are plucked from our path and presented with a different course. This new direction at the moment we are shown it is neither right nor wrong! It's what's in our hearts that make it good or not so good. This holds true for spiritual healers as well.

Though my experience with an Aboriginal healer/seer was not a favorable one, my belief holds strong that Aboriginal traditional healing methods play a crucial role in supporting the healing journey of our Aboriginal peoples. However, these healing practices should not be hidden, and they should definitely not create fear!

Integrating healing methods into mainstream Aboriginal health services encourages us to take a bold step toward demystifying healing and creating transparency. This is especially important for the development of young or novice healing apprentices who are new to their spiritual gifs and need to seek mentorship from more experienced healers.

I knew the healer as an acquaintance a year before this happened; he was somewhat aware of our lives through a couple of sources. That is why I took the messages to heart; I thought he could be trusted.

AFTERWORD

Exactly two weeks after I received guidance to write this book, I signed a publishing agreement with Balboa Press, a division of Hay House, Inc., to self-publish my book.

After I signed the agreement and returned it via electronic signature, I decided to relax for a few moments. Seated at the table where I had been writing, I closed my eyes. I automatically fell into a meditative state. The energies quickly surrounded me. My arms were moved to relax at my sides with my palms facing up. Energy pulsated through them. It shot through my body, arching my back. I began to weep; I keep repeating, *"I am in awe ... I am in awe!"*

Thank you for walking this journey with me.
Paula
Light from Creator

III

OUT FROM BENEATH YOUR WINGS (2016)

In her follow-up book to *Heaven's Wait*, Paula Sevestre delves deeper into the personal history of her experiences when she left her small Native community to venture out into the bright lights of the big city and beyond. Guided to share her story, Paula inspires others through providing humorous insights into her life experiences and the dreams that have helped shape her reality. Forever connected to her First Nation community in Cape Breton, it is Paula's hope that her journey will inspire healing in others who are seeking a deeper meaning to their lives and trying to heal from the trauma of their past.

"Could I overcome this revelation and continue in my work. Would it once again knock me into a sense of despair so deep that it would take another two years to overcome?...I began to waiver in my desire to visit the 'fathoms of my consciousness'..."

PREFACE

I walked the small beach, an inlet really. The rocks were smooth and shiny and covered most of the sand. I was feeling nostalgic; I was leaving Cape Breton Island for a second time. Even though I had recently moved to Halifax, which is located on mainland Nova Scotia, Cape Breton was just a short trip away. I had been married for eight months, and my husband, Mark, had recently been laid-off from his job due to funding cutbacks to the Aboriginal program which employed him. We decided to move to southern Ontario, where he had lived most of his life. We were taking this trip home to say goodbye to my family in Membertou, a small First Nation located near Sydney. This meant saying goodbye to my mother, who was just recovering from treatment for breast cancer, my dad, and my brothers and sisters and their families.

As I made my way back to the mainland, I took the more leisurely St. Peter's route. I don't know what made me stop, but I pulled over near a little beach I used to see all the time. Cape Breton Island is full of scenic vistas, but this one in particular seemed to beckon to me. The parking was somewhat difficult, so I squeezed as close as I could onto the blade grass that ran alongside the highway. There was a

PREFACE

church nearby, with a shrine dedicated to Our Lady of Guadalupe, and I used to love looking up at the shrine as I passed, often thinking of my mother. As I walked the beach, my mind raced. I questioned our decision to leave Nova Scotia, to leave the safety of my family, to leave friends that had supported us both in Membertou and Halifax. Images of my parents, my brothers and sisters, nieces and nephews, and my best friends passed through my mind. I came home to Membertou three years earlier to heal, to feel safe, protected, and to feel love again. I asked the Universe for direction, a sign we were making the right decision.

As I viewed the beauty of the Bras d'Or Lake, I cried. I could feel my people, my Nation in each and every sparkle off the water, in each wave that crested the shores, and in each rock laid out before me. I needed to know why I had to leave again. Why was I always on the move? I walked to the edge of the inlet and took a deep breath to try to calm myself. I looked down and there at my feet was a heart-shaped rock. I picked it up and marvelled at how much it looked like a heart. I smiled and put it in my pocket. If I couldn't stay in Cape Breton, then I would take a little piece of it with me. I felt its energy and love. I held it close all the way to Ontario.

My heart rock travels with me, a reminder of where I'm from, my people, my parents, and my family. One day, when I no longer need to live away from my community and from Cape Breton Island, I will return the heart rock back to that same beach where I found it. I will leave it for someone else to find, someone who is starting their own journey that takes them away from our beautiful and sacred Island, which for many is away from their people of the Mi'kmaq Nation.

INTRODUCTION

In the months following the release of my book *Heaven's Wait*, I was asked on numerous occasions how someone who was seemingly intelligent, worldly and well-read could possibly fall prey to what to them seemed like an obvious con man with an agenda based on manipulation and in their words 'fraudulent' activities. I too at times found it difficult to summarize what happened in my life that would compel me to take the drastic steps with the healer that I did.

For those of you unfamiliar with my book *Heaven's Wait*, it details my experience with a self-ascribed Aboriginal traditional healer in a First Nation community in southern Ontario. This supposed healer was known by many in the community, but was not thought of positively. Following the release of my book, it became clear from those whom I spoke with that many people were aware of his activities and the manipulative methods he used to gain a person's trust in his so-called healing methods but, unfortunately for me, this knowledge and insight came too late.

The nine months I spent with this healer changed my life profoundly. I went from being a confident woman, albeit high-strung and perhaps a little high maintenance, to a pathetic, frightened and

INTRODUCTION

bitter person. I was seeing or speaking almost daily to this healer from November 2010 to August 2011; he said this was part of a traditional spiritual healing process that was supposed to last a year. To my dismay, I also involved my husband (Mark) in this supposed traditional spiritual healing, regrettably threatening that if he didn't agree to the healing journey I would leave him and take our twin boys, who were seven at the time.

My life stood still for two years following the time I spent with the healer as I underwent an inspired spiritual transformation that was equally as profound. This healing journey was different. This journey was directed by my own spirit guides and, more importantly, from a place of love.

Initially, following the time when I severed my relationship with the healer, I wallowed in self-pity. I drank more than I should, trying to forget the shame and humiliation I felt for falling victim to the manipulation the healer used to gain what he desired and demanded: money, power, and respect. When I refer to this person now, I do not give him the respect that is associated with the term healer or medicine person; I have simply come to use the term 'charlatan', a person claiming to have special knowledge or skill, a fraud. He is what in some circles is referred to as a pseudo healer and is not even respected in his own community!

My spiritual transformation began in the local downtown library. I was drawn to the New Age section, but was unsure of the authors and so I read a collection of books from one author or genre at a time. At first I read for entertainment, but soon realized I was being guided to certain books and topics. Following some of the suggestions found in some of the more instructive books, I learned how to meditate and began a daily meditation practice. It was then that I recognized the gentle guidance I was receiving. I first thought I was simply selecting every book I came across; however, I realized as I ran my hand across the books, I was being stopped at a book or collection of books that had a particular feel or vibration to them. When I returned home from the bookstore I would often read through the night because I realized that each book focused on an aspect of healing I was currently experiencing. This realization opened my eyes to a whole new world, an unseen world of angels, guides and spirits!

I learned at a pace that was driven, guided and spiritually connected. All the knowledge gained from the books was easily integrated with my life experiences, lessons, and the wisdom gained from those lessons. During meditation I received healing energy that was previously unknown to me and even now defies description. It was like my entire being received a jump start, a boost of love so powerful it immediately heated my entire body and brought me to tears. I cried uncontrollably because this was the only way to express the intensity of the love that pulsated through me; love so healing it flashed white.

I read over 100 books on topics ranging from all things metaphysical (angels, guides, ghosts, mediums, psychics, psychic divining tools, reincarnation, past life regression therapy, meditation, light working, etc.), major religions and practices, spiritual healing, psychology, and finally, shamanism and ancient traditional healing practices. I felt rejuvenated by the works of these authors but also responsible for my own happiness, my own self-worth and my spiritual growth. I could not turn back, as once I became aware, the veil was lifted. The world is not as I once thought, nor will it ever be that way again!

My spiritual education continued on through 2013 and early 2014. I was now receiving a different kind of guidance; not only did it form in my mind accompanied with a tingling sensation, but it was also present in my writing. I wrote new ideas, strategies, and concepts without any thought given to the topics. I simply sat at the computer, put my hands on the keyboard, closed my eyes and typed. As the ideas took shape, and I typed paragraph after paragraph, I could feel my excitement grow. I could now visualize how a concept or strategy could be introduced, supported and sustained.

I was also picking up vibrations from those I interacted with on a personal level, whether in person or over the phone. Surprisingly, these messages often came when I was in the shower or doing my hair/makeup following these personal interactions. The messages

INTRODUCTION

were primarily insights on how a project/work/personal circumstance could be enhanced and/or shifted. They came in a fast, clear and precise manner, and needed to be written down quickly. However, this created another problem. I didn't consider myself a psychic, or anything along those lines, but how was I going to convey the message without appearing spooky or as some might say "out to lunch". I decided that using softer terminology in referencing the message was best so as not to overwhelm or frighten the individual receiving the message. I began to refer to these messages as inspired thought with no reference to guides, etc., and to my relief it worked. However, in time, as people came to know me, I began to feel more confident in sharing how I received the messages and that, as it turned out, was also okay!

By the time April 2014 came around and I was guided to write *Heaven's Wait*, I was prepared to accept the guidance and share my story. It was not an easy process and I deliberately knocked myself off the writing track a couple of times, unwilling to expose my true self. However, it was through this exposure of hurt, shame and guilt that I felt truly alive. For the first time in my life I was able to speak openly, and in turn, others felt compelled to share their own stories.

Our stories may differ, but dialogue is happening and that is the real gift of *Heaven's Wait*—inspiration. Inspiration to change, inspiration to heal, and inspiration to transform!

1

THE UNVEILING

A hawk soared outside my window. It was a majestic sight, and I was awed by the length of its wingspan and the whiteness of its feathers as it glided across the tree tops. I sat alone and went over in my mind the conversation I had just had with my husband. It was beautiful, one full of acceptance and love, and his support was unconditional. He recognized my need to write this book, knowing that what I was about to share had merit and each word would be written from a perspective of love and healing, a way to put my past behind me. "Go for it, don't be afraid to share your experience" he said, "You've hidden the hardships from your youth long enough. Let them go!"

In the months following the September 2014 book launch for *Heaven's Wait*, I traveled back to Cape Breton a couple more times to promote my book. On one of those occasions, I was asked to participate in a graduation ceremony for youth participating in an independent living initiative. I wasn't scheduled to speak at the event, so I didn't have a presentation planned, but I thought it would be easy enough to share some background about my book and do my usual book signings.

However, when I arrived, I realized most of the participants were in their late teens and communicated on a whole different level. Theirs world was one tuned to visuals, and I certainly didn't have time to create any such material for the presentation. As I sat there pondering my predicament, the moderator announced that she could assign 20-30 minutes for my presentation and in a panic I yelled back "I only need five!" "Okay, well five minutes for the author then" she replied. I scanned my table, looking for something on which I could write down a couple of notes. I had about 10 minutes to come up with something. I reviewed the Program Modules that were on the table and the one thing that popped into my head was, *wow... I surely could have used this when I was their age!* As I got up to introduce myself, I still didn't know what the focus of my presentation would be, but it seemed that my guides took care of this for me.

As I started my presentation, visions of my life in Toronto during my early twenties entered my mind. The words rolled off my tongue and stories I hadn't shared prior to that day came to life. I distinctly remember looking into one of the young faces seated at the table closest to me and having this intense need to convey to him, to everyone, the challenging times I experienced living in Toronto, many of which were due to my own lack of life skills. Unfortunately, when I lived in Toronto, my absence of life skills led me to make crucial misjudgements and poor decisions which spiralled into living conditions that were unstable at the best of times, and frantic at the worst. At these times, I could no longer trust myself to make sound decisions. I moved from crisis to crisis, trying to think up solutions only after getting deep into a problem and never really solving anything. If anything, I usually made things far worse.

I moved around the room, animating my accounts of woe and using humour to convey my messages. Time flew by, and when the presentation ended, I realized I had spoken for about 25 minutes. It was like I had flown back in time, and I felt rejuvenated when I finished. It was the first time I had shared these particular stories publicly, and they were told just as they had happened. I had shared stories with my family and laughed at my many exploits, but this time was different; the stories I shared were the real stories, the way I had actually lived them and not the stories I changed so as to reflect the way I wanted to live. I recognized that this time I was in a position to have a positive influence and I took this very seriously. For the first time in my life, I felt like an adult.

Today, as I write, my thoughts again return to my presentation to the graduating class. I think back to the person I was when I lived in Toronto. In my twenties, (I am now in my early 50's), I was more hardened to life than many people would have thought. How I appeared on the surface, attractive, out-going and compliant, did not in any way match what I felt inside and this miscalculation brought many problems into the lives of many I came into contact with. What raged inside of me was downright chaos. I created problems for no reason at all without even a thought to the turmoil I left behind. There was no pre-meditation to my actions; the chaos wasn't planned like some evil arch-villain as it was mostly spontaneous. I took advantage of situations, and the emotions of those involved, and harnessed the WITF (what's in it for me) mentality.

My life until that point had been a series of unplanned and spontaneous hits and misses. Nothing was done according to some great plan or knowledge of how life was to be lived. I grew up in a family that lived day-to-day. If there was money, it was spent. Keeping food on the table for a family of nine, eleven counting my parents (and then some) was not conducive to saving. Plans were for other people. We just lived. Most people we knew existed in the moment, existed without forethought to tomorrow, next week or next year. For many, that was just the way of life on the reserve, a lifestyle of simplicity created by poverty.

As my thoughts wandered again to Toronto, I remember standing at the window of a store near the intersection of Bloor/Yonge in the downtown core. It was a nice day and many people were shopping in the high fashion area of Yorkville. Everyone looked rich. How can so many people afford these things? What's it like to have money like that? I posed these questions to myself as I walked south, down Yonge Street and away from the Yorkville Shopping district. I didn't want to look anymore; it just made me feel too much want and desire for everything I couldn't have. I worked, but I made just enough to get by and when I did have money, it didn't last long as clothes were always a priority, sometimes even over food.

As I walked, I looked into the restaurant windows as I passed each one. I was hungry but didn't have any money to eat. I stood at a restaurant window where I had eaten before and imagined the chicken wings that I knew were so tasty! Oh what it would feel like to have wings and a beer -- when I get paid that is what I'm going to do first thing, I thought. I walked back the three miles or so to my little place because I didn't have any money for the subway or bus. It was a week until payday and I still had to get to my job every day, which was located in the same area as the high end shopping district. It would be cookies all week, I thought, as the office usually had coffee, tea, and cookies available for clients. I would just fill up on these and take some home for the remainder of the week.

I lived in this manner most of the time. It was always feast or famine. I had no plans beyond today if it did not include going to a night club or some sort of drinking venue. I didn't buy a monthly metro pass for the subway and bus lines because I didn't want to spend $35.00 up front, so each week I would invariably run out of money. When I lived in the city it was easy enough to walk, but when I lived in the suburbs, it meant the penny hunt was on. I would search for pennies all over the place. I would check and recheck places where I could possibly find any stray coins. Some days, I knew the bus driver noticed I didn't have enough fare, but he seemed to let it pass. I always had lots of pennies, so it at least sounded good. I know a few times I even threw buttons into the mix!

When I think about the city, it is a reminder of an unprepared life. Life skills were not even in my vocabulary. I came at life with both barrels blasting, only to get knocked down by the backfire. I lived a lie inside my head. Not all times were bad, and many were actually fun.

But this fun almost always involved drinking. I did not consider myself as having fun if I wasn't out somewhere having drinks and dancing the night away. I didn't own a television most of the time I lived in Toronto, so it was not something I could use to occupy my time. My time was spent in the bars and dance clubs.

Oh, don't think I had money for bars and night clubs most times, either. Usually, I would sneak in a six-pack in my purse and drink that in the nightclub. One place had a buffet, so I would head there as early as possible, buy one beer and sneak the rest out of my purse. I also sometimes had dates but I didn't usually go to nightclubs with dates. It was like I led separate lives. If I dated someone, I didn't want them around my other life. It would ruin everything when we broke up and I would need to find a new place to hang out. Maybe I didn't separate it enough though, as I was always looking for a new club, or a new bar!

What I came to realize later in life is that when living in a fantasy world such as the one I created for myself, it's imperative not to get too close to people. Invariably they want to know more about your life and they want to introduce you to their life. In relationships, once this process started, I wanted out. Because I lived in a strange web of my own design, I could not let others see the chaos. It was too much to keep a lie going when it was told to a third person, a fourth person, a fifth! Even though there were some I may have considered for longer term relationships, I couldn't let them get too close. It was too easy to see the tangled web from close up. Instead, I created distance any way I saw fit.

But each time I did this, each time I treated a person in a way that was less than what they deserved, I was forever linking myself to them. Without knowing it, I carried their hurt and their misplaced trust in me. This type of hurt is not something we can easily set aside, and it becomes more difficult over time to carry. Each face is imprinted on us, like a design on a blanket, face after face. For me, the blanket became almost unbearable to lug around as more and more faces were added, and it became dirtier with each passing year. Soon, hiding under the blanket became the only way to survive but all the while I was suffocating from the stagnant air, waiting to be exposed as a thief, liar, cheat, and fraud! I seemed always to be waiting for the shoe to drop, and for my life to come to a screeching halt!

But I digress, back to Toronto. It's amazing how people see you but don't see you. They see what they only want to see. I suppose this mirrored only that which I wanted them to see…the fun Paula!

One memory in particular is burned into my brain. I had been invited to an afternoon barbecue by an acquaintance I had not seen in a while. She was always inviting me to things even after I had hurt her. Her invitation surprised me, but this was one of the times when I was technically homeless, so I accepted the invitation; however, for some reason that now eludes me I said I would bring lobster! What was I thinking!? I had a job, but I got the job too late and couldn't pay my rent so I was trying to secure a place to live that day. It was taking longer than I thought and my options were limited. I could stay at the YWCA or the local women's shelter, but I didn't like restrictions these places had so I decided I would just figure it out later.

Having just got paid, I was miss Big Spender! I arrived bearing the lobster I had bought at the local fish market. It was freaking expensive! I was homeless, but I felt like a big shot when I arrived at the barbecue and everyone was excited about the lobster. Later, after an afternoon and evening of partying, I still didn't have any place to go and didn't let my friend know my circumstances. That's okay, *I'll figure it out,* I thought as I left that night. I rode the subway thinking about where I could go. It was too late for the two earlier options I mentioned and I spent a lot of money on lobster, so a hotel was out of the question. I eventually went back to the office where I worked and stayed there for the night. Fortunately, I had the key and the security code. But now when I look back, I realize that all this secrecy about my life was so unnecessary. One mention of my situation to my friend and a comfortable bed would have been laid out for me in her home. I see now that it was my self-destructive behaviour and pride that had me laid out on my office floor, mumbling under my breath about the unfairness of life and how everyone had it so much better than me. Those bleeping rich people! In my mind, I was never to blame for anything.

How did I manage to get through my earlier life, so crazy and full of missteps! I was fortunate enough to avoid any serious harm, but this lifestyle had its impacts. For the longest time, these missteps, both intentional and unintentional, were filed away in my mind, and were much too embarrassing to share. At that point in my life, it took numerous times for me to learn the lesson of planning ahead and creating balance in my life. I'm not talking long-term, save for retirement-type planning. I'm talking about how do I get to work next week and how will I pay my rent! Each time the lesson presented itself, it was in an ever-increasingly desperate manner. I simply wouldn't learn and as a result I suffered the consequences. These consequences shaped my life and put into play barriers and roadblocks that would hinder me for years to come.

Something as simple as grocery shopping was not properly learned. I primarily lived in my residence at university, so I was accustomed to a meal plan. I did have an apartment with my older sister one semester, but I relied on her to take care of preparing meals. I felt my job was to help carry the groceries, and didn't put any thought into the weekly meal plan or budget. The food was just there just as it always had been at home. It was incredible that I could reach my mid-20s and still not think seriously about what I was consuming and where the next meal was coming from! I lived on Kraft Dinner, Mr. Noodles, and peanut butter and some days just a small bag of chips or cookies for my lunch at work.

One time, when things got a little too desperate, a call was made to my mother for money. She sent $75.00. Most times, I bought food at the local convenience store, but this time I went to the grocery store. As I went about my shopping, I was loading up the cart with items, all the while not thinking about the cost. I bought anything I desired, like cookies I actually liked. Finally, as I went up to the cashier, the cart was full. For some reason, I had even bought tea towels. One by one the items were rung in by the cashier. I don't recall the total, but I was definitely over the $75 limit.

I started handing stuff back to the cashier to take money off the bill until I was under the limit. It was so embarrassing, as there were people lined up behind me. I finally finished and left the grocery store with a number of heavy bags. As I made my way outside, I realized that I did not have any money for the subway and I lived 2-3 miles from the apartment and it was a hot summer's day. "I'll have to take things back", I thought to myself, "I'll just tell them I didn't need the items after all!" I stood in the grocery store entrance going through the groceries once again, selecting items that I absolutely didn't need. I returned enough items to get tokens for the subway and some beer for the weekend; I had forgotten all about the beer and was relieved I remembered!

Unfortunately, a lot of the items I purchased were perishable that ended up going bad because I didn't cook them. I know $60 doesn't seem like a lot for groceries today, but 27 years ago it bought a fair amount. I had envisioned making healthy meals, but I was too used to slapping peanut butter on a slice of bread, folding it and considering my meal complete! If I didn't have peanut butter, I would do the same thing with ketchup or mayonnaise. My idea of food was to satisfy the hunger pangs and that was it. That is why I was satisfied with having a bag of chips for lunch. I had always associated prepared food with home, and I had never considered any of the places I lived as home. Making meals was for adults. I had a false sense of sophistication, while in reality I was barely getting by and my food choices reflected this state of mind.

What it comes down to is, I simply didn't know how to make a home for myself. I left my family home at 18 years of age and mentally that is where I stayed. Even though I had a job, lived on my own, and moved to Toronto, I still didn't know what truly made a home or what this would mean to my growth. As long as I bounced from place to place, job to job, friend to friend, I wasn't answerable to anyone and I certainly wasn't answerable for my actions. It was easier to pick up and disappear from someone's life than to stay and face the consequences of my betrayal and lies. So I ran, which created even more instability. Each time I tried to start over it was with less; perhaps even less than I had begun with because when I vamoosed, I left most things behind.

If I could only have said I was sorry or owned up to my actions my life would have stopped spiralling out of control. But I was so freaking proud! I would not admit to anything and this is where the majority of the guilt and shame originated from and why I was so easily manipulated by the healer. This chaos combined with my moral missteps seemed to engulf me into a secret world only visited by me. I held the key and refused entry to anyone that cared. It was like after having secreted away all my bad thoughts, actions, and behaviours I shut the door, locked it and I walked away. I walked away from Toronto and to a new life. But I knew I didn't hold the only key. There were many, and at any time the door could be opened by one of these key holders and I would be exposed.

2

A CHILD'S LOVE

I woke suddenly, startled by a dream I just had. It was the morning of January 8, 2015, a Thursday. In the dream I was asked by a lady from my community of Membertou to come with her, as a daughter I had given up for adoption wanted to meet me. *I didn't give a child up for adoption,* I told her. She was adamant it was my daughter and she really wanted me to meet her. I looked at the little girl and stared into her eyes for a long time. She was only about two, but she was lying down like a baby looking up at me. I continued to stare into her eyes. She was so beautiful. I sensed there was another child nearby as well, but it was this little one that held my attention. She was very familiar and had many of my facial features with a head of curly hair. "She just wants to get to know you" the lady said. I glanced back at the child. "I'm sorry, but I don't remember giving a child up for adoption!" I said.

I picked her up and looked into her eyes yet again. *This child is definitely mine*, I thought. The lady said, "She wants to know if you will visit again?" I said I would love to visit again and we could make arrangements. Then, I woke, wondering what the dream was about. I knew by the feel of it that it was different and it was not a regular dream. This dream was conveying a message to me.

The previous night, I had prayed that I would learn what emotional attachment I was not connecting with. I had felt like there was a lump stuck in my chest for days. The food I ate just seemed to sit on top of it. This was not a feeling I was familiar with. In the past, when I became nervous or fearful I would feel it in the pit of my stomach. This time it was in the area of my sternum. I was familiar enough with spiritual development that I knew it was time to deal with something—all I had to do was figure out what!

A week prior, I had arranged to visit a lady my sister had spent a couple days with and who had done some spiritual work with her office staff. She was a medicine woman. My sister said she had felt an immediate connection with her and that I really should arrange a meeting with her, but before I could send her an e-mail, I received one from her. She had read my book *Heaven's Wait*, which she had received as a gift from my sister, and was interested in getting together. As I read her e-mail the smell of sweetgrass permeated my bedroom, making me even more interested in meeting her! We arranged to meet a few days later and I decided to make the three-hour trip.

I looked forward to the drive. It was just after Christmas and I really needed to get out of the house. My boys, Bradley and Nate, were on their holiday break from school and preoccupied with their new video games and my husband, Mark, was watching yet another holiday hockey tournament on television. It seemed there were several hockey games each day and it was starting to drive me a little crazy. A nice long drive would certainly do a lot to restore our family harmony.

It was a beautiful day for a drive and I looked forward to connecting with someone that was on a similar spiritual path. My sister had commented that this medicine woman reminded her a lot of me and that she had similar views on spirituality. This interested me a great deal, and not because I wanted anyone to validate my spiritual beliefs, I simply craved an opportunity to have an open spiritual conversation, free of worry that I might offend. There was so much I wanted to talk about, and my mind raced as I drove towards our meeting.

I felt butterflies in my stomach as I arrived at the place we had arranged to meet, a Starbucks located just off the highway in a local mall. I tried to calm myself as I walked towards the mall, *it's just a get to know you coffee*, I said to myself. I walked towards a woman I thought was her, and introduced myself, but it wasn't her. *Okay*, I thought, *let's look around, who looks like she would be a medicine woman!* It was so crowded in the coffee shop. I looked around, wondering if she was able to make it. She said she would be journaling, so I checked out people with any type of book on their table. I finally found her after briefly making eye contact with a woman standing in line to order. I was relieved that she seemed normal. To tell the truth, I don't know what I was expecting! I guess after my last experience with a healer, I was a little weary. I felt an immediate sense of comfort with her. The nervousness I felt dissipated.

We talked from around noon that day until 9 pm that evening. We spent three hours in Starbucks, then three hours in Swiss Chalet and, finally, three hours in her van when she drove me back to my car. It was like I was starved for spiritual friendship. She talked about her life, and I talked about mine. Back and forth we went, with an ease I hadn't felt in a long while. I wasn't the teacher, and I wasn't the student. I was spiritually present. This connection was one of equals, with a shared knowledge of awareness and the Light Work we both accepted into our lives. Our work differs in scope, hers more culturally defined and mine in writing, but our paths were destined to intertwine.

During the last hour of our talk, she pulled out her totem cards and asked me to draw a card. I cut the deck and selected one from the top. It was a humpback whale, a water card (my sister, a week prior drew the same card). She asked, "Other than the description you see on the card, what else does this card, tell you?" I closed my eyes, then after a moment, I said "it's the water...healing comes from the water." She confirmed this and explained how I could tap into my humpback whale totem for deeper emotional healing by going deep into the hidden depths of the water, with the assistance of the humpback whale. In doing so, I may be able to uncover any emotional issues I may be holding on to. She asked me to research more on this topic in the coming days and think about listening to meditative humpback whale sounds. We also talked about grounding stones and she gave me a few types to research.

We said our goodbyes and I made my way home. It was another three-hour drive back home and it was getting late. I arrived home at exactly midnight. I was exhausted and looked forward to a good night's sleep. I was excited to talk to my sister the next day and fill her in on our meeting. However, the next morning, we only exchanged a few text messages since my sister was busy preparing for a New Year's Eve gathering, but she was intrigued that we drew the same water card from the totem deck. We talked about its meaning and agreed that it certainly warranted further investigation. (I should probably mention here that I do not include names in my writing, but I have four sisters and four brothers, one of whom is deceased; my parents are also deceased.)

In my research on spirit-animal totems, I learned that the humpback whale comes to help with emotional clarity. Some emotions are buried deep within the "fathoms of our consciousness," and the whale can help us understand on a deeper level the actions that have caused unrest in our daily lives. I had worked through many emotions during my spiritual healing journey. I felt there was very little I had not touched upon or at least was aware of. However, true to my character, I incorporated the meditative music into my daily practice. At the very least, I could say I gave it a try!

The meditative music was different. I could see how it could have a calming feeling, especially when stressed. I enjoyed the feeling of floating through the water, envisioning myself swimming along the whale, being carried in the current it created. I envisioned it diving deep, and us moving together as one. At other times, it was near the surface, allowing me to breathe. Down again it would take me. I could feel the pressure in my ears. I asked the whale to reveal to me what I couldn't see. I worried a little, wondering what if it was something I buried deep because it was too emotionally crippling! Could I overcome this revelation and continue in my work. Would it once again knock me into a sense of despair so deep that it would take another two years to overcome!

As I began to waver in my desire to visit the 'fathoms of my consciousness', I focused instead on researching the grounding stones the medicine woman had recommended. Research always seems to calm me and I reveled in its sanctuary. Each stone was meticulously researched, and its metaphysical qualities noted. The stones are very common and are readily available, but I had never taken the time to learn the metaphysical qualities associated with gems and minerals. I considered them pretty to look at, took interest in the monthly birth stones and made the odd crystal purchase, but that was the extent of my gem and mineral knowledge.

First, why do we need to be grounded? In meditation or spiritual and psychic development work we often open ourselves up to higher vibrations, so grounding is necessary to help bring us quickly back to a normal state. It will still happen, even without the grounding stones or going through the process, but it will take longer and the effects may create a sense of imbalance or a sense that we don't quite feel right. Grounding can be accomplished by using different techniques such as visual exercises, white sage or grounding stones. Due to my experience with spontaneous journeying in my dreams, the grounding stones were recommended to hold space for me and for protection during the journeying itself.

I was given four stones to research: Black Tourmaline, Black Obsidian, Carnelian and Bloodstone. Extensive material on the stones is readily available on websites dedicated to providing information on gem and mineral properties, so I will only provide a brief description of each. (1) Black Tourmaline: one of the strongest grounding stones and a powerful protection against negativity; it does not absorb negativity, but rather transmutes it to positive energy. (2) Black Obsidian: powerful cleanser of any psychic debris that is created in our aura and is used in psychic protection. Obsidian forms from molten lava that was cooked very quickly but didn't have time to turn to glass. This stone has a vibration for confronting truths and is known for bringing out attributes we may want to ignore, but once perceived, we can set about making changes. (3) Carnelian: a strong stone that gives us strength and courage to move forward on a new path in life. This orange stone will accelerate our motivation to help clarify goals. (4) Bloodstone: is a powerful stone to aid us in regaining our personal power. If we have ever felt fearful to take action, this energy will give us confidence and determination to meet all of life's challenges. It can help us face loneliness, and to make tough decisions.

Each stone resonated with my spiritual journey. I realize there are some that may roll their eyes at these metaphysical qualities, but for me, each one represented a milestone in my spiritual development and an area in which I was seeking further personal growth. I decided to move forward with purchasing the stones and visited a local gem and mineral supplier. The shop was quite large with a vast array of inventory, including jewelry. I walked around, notes and descriptions in hand. I wanted to find the stones myself and to feel that first connection. One by one I found the stones. There were so many more that I wanted to purchase, but I held off. It was important for me to be respectful to this entire experience; after all, I was about to ask for their energy to aid in my spiritual and psychic development.

I got home and examined the stones one by one. I recalled the properties of each stone and visualized how they may have looked in their raw state. I cleansed and dedicated each one and simply stated what I was asking for from each stone. I put one of each kind in a pouch to carry with me and a couple of others I laid out near my bedside as suggested in the research I had done. I purchased the stones on Monday, January 5th and had my dream the morning of Thursday, January 8th. By preparing the stones and practicing the new meditation technique, I had finally given myself permission to go deeper into my subconscious.

I sensed immediately upon waking from my dream that the connection to the little girl was accurate, I was her mother. She was the third embryo that was conceived during the In-Vitro Fertilization Process I had undergone in 2002. As many of you may know from my book *Heaven's Wait*, our 11-year-old twin boys were conceived as a result of IVF. I was 38 years old when I underwent the procedure and shared with readers the unfortunate reason for my infertility issue, which was a result of an ectopic pregnancy. I never did share that there was a third embryo. This was something my husband and I kept to ourselves.

It was easy to talk about the ectopic pregnancy. I could openly lament the loss of an unborn child due to blocked fallopian tubes as there was no moral issue linked to the loss. It was something that happened to me. However, the termination of the embryo was markedly different.

I won't go into the technical jargon associated with the IVF process, but following the egg retrieval procedure and sperm injection, nine fertilizations occurred. These then formed into embryos, but only three made it to the five-day incubation period. We paid extra to proceed with the five-day incubation period to try to take advantage of a slightly higher success rate. The morning of the injection, the doctor explained that two embryos were rated high on the scale, and the third was barely borderline. At this particular clinic, a maximum two embryos would be injected. They proceeded using the two highest ranking embryos.

The pregnancy was mostly problem-free and I made it to 38 weeks. When the boys were around six weeks old, we received a letter from the clinic. They were writing to inform us that the period of embryo freezing (part of our IVF treatment package) was near its end and asking if we wanted to renew it for another year! WE WERE FLOORED! I definitely signed off on embryo freezing prior to beginning the IVF process, but I didn't think we had any embryos to freeze.

We misunderstood their explanation of the borderline scale. They had frozen the embryo I thought was unusable and we didn't receive any notification of this until almost a year later.

We didn't know what to do. We were in the midst of surviving day-to-day with the twins and our emotional state was fragile. As new parents, we were just scraping by both emotionally and financially. We were definitely not in the proper emotional state to re-engage in the IVF process; in addition, the drugs needed to stimulate the body to receive an embryo are very costly and we were tapped out. But that wasn't the only issue at hand. The embryo had been at the borderline mark and my thoughts went to viability, especially considering the embryo had been frozen for a year. What could freezing do the embryo? There were just so many unknowns. This was a moral crisis of the highest regard and one I was spiritually ill equipped to handle. I simply wasn't connected to life in the same way I am now.

We went back and forth on the issue for days, and finally our decision was made. Mark and I sat at the computer and drafted our embryo termination notice to the clinic. It was devastating. Here we were with two beautiful baby boys and we were about to terminate an embryo that was formed at the same time they were. Even further still, there was a personal disconnection between us and the embryo in the lab. Not knowing of its existence until a few days prior allowed us to disassociate our feelings from its true being—the boys' sibling, our child. It was this very disassociation that I buried. I sent the letter and never examined our decision again. Not until the morning after my dream.

I lay in bed for a half hour feeling the memories, reliving my dream and trying to hold the memory of my little girl's face in my mind. I recalled that a medium I wrote about in *Heaven's Wait* asked me if my husband and I had three children. She explained that she could see a little one that was growing up on the other side and this little one was around us quite a bit and it liked to hide things. She wanted us to be sure to acknowledge this child on a regular basis. I thought she was talking about my first child that resulted in the ectopic pregnancy.

I recalled all the times I would jokingly say to the boys, "for some reason I feel like I'm going to have a little girl". The boys would laugh and say, "Mommy, you're too old to have another baby!"

My husband walked into the bedroom and I shared my dream with him. We talked for a while and I communicated with him my plans to commemorate our daughter's life. I would give her a name and engrave it on a heart-shaped box. We would then each write a letter to her and put it in her special box. It would be displayed in our family room, so she would never be forgotten again. Finally, a chapter of my book would be dedicated to her story and I would give voice to her brief life.

Yes, her soul was promised to us for only a short while, but she lived and she wanted us to acknowledge that, and to know she's still a part of our family, just in a different way. In her brief life, she allowed us to learn one of the most important lessons: we are here on this earth to learn that *Life is a Gift!*

I named her Rebecca Marie. I didn't think up this name nor was it ever in my mind when I selected names for the twins; I just felt it with every part of my being, and it was she who wanted to be named Rebecca.

God bless you my little one. I'll see you in my dreams.

3

SOJOURNS TO THE PAST

The phone kept ringing, but I wouldn't answer it. *It's those bleeping people again, why don't they just leave me alone*! I lay in bed, not having gone to work for a couple of days, and they wouldn't stop calling. "Is everything okay. Can we help you in some way?" Geez, I hated nice people, those do-gooders. *Why can't they just understand, I don't want their bleeping help*!

It was winter, but I can't remember the exact year, maybe 1987. I was starting to pull away from my job and the people at work. I was trying to make myself sick, opening my small room patio door and sticking my bare feet outside into the snow. I was tired of faking sick and thought a doctor's note would help. Maybe it would get them to lay off the telephone calls. In my own mind, I felt like they were looking down on me and I thought that, any time now, my false sophistication was about to be found out. I needed to get out before they would see the real me. *Oh, they think they're so much better than me*, I thought as my feet grew numb in the snow.

This seemed to be a pattern. I would get a job and fit in well, but inevitably I would do something to embarrass myself or I would take offence to a comment or criticism of my work. This would then lead me to self-recriminations that I would then turn outward towards my boss or co-workers. I'd constantly mumble to myself about those bleeping jerks, and what I would say to them the next time they dare say anything to me. These types of discussions and disagreements constantly bounced around my head and I always won!

I didn't get sick from sticking my feet in the snow and returned back to work after four days, but it was too late, I had lost their trust and was let go. Again, the internal dialogue raged. *If they think they can treat me that way, and get away with it, then they have another thing coming.* At the time, I didn't take even an iota of responsibility for my termination. It was always their fault. *Those freaking white people who think they're so darn important. I'm not going to put up with that crap!* Whenever I got going on one of my 'justified' rants, I always blamed the Caucasian race. It seemed they were the stick in my spokes. Just as I got going, boom…I was down!

The incredible efforts I put into marginalizing myself began to take a toll. The more I got into trouble the less I could tell people about myself. More than anything, I probably needed a good friend to be a sounding board for my crazy ideas and thoughts but I didn't allow myself that luxury. I simply kept doing what I was doing, showing only the surface and never connecting with people in a meaningful way. I met so many interesting people, people that could have mentored, listened, and guided, but respect was not something I yet understood and I didn't think I was worthy of anything at the time, especially respect.

Have you ever had that little piece of thread hanging down the back of your t-shirt or sweater and you pull a little bit to yank it off, but it only ends up longer and making a mess and getting all bunched up until finally you realize that you're in need of a pair of scissors! This was basically my life. I'd do something seemingly small, no big deal in my mind because I thought I could fix it later, but as the consequences of that one action played out, the situation became unmanageable and all that was left to do was get out the sharpest pair of scissors I owned and cut. But because I'd been yanking so hard and pulling on the thread with increasingly frustrated motions, the bottom of the shirt was ruined. At first I'd try to repair it but I could always see where I put in extra stitches, never quite matching the original stitching. Eventually it wouldn't hang right, so I would stop wearing it or throw it away. This was my life with relationships.

In these early years, I pulled and yanked at seemingly innocuous threads that only I could see. This was all relationships, not just the romantic type. If there was some way I could find a way out, without saying I wanted out, I found it. It seemed that normal scared me. If I lived a regular everyday life, what was the purpose of living in Toronto! Today, knowing what I do about angels and guides, I can only imagine their daily frustration at my antics; *Paula for crying out loud, get your feet out of the snow! Paula, you don't want to say that! Paula, that doesn't belong to you! Paula, please say you're sorry! Paula, LISTEN!!!*

I couldn't hear. I was oblivious to all guidance, both in this world and the spirit world. On the odd occasion I would go with my gut feeling or with a strange sensation that would wash over me, but I had a way of looking past these feelings. I would not back down. Once something got in my head, an idea (usually bad) or thought (usually contrived), I was on my way.

On more than one occasion, I really should have listened.

While I rode the bus to the airport, I realized it had been two or three months since I had last spoke to my family. As I said, whenever I got myself into trouble I stopped all communications, and this time was no different. I was leaving, but this time I wasn't going east, I was heading west, to Vancouver. I had made the decision just two hours earlier and here I was on my way, one little carry-on bag to my name and a paycheck I just cashed. That was all I had and it had to cover the cost of the airplane ticket as well as living expenses when I arrived in Vancouver. Fortunately, I still qualified for the cheaper stand-by tickets.

I didn't know anyone in Vancouver, which at the time I thought was the great part. *A fresh start* I thought. As I got closer to the airport, I fantasised about what a great new life I could make for myself in

Vancouver. I had never been there, but I thought I would figure things out fairly quickly. It couldn't be that much different than Toronto, and the further I was away from Toronto, the less I had to worry about. When I arrived at the airport, I walked towards the ticket counter, feeling fearless. One thing I haven't mentioned is, I didn't even tell my landlord that I was leaving nor did I pack up any of my things, I just left!

I arrived at my destination early in the evening. It was winter in Toronto, but looked like spring in Vancouver; everything was green and there were flowers everywhere. It was a little overcast, so I didn't see much else as I rode in the taxi towards a downtown hotel. I didn't have any accommodations in mind, so I had no choice but to go to a hotel for the night and I asked the taxi driver to take me to one that wasn't too expensive. I still had some financial resources left, so I was okay for a couple of days. (*As I write this my face burns with embarrassment. I cannot believe my ignorance!*)

The next morning I woke up and opened my curtains to the most amazing sight I have ever seen, the North Shore Mountains (not that I knew the name of the mountains at that time); I felt as if I was in heaven! *I definitely made the right choice in leaving Toronto*, I thought. I got myself together and decided to take a walk. As I walked around I was happy at the anonymity the city provided. No chance in running into anyone who had it out for me or who I had screwed over in some way. As I said, I lived in a fantasy world!

I walked around, happy in the warm sun. Toronto seemed so dreary compared to this place. I stopped in and had a beer at a nearby bar, it had an outdoor patio. I don't recall the name of the hotel where I stayed, but it wasn't far from the downtown shopping district. I returned to the hotel and made arrangements to stay one more night, but I really needed to find a place to live; I didn't have much money left. The next day I ordered breakfast in the hotel restaurant and signed it to my room. The hotel didn't have computerized updates, so my breakfast tab went unnoticed, but I had to leave the hotel quickly before I was found out.

THE FALSE HEALER: A TRILOGY

I left and walked towards the downtown district. It was time to find the nearest social services office; I think I had around 25 bucks left. I asked around and was directed to a place in east Vancouver. There were people everywhere, hanging around the outside of the social services building and many more lounging on benches and sleeping in the nearby park. I hadn't seen homelessness like this before, not in these numbers.

I met with one of the workers in the social services agency. I explained my situation and assured her I would soon have a job. I hadn't had a problem finding a job before, so I thought this would be no different. I also didn't have any identification with my picture on it and the worker had to make a phone call to my First Nation in Cape Breton to confirm my identity. The paperwork took a few hours to process, so by the time I left it was mid-afternoon. I was given two vouchers, one for accommodations and one for food; I would get a cheque for rent and allowance once I found my own place. Okay, I thought…now what?

The worker gave me a list of small hotels where I could stay, but they were located on the east side and there was no way I was going to stay there. I just didn't feel safe. I knew that YWCAs offered cheap accommodations, so I made my way to one located in a safer downtown neighbourhood. I was happy and relieved I was aware of this information; I had made use of the female dormitory at the Toronto YWCA on numerous occasions. I was pleasantly surprised when I arrived at the location; it was more like a hotel then a hostel. I met with the manager and negotiated five nights with the voucher I had received from social services. That would give me enough time to find a place to live.

I was shown my room. Many women made the YWCA their permanent home since it offered dormitory-like rooms at a cheaper price than what apartments cost in the city. Some were students, some were traveling in the area and some were seniors living on a limited budget. There were common areas on every floor to watch TV or to cook meals. In addition, there was a full-sized gym with a swim-

259

ming pool located just off the main lobby. I wished I had a bathing suit.

I was relieved as I settled into my room. I bought some groceries with the voucher I received and thought about my next moves. I also realized, however, that this was Vancouver and I wanted to party. I bought some beer and went out. I thought I would find a bar that had dancing. I put the beers in my purse and hit the town.

A fresh start…anonymity! I found some place (don't ask me where, it was just too long ago), and spotted a place to stand where I could safely pull out my own beers to drink. I was having fun watching the crowd. I talked with several different people as was my habit and I was slowly getting in the mood to dance. The bar was crowded, so it was necessary to slowly maneuver myself towards the floor. Just as I was about to step onto the dance floor, I heard someone say my name. As I turned around, there, standing right behind me, were two girls I knew from Toronto. CRAP!!!

I hadn't had a bad relationship with these girls, I just wanted my past wiped out. So here I was, having to be the same old Paula. They were happy to see me, and bought me some drinks, but invariably the questions started: Where are you staying? What brings you to Vancouver? Are you working! You must come to dinner! Fuck, I thought that I left this all behind! I didn't want them to know I was staying at the YWCA, so I made up some lie about staying with friends. Of course, this then led to other lies and, before I knew it, I was accepting an invitation to their place for dinner that weekend.

Time was ticking by and the five days I had negotiated with the YWCA were almost up. A couple of those days I was too hung over from partying to give any thought to apartment or job hunting. I just lazed about like I had all the time in the world. Then, the time came to go to the dinner I was invited to, so I caught a bus to their apartment on the west side.

It was a fun evening and I remember laughing a lot. They were very friendly and down to earth, but that was the last time I would see them. I just didn't want my past in my life; after all, I was trying to make a fresh start. I never made contact with them again and didn't go back to the bar where I ran into them in the first place. I convinced myself that it was time to move on.

My five days soon were up and I still didn't have a place to live. I just pretended to check-out, but the YWCA was so big that I just hung around on different floors. It had to be at least 15-20 stories high. This went on for about a week, as I slept on the sofas in different common areas. There was security, but only one person at a time and most times they were easy to evade. It felt weird, but at least I wasn't out on the street. I finally managed to find a small place that was in the price range I was allotted by social services. It was in the west end, in a nice neighbourhood. It was only a room, but it suited my needs.

I immediately hooked up a telephone for my job hunt. With no subway system like in Toronto, I found it more difficult to get around. Everything seemed to be far from the bus lines. I went to one job interview and after talking with the hiring director for some time he asked me what my favourite colour was. I was going to say blue, but I switched and said black. "Black isn't even a colour" he said. In my head, I just heard *you're so stupid you don't even know what a colour is*! My mood quickly changed and I left. As I walked back to the bus stop, I kept mumbling about the white bleeping jerk. *Thinks he so fancy*! I hated Vancouver's snobby and uppity attitudes! What do you think came next in my thought…*they think they're so much better than me*!

Not long after that, I got a cheque from social services and decided to treat myself to lunch downtown. I had previously struck up a conversation with some people at small bar where I had lunch and decided to go back to the same place. It was homey and reminded me of a place in Toronto I used to frequent. I sat at the bar enjoying my beer and pizza. I was talking with the bartender about being new to the area when I caught a glimpse out of the corner of my eye of a person standing on the sidewalk about to get into a taxi cab. I quickly said to the bartender, "I'll be right back, I think that's my brother right there!"

I rushed out of the restaurant, and ran over to him. "Oh my god what are you doing here", I asked him. He looked at me kind of strangely at first, not realizing it was me. We hugged, and he finally said he was attending a meeting in the area. "I have to leave, I'm late for a meeting," he said. "Come meet me at my hotel later," he said. "Okay, that sounds great" I replied. "What's the name of your hotel?" He gave me the name of his hotel, but it was the same one I had stayed at when I first arrived, and I knew I wouldn't see him again. "Bye, I'll see you later" I said, even though I knew I wouldn't. The taxi door closed and I was left standing on the sidewalk. For those few moments I was so excited, but my mood was quickly deflated. I walked back into the bar to finish my beer and went home soon afterwards.

I only lasted another couple of months in Vancouver. The rain and overcast conditions depressed me and the job hunt was fizzling out. I simply didn't have the funds to run all over the city to go on interviews. I could disappear and nobody would know anything about me and that was a scary thought. I went back to Toronto the first chance I got and immediately called my family to let them know I was okay. They were relieved to hear from me, but also angry. I didn't fault them their anger, as they had every right to be upset. I promised it wouldn't happen again.

4

A TANGLED WEB

I lay on the couch, heavy with self-pity. I had put myself into a state of nothingness. I was worth nothing, and would always be nothing! My mouth felt dry. I stared straight ahead, not seeing or registering anything around me. I had been in this state, for two, maybe three hours. Not quite laying, not quite sitting, just in a lump where I had fallen over from a sitting position. I picked up my cellphone and saw the little kitty I had uploaded as my wallpaper. The kitty was standing and wearing a cute little fur hat tied around its little head. Usually when I saw this, I would crack a huge smile. On this day, I thought to myself *oh don't you try to cheer me up*! I deleted that little kitty right off my phone. I wanted to be depressed; I didn't want to deal with anything or anyone. *Just leave me the hell alone!* I thought, not really knowing who I was referring to.

Most days I was happy. I didn't need a lot of outside influences to affect my ability to enjoy life, I just did so naturally. But this day was different. This feeling had carried over from the previous day and I had allowed it to intensify. I actually gave myself permission to intensify it. I wanted to feel angry, I wanted a fight! The question was, with whom? I knew I was losing control, but I didn't care. I just didn't want to do any more self-analysis or healing. I had enough. I had every right to be mad --look at what I had gone through! Who wouldn't be mad…right!

I thought about that morning when I gave myself permission to act out. I started slamming the cupboard doors while making the kids their lunch for school, mumbling under my breath the entire time. If I had fire-breathing abilities, my whole kitchen would have been scorched. On top of that we only had a little bit of milk, so I mentioned to my one son who was getting some cereal to save some for my coffee. "Okay mom," Nate said. I continued with the lunches, but now I was throwing in swear words and saying to my husband that I would punch out anyone who ever tried to do anything to me again. "What are you talking about" he asked. "Oh, that bleeping healer, if he ever does anything to me again, I'll burn his house down or punch him in the bleeping face" I said. "Why, did you see him?" he asked. "No, I didn't see him; I'm just saying if he ever gets in my face again, I'm going to punch him the bleep out!" I finished.

In my peripheral vision, I could see my other son, Bradley, put down his glass and heard him make a satisfied "ahhhhh" sound.

"Bradley, did you drink all that milk," I quickly asked. "Yes," he said. "But I asked you guys to save me some for coffee," I stated. "You didn't ask me" he said, "I guess that's too bad for you!" he replied and walked away.

I was fuming, I felt like I was a kid again and my older brother, Bradley, was making fun of me. My brother used to embarrass me all the time and knew just how to press my buttons. I was thinking in my head of a mean comeback, but in an instant I realized he was my son and not my brother. I sulked and didn't say my usual goodbyes as my husband and boys left to go to school.

Finally, I was alone. This was usually the time when I would read the daily newspapers and have my coffee, but today it was not to be. I walked over to the couch feeling defeated, *doesn't he know what I did for him* I thought.

Like most instances such as these, the minor issue with the milk didn't lead me to despair. It was more profound than that, but I wasn't ready to face it. The day before, October 16, 2014, I had received a call from the school board responsible for administering funds to the school the boys attend in Brantford. We live about a 25-minute drive from the school on a First Nation where my husband is a Band member. The school board was calling to confirm our address. They indicated to us that since we didn't live within the school district and we didn't pay taxes anywhere in the surrounding catchment areas, tuition was an issue, a $12,000 a year issue for each of the boys. We had not lived in the school district for three years, and we were only now being flagged. Actually, we had been flagged at the end of the previous school year, but we didn't hear anything from the administration. My husband worried throughout the summer, but I finally convinced him that everything would be okay. *I'm sure things will be fine, we've been through so much already*, I told him.

I didn't want Mark and the boys to worry; I believed we would be guided through the process and whatever was waiting for us ahead would be divinely supported. I trusted that the situation with the school would be worked out as long as we stayed positive. My spiritual healing had brought with it much peace and I knew in my heart we were safe. My angels and guides sent many messages of support and I trusted their guidance. I knew we would not be given anything more than we could handle. But on this day, I did not heed my own guidance.

When the boys started school in September, I scheduled a meeting with the principal since my husband was still worried about the tuition. The meeting went well and we were hopeful for a positive outcome. However, in the end, the school board again flagged our address and we were now stuck between a rock and a hard place. I won't go into all the details about education funding, but we were caught in a proverbial "no man's land". First, we live on a First Nation where my husband is a Band member so we don't pay municipal property taxes; therefore, the School Board cannot access Provincial Education Funding as is the norm. Second, the boys are not registered

Band members in the First Nation where we live and have never attended school on the First Nation, so access to First Nation Education Funding was unavailable to the School Board; this type of funding is sometimes made available for transfers between local on-reserve schools and nearby off-reserve schools to cover tuition.

Finally, I had a great conversation with the School Board and explained the situation we were in and we ended the conversation on a very positive note. They were going to look into what options were available to them and they would get back to us soon. My despair was not necessarily due to the call from the School Board, it was the fact that we found ourselves in yet another situation fueled by the negative experience we had with the healer. *When would this connection ever end* I despaired.

As revealed in *Heaven's Wait*, we sold our house in the city because the healer informed us he had a spiritual vision that our boys would be kidnapped and horrible things would happen to them as a result. He told us we had to move, but the move could only be to the First Nation where my husband was a Band member. At the time, his vision absolutely terrified me and I convinced my husband to follow the healer's instructions. He assured us it was the only option available to keep the boys safe. These instructions meant we had to sell our current home, move to my husband's community, and build a house and move in by the Christmas holidays, which were less than a year away. The move in date was initially in September, but I said we just couldn't do it because, according to his instructions, we could not get a mortgage. We had to use what limited cash we would get from the sale of our home in the city to complete the build, so that meant my husband and I would need to do the majority of the interior work ourselves.

Now, a couple years after we had moved into the house, I sat on the couch and I let the wave of negative thinking wash over me. I allowed myself to go down that path, to feel absolute despair. I fell over in defeat. It would never end; I am forever tied to the terrible decision to work with the healer. Hours passed and I slowly got myself into a seating position again. I knew in my heart how to heal myself and I finally gave myself permission to take the necessary steps. Just as I allowed myself to despair, I now allowed myself to move forward.

We all have choice and I was choosing to use my spiritual development to guide me. I took out my computer and started to write. At first I wrote nonsense that included a lot of profanity and self-denigration. But then a prayer kept calling out to me...*You are the sum total of all your experiences, to love from one heart, never to be diminished in any way*

It was the prayer the Angel had told me during one of my meditative healings. I repeated it over and over and took the hand that was extended to me: the hand of love, the hand of light, the hand of God.

I didn't need to suffer alone; I didn't need to suffer at all! I remembered my soul's true self, the true self that exists beyond this physical world. I rose to that level now. I saw my soul step outside my physical body, existing only as energy. As I maintained this image, my energy source vibrated beside my body; it is energy that is old, knowing, and in the likeness of its creator, the source of all life.

This energy is my soul and it has been through many lifetimes and incarnations, and has been spiritually renewed following each of these lifetimes. In this knowing, I am aware of the need for life lessons, the need to realign my path, and the need for growth. I have a soul mission to be a Light Worker, and the pathway to that light needed clearing. I reached out and embraced other energy forms around me. I saw my family. I saw each face as we all joined hands. I continued this visualization until every person in my family was in the circle. I recognized that we had committed to share our lives, to help each other grow spiritually in this lifetime and to help each other meet our spiritual goals. Our energy forms looked etheric as we held hands. We were enveloped in a beautiful blue and white sky and then something else started to happen. My deceased parents connected in and joined hands, and then my brother, our grandparents, and many more. They were all the souls connected to us. They were joining in our circle of commitment, helping us from the other side. Love emanated through the circle and I reveled in the beauty of all our souls. We were all free of the debris of our physical bodies and the ego of our human existence. I knew my state of mind had shifted. It was back in the light and I was ready to work.

I think every once in a while I need to remind myself of the suffocating despair our minds are capable of conjuring as it much of my work is related to this issue. I often get calls for spiritual guidance when people sense change is near or when they are in a bad situation or crisis. They are usually reaching out for reassurance, direction or purpose. So if I couldn't empathize with their situation, I wouldn't be able to offer genuine and useful guidance to shift their thinking, or offer a more positive way of looking at their current circumstances.

When I'm not writing or promoting my book, my focus is on the practice of numerology. It is here that the connection with the spirit is sustained and where I tap into the guidance I draw on when I'm writing or presenting. Words seem to leap from my mouth and energy washes over me as I review birth charts with clients. This is not something I am able to spend a lot of time doing because of the length of time it takes to complete a full birth chart, but when I do, the experience is an uplifting one. Numbers can uncover much mystery and guide in a way that is clear, concise and without judgement. Using them to help guide others along their spiritual path is something I take seriously and approach with a profound sense of responsibility. Each chart is like giving birth to a new life and a new future.

It's in this work with numbers that my first spiritual business was born. It was my desire to launch a site to help those seeking awareness come to know their true soul-self and to take responsibility for their own spiritual growth. Through the use of numerology, I am able to help guide others to understand their life purpose, their soul's need for spiritual growth and what that spiritual growth involves. By using the Pythagoras method of Numerology and the work expanded on by David A. Phillips, Ph.D., in his book *The Complete Book of Numerology: Discovering the Inner Self*, I construct birth charts designed to help others interpret his amazing work. It is one thing to read about numerology and do a few exercises provided in the book, but the purpose of the book is to bring all the exercises together in a clear and concise manner that allows us to see the complete profile. Unfortunately, this point often gets lost in flipping between the chapters and pages for our own personal interpretations and doesn't allow us to see other character traits that may be missing from our chart, and why that is of importance to our spiritual growth.

I decided a template based on the exercises in *The Complete Book of Numerology* was needed. This way, I could easily personalize each chart and apply the interpretations below each exercise and explanation for its purpose. I requested permission from the publisher/copyright holder to utilize the template and permission was granted. The only question remaining was how do I use the template without copyright infringement on the interpretations? I could use my own interpretations, but the ones in the book were to the point and already in a summary format, although at times, further simplicity was needed on some points.

I figured that the best way to teach Pythagoras Numerology and David A Philip's interpretations (and maintain copyright integrity) was to share these numerology concepts in a workshop format. This way, the spiritual purpose behind each exercise such as the Life Peaks Pyramid could be easily explained and the calculation methods demonstrated. Further, I could offer my own personal interpretations as gleaned from studying Philip's book and other numerology sources without relying on any one author's written interpretations. In addition, each workshop attendees would receive a ready-to-go template to record their own relevant information as provided in *The Complete Book of Numerology* should they wish to purchase their own personal copy for further study.

Connecting to our life purpose, such as we do in numerology, is about opening a door to awareness. For me, the connection to my soul purpose involved several stages of spiritual development that lasted several years. I did not nor could not immediately see or understand my connection to the unseen world which our soul calls home.

It seemed simple enough to understand that our soul leaves our physical body when we die, but where does it go, and how does it exist? Does 'it' know who it is! I was also confused with the word 'spirit.' Who was a spirit, what was a spirit, were spirits good, bad or even worse... demonic, and where did spirits exist? Are spirits the same as ghosts! Then, there was the world of angels, guides and guardian angels; are they spirits too, perhaps loved ones that have died! I had so many questions and I was put on a journey to find answers that would work for me. I didn't know it at the time, but I was being guided on this journey to help others find answers, too.

5

WHAT WENT BEFORE

I opened my eyes, blinking away the fog that had built up around my contact lenses. I hadn't taken them out the night before; I couldn't, as I didn't have any contact lens solution or a case. I tried to stretch out my legs but there was not a lot of room, the little red car was too tiny. I had found it open the night before and it looked like it hadn't been used in a long time. *Perfect,* I thought. The car was located on a lower level of an apartment parking garage in downtown Toronto. I could hear some people moving around, so I made myself smaller in the back seat and covered my head so as not to be seen. Fortunately, the windows were dirty from sitting unused in the garage for some time, and it provided a little camouflage. I needed to go to the washroom; I would have to make my way to a nearby office building that had public washrooms. This apartment building had a bar located on the main level, but it wasn't open yet.

The night before, a nice couple had dropped me off at the building after I had struck up a conversation with them. They were friendly and offered me a ride home; at least to where I told them was my home. I just pretended to go into the elevators, but then went down to the underground parking garage. At least it was somewhere safe to stay until the morning. There wasn't anything I could do until then anyway. I would make my way back to the YWCA when they opened for regular business hours. It was getting cold out and the clothes I had weren't very warm and I didn't have my jacket. I was back in Toronto.

(With all of my heart, I resisted writing this story, but I know it must be written to release me. Not many people know this story from when I was in my 20s and I only recently told it to my husband. While writing I got up to eat, to stall perhaps, but the food went down hard. I gave up, and sat back at my computer. I thought to myself, *its okay, Paula, you've come a long way, just write -- you have already lived the judgements, the punishments, this is just the telling, its the easy part!)*

Six weeks prior to ending up in the garage in downtown Toronto, an incident occurred that led to me being arrested. Unfortunately, for me, I had a previous charge and could not sign myself out on a promise to appear. I would need to post bail until the matter could be investigated. But as I have already explained, there were many times when I didn't communicate with my family and this was once such instance. The bail amount was very little, just a few hundred dollars, but I refused any help in the matter and I most definitely was not going to call my parents. I was extremely stubborn and didn't care what happened to me. I wasn't about to go crying to anybody for help and hear their recriminations for the predicament I found myself in. As a result, I was sent to the detention centre until I decided what to do about the bail. A lawyer came to see me, "are you sure you don't want to call someone", he asked. "No, I'm alright, I'm not scared" I said and off I went to the detention centre.

Believe it or not I wasn't scared. I had seen enough and experienced enough that this didn't seem like too big of a deal to me. I settled in rather quickly. There was another native girl in there, so I chatted with her first. Then, I met another girl that was on an immigration hold from China. She had been there for a while, and her English had improved quite a bit. She shared a lot of her things with me as I didn't have a concession account since no one knew I was there to help with such things. Each week, I would go back to see the judge about the bail. "No changes" the lawyer would report and back to the detention centre I would go.

I liked the routine. I played cards quite a bit with the other girls and helped out with things when I could. I decided to sign up for work duty and went painting with some of the other girls during the day. It was in another part of the detention centre, but we were mostly on our own all day and did a lot of joking around. Our lunch and snacks were brought to us and we enjoyed the quiet of being together; there were usually six to eight of us assigned to a particular project.

Some of the girls seemed a little rough compared to my personality, but I had grown up on the reserve accustomed to circumstances in which all manner of personalities were encountered and this was no different. Some were just a little more aggressive than others, especially the ones that were coming down from serious alcohol or drug addiction. Usually, they were placed in a different area until the worst of the withdrawal was over, but they were still fairly agitated by the time they were released to the section where I was being held. This section was for people waiting for a court or bail hearing, a short-term transition area.

One day, a woman in such an agitated drug withdrawal state was put into our area to await a hearing of some sort. She was bigger than I, with a heavier build, and she was not a happy camper. I could tell right away that I rubbed her the wrong way. Maybe it was my size or my quietness, I'm not sure. But she thought I was an easy target, that I knew for sure. Every time I walked past her she would say something to me or she would sit across from me and mimic what I said. I had been there for about three weeks now, so there were a few people I had made friends with but she didn't know this.

That evening I sat down for supper and as usual I chatted with some people around me. This same woman decided to take the seat directly across from me and started to taunt me again. At first I laughed it off and let it go, but she continued and I could see she was starting to get more aggressive. I knew at that moment I would have to do something, and without thinking, I was across the table and we tousled for a few moments and she was knocked off balance and fell down. Since she wasn't expecting the attack, and was still in chatter mode, she didn't have time to prepare and in those couple of seconds, I was able to gain a slight advantage.

The people around us broke the fight apart. But it had the effect I needed. She knew I wasn't scared of her and she also knew I had friends. The taunts subsided after that, and she was actually a nice person once the harsh effects of the drug withdrawal wore off. "Holy cow" one girl said, "I just saw you flying across the table like a mad woman!" I laughed and thought to myself, *I guess all those childhood wrestling matches with my brothers and sisters finally paid off...I was usually pummelled!*

As the days went by, I didn't give much thought to my predicament. I was comfortable and felt that any punishment was due anyway. I just made the best of it. What I didn't know was that my mother was getting quite worried about me. She was calling around trying to find out my whereabouts. I'm not sure how she finally found out about my circumstances, but she did; however, not before I was released.

I enjoyed making the girls laugh. I would tell funny stories late at night, and sometimes I would laugh so hard while telling them about one of the embarrassing predicaments I found myself in that the whole range would be in hysterics as they awaited the punch line or the conclusion of the story. Sometimes, the laughter was so loud we would be told to quiet down. This is the way I remembered my last night in the detention centre. The next day I was released. The judge finally just let me go on a promise to appear and I was scheduled for court the following week.

By the time I got back to the detention centre for processing my release, it was past 11 pm. The detention centre was located way out in the suburbs. They had only one or two buses that ran during the day, but none at night. Once you were let out that was it, you had to leave. Fortunately, a nice couple who was there to pick up someone else also gave me a ride downtown. They went out of their way to take me home (or where I told them was home) and I was grateful for their thoughtfulness.

I found my way back to the YWCA dormitory and went to court the following week. The theft charges the person had laid against me were dropped. The other charge was dealt with through time-served, though it probably wouldn't have been that harsh. In fact, my sister showed up at the courthouse, so my mother had found out anyway, making my stay in the detention centre completely unnecessary all because I didn't want my parents to know the truth. Go figure! But I don't blame anyone for my circumstances. I created the problems and I had to live with the consequences. If I hadn't been so bent on destroying my life and living in such an "inferior" driven vacuum, I would not have suffered such a fate. I also know that the time I spent in the detention centre could have been easily avoided with just one phone call, but I insisted on doing things my own way, even to the detriment of my own safety.

As I mentioned in an earlier chapter, when lessons are not learned they will continue to come back to us time and time again, and with increasing intensity. I had to get my life together and this is what I refused to do. I continued to hold on to my old ways of doing things and remained willful and hardened in my assertion to do as I darn well pleased. So, around I went for another experience, another hard knock. *Learn Paula...for crying out loud, LEARN!*

I sat at a bus stop. It was 3 am in the morning and I was pretty shaken. *That fucking asshole!* I thought.

Bus service was finished for the night, but I was way out on the outskirts of the city and I didn't have any other choice but to wait the three hours until service resumed. A taxi was way too expensive and I only had about $25. I was trying to get back to the YWCA where I had been staying. Fortunately, a delivery truck that was filling the newspaper vending machines came by and offered me a lift to a section of Toronto that had 24-hour bus service, as it was along his route. I had to sit on the newspapers, but I didn't mind, the area at the time was being hit by serious rape crimes and I was happy to get out of the area. (Yeah, I know serious rape crimes and I get in a delivery truck!)

Earlier that day, I went over to the place of a guy I had been dating for a few weeks. It was nice to get away from the dormitory every once in a while, so things were good. I brought an outfit with me to change into for a wedding reception he had invited me to attend with him. I didn't want to attend the ceremony and said I would wait for him at his apartment and meet him later. He wanted me to get a taxi (he would pay) to the venue as he planned on having a few drinks. I didn't know any of his friends, so I didn't want to hang around with them during the afternoon ceremony. I always found that type of interaction much too awkward and there were always so many questions.

It was nice at the apartment. I watched some television and then decided to meet another friend for wings. I was gone most of the late afternoon and early evening. He had given me the key to lock up when I left. He phoned and phoned. When I arrived back at the apartment it was late and by this time I had no interest in attending the reception and I refused to get dressed and meet him.

He was furious when he arrived back later that night. I didn't think it was that big of a deal. We weren't even dating that long…why did he care so much! I thought I would wait for him since I had nothing better to do and hear all about the evening. But he was in no mood for niceties. He was getting angrier and angrier as I explained my reluctance to attend the reception. It wasn't long before he started to threaten me. He pulled some papers out of his briefcase.

"I know all about you" he said. "My friend is a cop and he gave me some information about you. You're nothing but a criminal" he continued.

"So then why are you so angry I didn't show up tonight!" I replied. "Are these the same friends you were going to introduce me to," I asked.

"You're nothing and that's all you're ever going to be," he continued.

"Well then let me go," I said. He was blocking the doorway and I couldn't leave. "I'm happy I embarrassed you if that's what you think about me!"

On and on it went for about two hours. He was getting more aggressive as time went on. "I should fucking kill you" he said. He burnt my leg in several places with his cigarette.

I backed towards the balcony. It was a high rise building and we were on one of the top floors. I continued to back-up towards the railing as he continued trying to burn me with the cigarette. He started to threaten to push me over the railing. Then he pushed me very hard and I hit my back. He grabbed my neck and made a move to lift me over, but I held strong. I managed to push him away and I got back into the apartment and made a run for the door. I grabbed my bag as I left and he was yelling at me from down the hall. I got into the elevator and went down to the garage. He loved his car, so I went over to it and punctured the tires and gave it a good scratch. He suspected I was up to something, and I saw him come around the corner, but he didn't catch me. I managed to get away and find my way to the bus stop and onto the delivery truck.

It was a long night and I was tired and also very sore. Later that day I thought *what if he did push me over!* Fortunately, he didn't know where I lived since he never picked me up; I always met him at whatever place we had arranged since I didn't like people knowing I lived at the Y dormitory.

However, soon enough I was back on my feet with my own place again. I wasn't about to give up, not yet anyway; I still had the will and determination to make a go of it in Toronto. All I needed was a little luck. *Hey*, I thought, *if I could survive all that happened this year, I think I can survive almost anything!* One thing I knew for sure, there were a lot more people worse off than me in Toronto and I was not going back home; at least not before taking a few more kicks at the can.

6

WHEN ANGELS BECKON

As I wrote on that cold morning, my eyes kept wandering over to the river that lay beyond the sparse tree line at the end of our plowed field. It was still, as a layer of ice had formed from the cold weather that had developed overnight. My thoughts kept going back and forth over the stories I had already written, uncertain as to the effects they might have on my future as a writer and spiritual worker. I felt a little uncomfortable, as the magnitude of my poor decisions during those years weighed heavily on my shoulders. Was I making a mistake by sharing too much!

For people like me, shame and guilt compel us to take all sorts of misguided steps. Our actions may not be what we originally intended, but they have real, life changing consequences that create even more self-hate and self-blame. Yes, for some they don't feel the weight of their actions, at least not yet; but for many, it is a road traveled in a cloak of disgrace, our faces hidden, mortified by of our actions. We hide this in any manner available to us, often resulting in further negative consequences. Some, like me, choose to run, as I did in my youth. We don't think about where we're running to, we just want to get away from the feeling of letting others down, especially those that gave a damn in the first place. So we pull away, deeper and deeper into our own thoughts and recriminations and, unfortunately, this is what truly damages us. There is no light; we won't allow ourselves any light to help guide us, it is not deserved.

So I write, continuing my story. I hope to share and inspire in any way I can. I want to share the knowledge that no person is a mistake (there is purpose for all souls), that we deserve love and that we have guidance around us at all times whether we want it or not, as in the case with angels. Angels are sent directly from God, and it is their mission to serve humankind. The protection given by the angels is real; however, angels cannot protect you from yourself as far as the choices you make because they cannot interfere with free will; however, they can and do help protect and guide you to lessen the impact of your choice or prevent you from death if it is not your fate.

For example, when I go off on a rant and I am moving in a direction that is undesirable and not conducive to living in light, I will sense their gentle prodding. I sometimes ignore it because I can be stubborn at times, but it's there. I feel it in my gut and I feel it around my head. I usually sense words that seem to come from outside the top of my head and travel along to my forehead. This is when my forehead starts to tingle. Do I listen or do I ignore!

Sometimes I choose to ignore their guidance because I do not want to deal with the consequences of my actions or I want to continue to feel upset and justify my objectionable behaviour. This one particular time I refused to meditate and allowed angry and suspicious thoughts to rage through my mind. *No, I won't meditate*, I kept saying in my head; *you can't make me!* I paced throughout the living room, sending text messages full of anger and jealousy. I was not a happy camper to say the least.

Earlier that morning, I had blasted my husband for going out while away on a trip. I saw a photo of him on social media with a couple guys I didn't know, and I wondered who took the picture. There it started.

"Who took that bleeping picture, and why are you out partying with her; don't you know how disrespectful that is to me!" I said. "You know I'm from that area and people might think that you're cheating on me!"

My husband didn't know where my anger was coming from, he had been friends with this woman for years, so why the jealousy now. "I'm sorry", he said, "we went out for dinner and ran into these guys and they were so interesting and funny to talk to. Time just flew by, I didn't think it was a big deal."

"No, you didn't," I replied. "Why don't you just grow up and stop living in the past for crying out loud", I continued. My anger was escalating, and this is when I started to hear, *stop...go and meditate*! But I continued.

Texting like a mad woman, I hurled words at him that he couldn't make sense of and finally he called. I answered the phone and I swear, I was so deeply furious that I felt like I had steam blowing out of my ears. "Babe, what's wrong," he asked.

"I'll tell you what's wrong," I said. "You're not going to hang out with that woman again, and you are not participating in that crap again, for crying out loud, it's only volunteer stuff," I screamed at him, "how dare you embarrass me!" I hung up the phone.

He was on his way to the airport. His flight back to Ontario was around noon. Later he told me he felt really sick and was not looking forward to the hour-long drive home from the airport.

I was back to texting and pacing. At the same time, I was going over in my head the reasons I felt justified in spewing so much anger towards his friend because in my mind it was really her that was the problem. In that moment, I knew my anger had gone too far and I had to regain control. I had no other choice but to meditate.

It was difficult to ground myself, as my breathing was way off. It took me almost 10 minutes just to stop the rant that continued in my head. Slowly I relaxed, but my thoughts continued as I tried to look at what made me react in such an objectionable manner. I did some more exercises to break down the walls I had so quickly constructed. I attempted to find the root of the jealousy and insecurity I felt. I walked through the stages, examining each one. I knew that I was reacting to something I conjured up, but what? I felt the heat form within me, a familiar feeling. I knew in that moment I was being guided. I relaxed.

Images began to appear in my mind; they were images of other times when I had blew up at Mark. In each one, it was because of a woman; not always someone he had direct contact with as it could have even been a story he shared that related to an outing with his buddies. But each one had a common link, which was that the woman always had blond hair. Guess who had blond hair?

I was taken further, down into my stomach. I was shown another image. It was of me standing at a bar when I was 20 years old and a friend of my ex-boyfriend giving me an update on him (not that I really wanted to know, but curiosity compelled me to listen). My boyfriend had unceremoniously dumped me a few weeks before and I was having difficulty recovering from the shock of it.

All I remember hearing from this friend of my ex-boyfriend was "isn't it crazy, he eloped with her over the holidays, they knew each other only a week; you know she's a blond…!"

You know she's a blond is all I heard, and that is what I held on to. I was devastated when his friend told me of the elopement. I realized in that moment that it wasn't my husband's friend that I didn't trust, it was the colour of her hair. Blond hair is all I heard and had to go on and that is what formed the basis of my rejection and deep sorrow so long ago. Each time I felt the least bit threatened in my relationship with my husband, I unconsciously associated this threat in some way with this particular hair colour, regardless of who the woman happened to be.

I also learned in that same meditation that there is a time for healing. That is what the angels wanted to show me. It was time to let this go, time to heal from the sorrow of that broken relationship. I couldn't continue to carry the residue of it any longer and they comforted me as I cried. I wept for a long time as I released the sting of that hurt out of every cell. I was cradled and could feel their energy around me; but as I settled, I knew I had some apologizing to do.

How could I have been so cruel? I thought.

I immediately apologized to both my husband and his friend and gave him an account of what had just happened. Of course he was hurt, and it took a little time for him to recover from the events of that morning; after all, his integrity and honour had been called into question and we needed to sort through these emotions and set a new path forward. I accepted my role in this realignment and understood the purpose of the lesson and what it meant to my spiritual growth. However, I also know that we have equal responsibility to keep our paths free of debris and situations that create disharmony and imbalance in our personal relationships and with others whom we interact. If not for the gentle guidance of angels, I most likely would have continued to rant and do even more damage.

Angels it seems are around us always, from the time of our birth until the time of our death and even thereafter. The number of angels we have around us depends on the difficulty of our charts and the lessons we are on this earth plane to learn. We can also call additional angels to ourselves anytime we deem it necessary and these too stay with us. The angels, from what I understand, are of various orders. They have never lived life as humans and never will. Their existence is meant purely to serve and in this service to humankind they serve God, thus fulfilling their spiritual purpose. Because they have never lived an earthly existence, they know only love and it is in love that they serve.

From what I understand, angels are of various orders, with a specific spiritual purpose for each order, and angels stay within their specific order until such a time when advancement occurs. The word "time" is only a term used on earth, and has no meaning in a world that exists in infinity. So, let's just say at some point, the angels ascend to a higher calling. Some of the orders of angels that various writers have included in their books include: The Ministry of Angels,

Archangels, Cherubin, Seraphim, Powers, Carrions, Virtues, Dominions, Thrones and Principalities.

I have found commonalities amongst authors who write about their experiences with angels or have received information through their spirit guides. Some of these common characteristics are: Angels have colours associated with their order; Angels can take human form when needed; Angels can facilitate divine healing; Angels do not judge in any manner, as they are pure love; Angels can help us without us needing to ask for their help, like in arranging a serendipitous meeting that will assist us on our life path; Angels work with our spirit guides to help fulfill our destiny, but they cannot change our fate; Angels cannot circumvent our free will; Angels can make their presence known in what feels like a light, wispy touch; Angels often make their presence known to children; Angels can protect us from that which is not part of our life path or decrease its intensity or severity, such as a car accident or illness that may have resulted in death; Angels perform specific functions related to their order, and all the angels within this order are known by the same name; for example, Archangel Michael; Angels are not known by gender, and although they may occasionally appear in human form as either female or male, it is only for a short period until their task is complete, and; Angels have been known to communicate without speaking and many who have reported such experiences indicate they just knew what was being communicated without the need for words.

There are many fascinating books on angels and I encourage you to discover the angelic realm for yourself. At the same time, however, try not to get caught up in all the orders and specific purposes of each order. At the end of the day, when we call upon our angels for help, the angels know in a heartbeat our specific prayer and circumstance and direct an angel to our cause – this is all done without even a thought, for they already know our heart and our needs and are just waiting for us to take notice.

A simple *Thank You* at the end of the day before we fall into sleep brings so much joy. In this simple acknowledgement to the angelic realm, we are accepting their service to God and their service to us and all humankind. Whether we realize it or not, angels assist us in our lives on a daily basis and they wish to help us with so much more, but this is when asking comes into play. We must ask for their help, but please, do not demand it; a gentle request will do.

When I finished writing *Heaven's Wait* I sent an electronic copy home for my sister to review. I was very nervous because the book included a lot of stuff from our childhood and I didn't know if her reaction would be one support or dismay. As I drove to pick up my boys from school, I prayed to the angels and my mother to help my sister understand the reasons why I had written *Heaven's Wait*. After I finished praying, I turned the corner near the school and a car stopped at the intersection with the license plate RUTH; this was my mother's name. I sat there in amazement, and thanked the angels and my mother for the message. My sister loved the book and encouraged me to publish it. She said, "Paula, although this is about our life it can help so many people!"

7

THE LAST STAND

*D*amn, why can't I get this bleeping bottle open! It was one of those rare occasions when I felt good about life, and I wanted to celebrate. I bought myself a bottle of red wine and some of the Babybel cheese I had seen in the fridge at the office where I worked. I also got some crackers and grapes and settled in for the night. I felt grown up laying out all the stuff on the small table in my room; I even had a television I had borrowed from one of the other girls that lived in the rooming house where I rented a room. It was very cozy and I was happy.

I bought wine, but because I rarely drank wine I didn't have a corkscrew. I tried everything. As I paced in my room I was getting angrier, losing the earlier high I had from a great day at work. An hour passed and I still couldn't get it open. I thought about going to the store, but that meant I would have to go out into the cold. I thought I would try one more thing. I placed a knife over the cork and pounded it with my boot. It's working, *yay* I thought. As I hit harder the cork started breaking apart into tiny pieces. It took some time, but I finally managed to push the cork all the way through. It was now an hour and a half since I had started and I really wanted to enjoy this wine. I poured a glass, well not into a wine glass but a coffee mug, and sat back to enjoy my hard earned efforts. *That's good wine* I thought, as I pulled pieces of cork from my mouth. *What an excellent choice!*

I no longer focused on the trouble I had opening the wine. I had a good day and I was going to celebrate. I opened the box of crackers and then removed the wrapping from the individual cheese pieces. *What the heck is this*, I thought. I tried to take a bite of the cheese but it was hard. *How can people eat this crap?* I examined it a little while longer and placed it back on the table. I took another sip of wine, the pieces of cork becoming increasingly frustrating to deal with. *Darn wine bottles!* Again I went back to the cheese, and thought *what's wrong with this cheese!* I looked at it again and noticed there was a little piece of a pull tab poking out. I started pulling and realized the cheese was splitting in two; *it's another freaking wrapper, what an idiot* I thought. I laughed at my stupidity and slowly the buzz of the wine washed over me. I relaxed and went over the events from earlier that day.

I was quite pleased with myself and my new lease on life. I was finally making progress. I had been working steadily and actually had a friend or two. Well, not real friends like ones I would confide in but people I hung out with regularly and whom called to ask about my plans. We often would meet up for drinks and the occasional Sunday brunch. This was about as friendly as I got with people that weren't family, so I didn't feel quite as lonely.

I was given more responsibility at work. Throughout my work history, I usually completed my work tasks without problem and worked easily with people, but it was inevitable that my lack of self-confidence often led me to sabotage my jobs. This time, however, I had held on. I was going to work with another person on communications-type projects that involved a lot of creative input. I was happy with the confidence they had in my abilities and I loved working with the team. Then, almost overnight, there was an internal structure change, and the director who promoted me left for a new job.

The new director was not as experienced in the creative functions that were necessary to complete projects quickly and the need for almost weekly turnover in creative materials weighed heavily on the department. I wasn't formally trained in this type of work and learned a lot through working with the previous director, but not enough to keep the projects moving along on my own. I was embarrassed by the feedback the new director and I received on work submitted to management. Unfortunately, I didn't take well to this type of negative feedback and didn't know how to fix the problem. The director seemed to take it in stride, but I took everything personally. After one such devastating session, I didn't want to return to work. I called the human resource manager and set up a meeting. I decided to quit.

"I have a great opportunity and I'm going to go for it," I said to the manager. "I know this is short notice, but I'll take the rest of the week and wrap-up projects with the team," I assured him.

"Are you sure there isn't anything we can do to change your mind," he said.

"No, I'm pretty certain and have already set things in motion for my new job," I replied. "I'm so thankful for the wonderful opportunities you have provided me," I continued.

"Do you want me to write you a reference in case you need one in the future," he asked.

"That's so nice of you, but no, I'm okay," I concluded.

I went back to my department and notified the new director of my imminent departure. I felt great relief that I didn't need to go through another project submission with management. At the end of the week they had a little cake for me and I said my goodbyes. It actually seemed like they were sad to see me go, but there was no turning back; I had already said I had another job, but I really didn't.

I was on the job hunt again, but I really should have accepted the reference the HR manager had offered. I signed up with a temp agency and found some short-term work assignments. This kept me financially afloat, but it wasn't long before I began to slide. I didn't have the discipline to maintain a budget with sporadic payments based on work assignments. Soon I had missed a couple weekly rent payments and couldn't get caught up. The landlady gave me a few chances when I explained my situation to her, but she soon grew weary of my excuses.

I temporarily moved in with one of the friends I had met in the previous months, but this put stress on our friendship. I really liked her, but I also went into self-defence mode when criticized. Her place was small, and these close quarters drove us both mad. I was finally able to get another job, but it took some time for the paychecks to process through the usual pay schedule and by the time I had the first and last months' rent, our friendship was over. We were unable or perhaps unwilling to recover from the resentful feelings that arose during my stay with her, and we never spoke again.

I still had one friend, but as my life spiralled down I eventually stopped calling her, too. At the time this seemed to be for the best, as they were all intertwined. Once again, I started anew: new friends, a new place to live and a new job all within a couple of months. Yes, this type of renewal was sometimes downright exhausting, but that was all I knew. It was normal for me to feel heavy, almost like I carried barbells in my coat pockets. If I moved steadily, it was fine; but one quick move or knock to the side and I lost balance and, as usual, I hit the floor with a great thud!

So, I had a new job and it felt good to be working again. I probably had about 10 different jobs when I lived in Toronto, not including my time as a flight attendant for Saudi Arabian Airlines, which I wrote about in *Heaven's Wait*, so it was easy for me to adjust to a new work environment and the office culture that accompanied it. I probably had as many places where I lived, all spread out in different parts of the city. The jobs, however, were usually in the downtown core.

I was constantly moving in and out of people's lives, and this time was no different. However, this last bout of hardships seemed a little more surreal. I had met some people that were all connected by friendships, and once I was accepted into that group of friends, it was difficult to extract myself. On the one hand, I was engaged in this high living lifestyle that had all the comforts one could hope for as far as the material aspects of life are concerned. But on the other hand, I was shielding my real life from being discovered and that required a lot of lies and maintaining a safe emotional distance. I really liked them all and this made it very difficult.

I couldn't let them know what a loser I really was. They enjoyed the company of no hassles Paula, who was always upbeat and fun to be around. I was a lot younger than most in the group, so they often got a kick out of my stories and they loved the fact I was Native. They were of European descent and being Native appealed to them a great deal. We went out to a lot of nightclubs and restaurants, never worrying about money, at least not for them. I was always worried about money and I still had to dress the part.

In the beginning, it was easy to move between both worlds. There was their world, and there was mine; no intermingling and no confusion. I would meet them at a club or restaurant as it seemed they preferred to stay around their own group of friends. They all would take turns paying the restaurant or bar tabs. They had been friends a long time, so this was a common practice. But as I got more drawn into their world, my world started to collapse and they had no idea what was happening in my private life. You see, by living in their world too long, I couldn't maintain mine or continue what I had managed to put together in the previous months.

I made choices that affected my work and which severely reduced my ability to pay my bills. I couldn't ask them for any help, because I led them to believe that I was a capable and independent person who was quite used to looking after myself. I was stuck. Here I had these friends I really liked, yet I was on the cusp of losing the little independence I had that made me interesting to them. I scrambled to hold on, but one by one the dominos fell and I was at the mercy of social services again.

The surprising thing is, even while going through this fall I still managed to maintain my friendship with the group. I just had to be a little more creative in my interactions with them. If I couldn't make it to some event because of time restrictions at the dormitory, I would say I was volunteering. If I couldn't go to lunch or shopping with some of the girls because I didn't have money, I would say that I had extra work that kept me busy.

I remember once being out on a large, expensive boat at the Marina. Here I was, technically homeless, laughing and hanging out at the waterfront with people that didn't even really know what was really going on in my life. I have just a couple of pictures from that time, and I cringe when I look at them because I know the circumstances I was going through. The girl in the bikini smiling back at the camera was not real. That girl snuck back to the boat later, and spent the night there because she had stayed out past the curfew at the YWCA. Oh, how embarrassing!

On and on it went, hiding in plain sight. The strain of living a double life was incredible. Finally, after riding the Toronto transit system all night one time because I didn't have anywhere to go, I finally realized I wanted more out of life. I wanted to have a real life, free of pretending. I didn't want to live this way anymore, but I knew I couldn't stay in Toronto and achieve that. It was time to move home.

But this move wasn't without its perils, and the first attempt was a complete bust. I missed the fast-paced life of Toronto and I missed my friends who I had managed to maintain a connection with, even from a distance. I moved back one more time for about three months, without success. It just wasn't meant to be and I ended up hurting even more people. In addition, I was beginning to change. It was time.

I was around 28 years old when I finally moved back to Nova Scotia for good. I still visited my friends in Toronto on occasion for two years following my move. It wasn't like the move magically transformed me. I had to come to terms with a lot of issues and the wall I had built up around myself was solid ice. I had walked away from home at 18 years of age, full of hope and aspiration to have a successful life. I returned nine years later, definitely not in any way like the girl who had left and with a wall that shielded my emotions. My feelings and my very essence were frozen.

Little by little my family chipped away at that icy exterior, but I fought it all the way. I didn't want to be there, but I needed to be there. My very survival counted on it. For two and a half years, they persevered even though they may not have truly understood the healing they were offering. We confronted a lot of attitude issues together I had developed throughout the years, even if this meant having a few blowouts. By the end of it, I cut my last connections to Toronto and never looked back. It was too painful and too embarrassing to continue my now limited forays back into that life.

I was ready for a new chapter and in this new chapter, my family walked beside me. I was honoured to have such a supportive family and I am truly grateful they have been part of my life. I was now proud to be a daughter, sister, auntie, niece, cousin and friend. I no longer had a need to run and the Creator had a gift for me...my husband!

8

TO KNOW THYSELF

I must return to my study of Pythagoras Numerology because it played an important role in helping me link my past with my present and, perhaps to a degree, my future. I'm not saying this concept of numerology can explain away all my experiences and lessons, as these involved a great deal of free will on my part, which in turn, for me at least, increased the intensity of the lessons being experienced. However, it does provide insight into my character traits; additionally, it provides reference points for significant milestones in the process of my maturity, which is still undergoing.

Just to review briefly, my Ruling Number is 8. What is a Ruling Number and how did I calculate this number?

First, your Ruling Number is the purpose for which we are on this earth plane. It provides a means through which to illuminate our Path and is in total harmony with the Spiritual Laws of the Universe. In our life journey, we must evolve through the Ruling Number to undertake further spiritual teachings. Some people only reach the purpose of their Ruling Number and stay there; others don't reach it at all. Others still surpass it and this is where higher spiritual teachings await us. It's like a process of removing layers of yourself until your true self is revealed and the reason for our being is understood; this is how we want to meet the Creator.

"Before a tree can bear fruit, it must grow in strength and maturity. So it is in human life. Our strength and maturity emerge as we fulfill our primary purpose in life, as simply revealed by our Ruling Number." David A. Philips, Ph.D.

As for calculating the Ruling Number, it's quite simple; just add together all the numbers in your full birth date. My birth date is May 10, 1964. The month of birth is usually converted to the number sequence as it appears on the calendar. For me it is the month of May, so I would convert the month of May to a 5.

So my birth date would look something like this as each component of the birth date is broken down into digits: Month: May = **5**; Day: 10, 1+0 = **1**; Year: 1+9+6+4 = **20**

Next, add these numbers together: 5 + 1 + 20 = **26.**

Further, 26 is broken down to a single digit: 2 + 6 = **8.**

The Ruling Number is 8.

In Pythagoras Numerology, the Ruling Numbers are as follows: 2,3,4,5,6,7,8,9,10,11,22. Ruling Numbers 10, 11, 22(4) are never broken down to single digits, except for some analysis like in the Life Pyramid.

Now, moving on, my Ruling Number is 8 and the primary purpose of the Ruling Number 8 is to learn how to express and appreciate love. This may sound simple enough, but experience has shown me it is far more complicated. In fact, we often make it more complicated than it has to be and these complications arise from our individual character traits. For me, I fought tooth and nail for my independence and shunned love because I didn't believe I could be independent and express love. I felt that everyone weighed me down and judged me, and I had to get out from under that self-perceived weight and judgement.

In the end, I had to understand that love did not make me weak, or require an end to my independence; it was quite the opposite actually.

Love helps us grow and strengthens the confidence people have in us and their willingness to share. This in turn provides a basis from which to grow. The Ruling Number 8 also represents wisdom, and until that wisdom is gained, a life may be lived in great disorder with a poor foundation on which to grow.

The word "independence" and how it is used in the above context is appropriate for explaining the purpose of the Ruling Number 8. However, "independence" when used in numerology is far more profound. When we speak of independence, it is not the kind that can be gained from earning more money, releasing yourself from a relationship, or even opening your own business. Independence is about understanding who we truly are in our connection to all creation and to know that this connection is above all else! When we release ourselves in this manner, we no longer need to identify with things, status or people to feel whole. We have matured to a point at which we recognize love in all its forms, especially love for ourselves. This is the true purpose of our lives, for it is in this love that we respect all living souls, including our own, and find peace in our lives.

So, what is it about my character traits that pushed me to experience the extreme of the Ruling Number 8! I will break the numbers down using a brief overview. Let's start with my birth date, which is May 10, 1964.

The numbers I place in my Birth Chart are derived by breaking down my birth date. Picture, if you will, a tic-tac-toe box. Now, in that box, picture numbers, moving from the bottom upwards: the bottom row has the numbers 1, 4, 7; the middle row has the numbers 2, 5, 8; and the top row has the numbers 3, 6, 9.

My total birth date numbers are two 1's, one 4, one 5 (May is the fifth month), one 6, and one 9. I do not include the "0" as this is not considered a number in Pythagoras Numerology, but a symbol.

A description of the "zero" as provided in *The Complete Book of Numerology: Discovering the Inner Self by David A. Phillips, Ph.D.* is as follows: *"...The 0 is present in many birth dates and has an important symbolic significance. Philosophically and mathematically, it represents* nothing (as the numerator) and everything (as the denominator), the two infinite ends of the finite, neither of which is physically attainable. Thus, it is a totally mystical symbol, indicative of the degree of spiritual mysticism inherent (but rarely developed) in the individual. Anyone who has one or more zeros in their birth date has an inherent spirituality that they should recognize, for it has the potential to assist them in understanding many of the deeper aspects of life (such as life's purpose, the power of thought and the process of reincarnation)."*

If we were playing tic-tac-toe, we would be able to strike a **slanting line** across the **11-5-9**, and strike a **vertical line** up the **4-5-6**. These lines where all our numbers are represented are considered our strengths. In my case, the *1-5-9* represents *Determination*, and the *4-5-6*, represents *Will*. (If we had a complete line on our tic-tac-toe box <u>without</u> any numbers, these would indicate our weaknesses.)

For me, *Determination* and *Will* are both positive character traits to have, but when living negatively they can shift and the bearer experiences the not-so-good side of these traits.

For example, *Determination (1-5-9)* is a powerful trait as it is usually coupled with persistence. It is used to carry out such things as plans or projects that the bearer has determined to be of importance. However, with this line of *Determination*, the bearer often becomes stubborn and is unwilling to consider any other way of carrying out their objectives. They usually have already determined that their plan is the right one and will consider obstacles, when encountered, as something they must overcome by any means possible. Unfortunately, they have not yet recognized their ability to use their innate intuition to consider another direction or a different path to reach that same goal or if that goal is even something that is right for them. They have already determined it is!

Also, the same applications apply in the line of *Will (4-5-6)*. "*This line represents our spine and the life force that flows through it,*" David A. Phillips, Ph.D. It is exactly as its name indicates. There is fortitude and courage represented here. However, when living negatively, the bearer often forces their opinions onto others without taking into account the other person's feelings or point of view. If not rectified in childhood, this can give rise to an opinionated individual who only has their self-interest at heart.

In both *Determination* and *Will*, it is important not to use manipulation as a form of getting one's own way. Unfortunately, it took me a long time to learn this lesson and as a result it surfaced many times before I recognized its negative influence on my life. When I finally tapped into the wisdom contained in my numbers, I recognized it was one of the most important lessons I needed to learn.

But all is good; I managed to finally strike a balance in my life and that is the whole point of wisdom. It comes at us gradually, gently taking us by the hand. If we listen, we have the capacity to help create miracles. These miracles are not in the form of some big, awe-inspiring display. They take the form of good deeds, balancing our ledger. Gradually, we are no longer in the red and a transformation has taken place that is truly magnificent. This transformation provides us the strength and courage to continue on our path and to awaken to our spiritual journey.

All the numbers individually also represent traits and have various meanings, depending how they are analyzed. However, if I had to describe them each in one word, they would be: 1-Ego, 2-Intuition, 3-Trinity, 4-Order, 5-Balance, 6-Creativity, 7-Sacrifice, 8-Wisdom, and 9-Idealism. Each number of course has a complete definition, but these are the brief one-word meanings I use to aide me in remembering the key aspects of each number, which are often quite detailed.

When numbers appear on our Birth Chart they are considered innate qualities. As such, they are a part of our make-up and are often easier for the bearer to integrate into their personalities. But when they are not on our Birth Chart, they are considered a trait which we need to develop. Though, for one reason or another, many people don't recognize these missing links and usually need to repeat lessons over and over until a balance is attained. They may not be able to pinpoint the exact word or lesson learned, but they know a positive change has occurred when they start to look at life differently and make different choices. Unfortunately, some never do and their entire lives are lived in one form of upheaval after another, never quite understanding why life has dealt them a losing hand.

Another more interesting way to understand our character traits is through our Life Pyramids, which are also part of Pythagoras Numerology and described in *The Complete Book of Numerology: Discovering the Inner Self, by David A. Phillips, Ph.D.*

Pythagoras Numerology defines three stages of life: Adolescence, Maturity and Fulfillment. The Life Pyramids help us to identify the age at which we will reach our *Age of Maturity*. Usually, we reach this *Age of Maturity* between the ages of 25 – 34; depending on our Ruling Number and it lasts 27 years. However, some may inadvertently delay the onset of this milestone and increase the chances that more lessons will be needed.

What can these Life Pyramids tell us? The Life Pyramids help us pinpoint the following: 1) The time at which we will reach our *Age of Maturity*; 2) Three successive peaks which indicate periods of extra energy to help us achieve our goals during the *Maturity* stage. These peaks are nine-year cycles calculated from the age at which we reach our *Age of Maturity*, and: 3) The type of growth that is required in each of the three Nine-Year Cycles in the Maturity Stage. For example, one peak may represent a period of pronounced humanitarian activity and based on your Ruling Number, may indicate how to achieve these humanitarian goals.

I will not demonstrate how to build the pyramids here as the information is too voluminous, and could possibly result in copyright infringement; so instead, I will only include the *Age of Maturity* and the three successive peaks in the *Maturity* stage. As you can see, once the *Age of Maturity* is defined, it's easy to calculate the rest as they're nine-year cycles.

Using my Ruling Number 8, my Age of Maturity is as demonstrated: **Age of Maturity** - Age 28;

First Peak - Age 37; **Second Peak** - Age 46; and, my **Third Peak** – Age 55.

I will help you out a bit in calculating when you will reach your Age of Maturity. You will need your Ruling Number, so please go back to the previous page and calculate it if you haven't already. Now, deduct your Ruling Number from "36". Remember, my Ruling Number is 8. So when I deduct 8 from 36, I end up at age 28 – my Age of Maturity.

For ease I have provided the Ruling Number (italics) and the Age of Maturity (bolded italics): Ruling Number *2* = ***34***; Ruling Number *3* = ***33***; Ruling Number *4* = ***32***; Ruling Number *5* = ***31***; Ruling Number *6* = ***30***; Ruling Number *7* = ***29***; Ruling Number *8* = ***28***; Ruling Number *9* = ***27***; Ruling Number *10* = ***26***; Ruling Number *11* = ***25***; and, Ruling Number *22/4* = ***32***.

Remember, to calculate the three additional peaks, continue to add nine years starting from when you reached your Age of Maturity until you have calculated three additional peaks.

As you can see, I reached my Age of Maturity at 28 years of age, just as I moved back to the East Coast. This was important, because had I continued on the destructive path I was on in Toronto, more lessons would have presented themselves. What these lessons would have been, I don't know. I do know they would have been challenging enough that I would have had no other choice but to change. However, there was always the alternative, keep on doing what I was doing and find out; after all, we all have free will.

I reached my second peak when I was 37 years of age. At this time, my husband and I decided to explore our options with in-vitro fertilization. It was a success and we had twin boys. The third peak I reached at 46 years of age. This peak coincided with the time I started to pull away from the traditional healer and the reason I wrote *Heaven's Wait*. The fourth peak is yet to come, but it will mark the end of my maturity and lead me into the years of *Fulfillment*.

In these years of *Fulfillment*, I will share all that I learn, and continue to teach in some spiritual capacity. That is the growth indicated in my Life Pyramid. *Fulfillment* is a time to live and a time to experience all life has to offer with as much joy as is our right as creations of God's infinite love. More importantly, it is a time for continued spiritual growth, not just for me, but for all of us in these exciting years.

When I finally returned home for good at 28 years of age (remember, it took a couple of attempts), I managed to attain a sense of normalcy, but I was not balanced by any means. When I say balanced, I am referring to the mind, body and spirit. Certainly, my immediate physical needs were satisfied; however, I was in no way healed from all my experiences or in any way capable of understanding the extent of the damage I had done to myself and to all of those whom I had hurt. This of course came later, and my books are witness to this spiritual awakening and healing.

Today, right this moment, I see the silver lining in these experiences. Yes, we can go through life without creating so much pain and suffering, but I needed to experience this chaos to know what I didn't want or need it in my life…ever again. It helped me grow and to truly appreciate the stability of a loving and nurturing relationship and to put the needs of my children in proper perspective. In addition, these experiences, lessons and the wisdom gained helped lead me out of another kind of darkness, and I was able to use the same determination I put into ruining my life in my twenties into healing it when it was time.

I know I have shared a lot of information with you on numerology, and it is my hope that you too will take the time to discover more about your own Birth Charts and Life Pyramids. There is so much information to share, but of course, this is not a book on numerology. I thank you for allowing me to share this chapter with you and I believe it is wise to give pause to our life and realize for better or for worse that we have set our lives in motion and nothing in life is a mistake, especially life itself.

9

UNDERSTANDING THE UNKNOWN

It's sad really. Other than the memories in my head and a few pictures taken when I traveled home for a visit, I really don't have anything left of that time in Toronto or even before I moved to Toronto, the whole period of my life between 18 – 27 years of age. Every time I moved, it was with fewer and fewer things, until there was nothing; no pictures, no furniture, no little keepsakes, absolutely nothing. I look at social media now and entire generations are capturing images of their day-to-day life, even what they eat! Yet, for me, this period is captured only in my mind. Perhaps, in a way, that is best.

It was in my mind that I wrestled with the demons of my past and it was these that I needed to lay to rest in my healing journey. I attempted to begin this process with the healer that sought me out, but that process was ill-fated from the beginning and I had to begin anew in my own way. But first, I had to get something out of the way; my fear of the spirit world.

This fear of the metaphysical is what the healer used to manipulate me. He had projected many of his own spiritual fears and his preconceived notions and prejudices on to me and, to a larger extent, my husband. In my husband's case, he did not experience a life similar to mine or to the healer; my husband's life experience was one of multicultural interactions, a middle-class socio economic upbringing, and he had a healthy focus on sports and creative outlets like music and drawing. We grew up worlds apart and this was evident in how the healer interacted with him. It seemed the healer was always trying to punish him for who he was and what he represented to the healer, everything the healer wasn't; a university-educated person in the financial field that seemingly had everything.

Regrettably, this too was how I sometimes felt about my husband and his upbringing. I often imposed my feelings and insecurities on him and his interactions with friends, colleagues and to a small degree his family. I would sometimes say to him that I didn't think he was Native enough; after all, he didn't grow up on the reserve and knew nothing about our life! I was also suspicious of when he wanted to hang out with friends, especially hockey buddies after a game, because in my world this sometimes led to days of drinking, or family disharmony of some sort. In my family, it was sometimes difficult to distinguish between alcoholism and happier social interactions that involved drinking. I had to shift my understanding to realize that not everyone who drinks becomes an alcoholic or destroys their life with its use. However, the healer punished my husband financially for drinking, and implied there was no such thing as social drinking with Native people. The healer's past personal experience and use was one of intense alcohol and drug addiction and he felt it was the root of all evil and had a strict black and white view of alcohol consumption that he, inappropriately, projected onto us.

In addition to his past addiction issues, he was intent on removing himself from any situation that might trigger his addictive behaviours. I now see that the healer's struggle with maintaining sobriety was related to his lack of faith in himself and the true intention of sacrifice. As I mentioned in *Heaven's Wait*, I abstain from alcohol as part of my spiritual growth, but I am not adverse to its use around me as long as it is not in an out of control manner and I certainly don't remove myself from all functions where alcohol is served.

   The importance of sacrifice is one of the lessons we must learn in our life. It is a fact of life. Although we can sometimes choose what we will sacrifice, this intention must not be as a reward for something we desperately want and feel we need. Our body is very capable of providing us clues as to what no longer works for us and should be given up. For instance, when I decided I no longer wanted to eat pork or beef products, it was just a very intense thought that came over me. That previous weekend I asked my husband to purchase steak for a beef stir fry and I enjoyed the meal immensely. Then, the next day, I made a choice to not eat pork or beef. It just entered my mind and my decision was made. The same goes for sugary treats. I loved having a cookie or piece of pie with my evening tea. Then, one day I had a craving for my favourite lemon meringue pie, which I enjoyed a slice of each evening. The next morning I awoke and announced to my family that I would no longer eat sugary treats. This process was the same with caffeine, though it took a week to completely let it go. Each day I made my coffee weaker and weaker until it was nearly water. I replaced my coffee intake with warm lemon water and my tea with herbal tea.

   A while later, while in thought, I asked myself if I felt there was any benefit to the changes I had incorporated. The next day, as I was making my bed, I had the sudden realization that I hadn't had a hot flash in about three weeks. I am not saying consuming any of the items I had given up caused me to have hot flashes; what I'm saying is that the sacrifice I made out of a moment of inspiration had a balancing effect of eliminating an annoying symptom that is a natural result of menopause. In being willing to give up without expecting anything in return, I received a small miracle of healing. This can apply to anything which we choose to sacrifice, but we must be mindful that we do not make sacrifices out of fear or some new article that we read, but out of love for the act of sacrifice itself and what it means to our spiritual growth. Remember, your sacrifice is personal and there is no need to continually beat your own drum about your new way of thinking/living as this only creates followers who look to you to decide what to sacrifice in their own lives in the hopes of achieving the same benefit.

In researching metaphysical and/or paranormal activity related to spirits, I noticed that it is sometimes suggested that our energy field (aura) may be weakened as a result of the overuse of alcohol or any substance that is used in an abusive manner. It has been suggested that in this weakened state, spirits not of the "light," may influence behaviour and thought processes in a negative manner, often resulting in actions that may have regrettable or dire consequences.

I don't believe all negative actions transpire in this manner, but I think we are capable of creating the right conditions and/or environment for influences not of this physical world to seep into our energy field and worsen our already weakened state. In particular, an already weakened state of mind that is artificially and repeatedly comforted, toughened or pumped-up by things such as alcohol, drugs, sex, food, or a host of other behaviours equally as numbing may be prone to the influence of such negative energies.

In order for this affect to be understood more clearly, I will need to provide a brief overview of what I have come to learn about the spirit world. Just so you know, my personal experience with angels, spirits and guides is limited to intuitive thoughts, dreams, guided writing, meditative interactions, prayer and sensing spirit energy. I have not seen spirits or communicated with spirits, but I have been with people whom are able to facilitate the channelling of spirit energy. So for this section, I must again rely on research I have conducted over the past three years.

Where do I start? First, I'm basing this section primarily on books written from a Western or Christian New Age perspective by a wide array of authors from many different professions and backgrounds. Actually, just so you are aware, my books are classified in bookstores under the section *New Age and Occult*. The word "occult" freaks me out a bit, but I am not the one making these classifications. However, in the publishing world, my book is referred to as one that relates to *Mind, Body & Spirit*. I think I prefer this classification.

I am writing from memory, so obviously these perspectives resonate in some way with me and help me in a particular way understand and gain a comfort level with the world of spirit. To make my writing a little easier and to help you differentiate, I use the word "spirit" to refer to a deceased person that has crossed over and is in or from the "light." I use the word "soul" to talk about our life as it currently exists here on earth in human form. Then, I will use the term "earthbound spirits" to talk about deceased persons that have <u>not</u> gone through the "light." Some of these "earthbound spirits" may or may not interact or interfere in our lives, and often are referred to as ghosts.

Often the words "soul" and "spirit" are used interchangeably. The word "soul" is considered more of an Eastern world term which essentially means the same as how the term "spirit" is used in Western society. But I have borrowed it and use the word "soul" for my own personal discernment as described above.

For individuals who may be sensitive to metaphysical energy, spirits are often noted by different names; the most common of these names are, "spirit" "angel," or "guide." But for me, they do not mean the same thing or actually do the same thing. Just as I described angels as being of different orders, so too are spirits and guides. Always keep in your mind that, as soon as we die, we too become a "spirit." So please do not let fear overcome you when this topic is broached.

Many of us have experienced death up close and have witnessed our loved one's soul no longer be a part of their physical body. This is usually not actually seen, but is "felt" by the release of our personal connection to the body that remains. Not that we want to accept this disconnection immediately; it is necessary for many of us to say our final goodbyes in a more formal manner, which usually involves family and friends. But for the deceased, their spiritual journey has already begun.

For spirits that have recently died, the cross-over may be quick or it can linger a few days. Some may choose to stay around and view their services, then go through the *light* a few days later; while others immediately go through the light and onto the next stage of their spiritual reconnection or renewal. Further still, some spirits may simply get caught up in the crisis of their death and the grief of the family, or the anger of their untimely death; and, in these cases, they choose not to go through the light and become what are known as earthbound spirits.

In the book *When Ghosts Speak: Understanding the World of Earthbound Spirits*, 2009 written by Paranormal Investigator Mary Ann Winkowski, the author makes reference to the timeframe in which recently deceased spirits have until they can cross into the light, and that period is approximately eight days. She maintains that spirits may still cross over after that time period, but may need assistance or an awareness of other "light" sources such as light that appears for the recently deceased.

Going back to the spirits that have crossed through the light, I will need to back up a little. From the numerous accounts of books on the topic of death and the afterlife, a few commonalities appear. Yes, this doesn't cover all souls, but I am only focused for the purpose of this brief chapter on souls that have entered the light. Commonalities include: *(1) Upon the death of our physical body, we hover over our bodies and travel through the tunnel to the light. At this, the time of death, we feel no pain, anxiety or fear; (2) After we travel through the tunnel we are met by our Guardian Angel and then are greeted by all our loved ones who have passed from this lifetime and other lifetimes we may have lived; (3) We are still in what is known as an "ethereal" form: (4) Then we are taken by our Guardian Angel to review the life we have just lived; (5) Following this, there may exist a time of spirit renewal to reconnect with our purpose and our true being. Depending on our life, the circumstances of our death and other factors, this renewal period may vary, but it is always a period of intense love, and; (6) Following this period of spirit renewal we enter the light as our true spiritual self and are no longer in an "ethereal" form.*

So, who communicates with us and why! This is where it gets a little tricky.

Various levels of energies communicate with us for any number of different reasons. We'll start with the spirits who have finished viewing the life they just lived and are in the renewal process. During this time, they are usually accompanied by their guide and continue to remain in the ethereal form. In their renewal they may need to communicate a message to an individual they may have harmed in their lifetime or created an emotional scar the individual on the earth plane is still unable to release. In these times, those on the earth plane often feel compelled to seek out mediums, psychics or may run "into" a person with these metaphysical abilities. Souls who may still be in the renewal process following their "life review" sometimes may be brought through by Angels in our dreams. For example, I had a dream in which an old boyfriend visited me. In my dream, I introduced him to my husband and boys. He was considerably older than me when we dated in my twenties, so he looked the same as when we had dated. He asked if he could speak to me in private, to which I agreed. We went into a room and we sat across from each other. He asked me if I would forgive him. A tear rolled down his cheek when he asked for forgiveness. I said, "of course, yes!" When I said yes, his face turned from an older face to one that was much younger. We hugged and I woke up. That morning I checked the obituaries and learned he had died nearly two and a half years earlier.

Though I hadn't thought of him for a long time and didn't feel there was anything to forgive on his part, I realized that in our time of renewal we are shown things that are linked to the Universal Spiritual Laws. In this case, I believe it was related to respect and love and how we treat each other in this regard. I am happy that our connection is now healed and his journey through to the light can continue.

In these sessions the spirit who is being guided through their renewal will utilize the abilities of the medium and come forward to voice their apologies to the individual that was harmed. It is hoped that with the apology from the departed spirit, that both the spirit and the individual on the earth plane will now be able to advance on their healing journey. Sometimes it works for the individual on the earth plane and sometimes it doesn't and they may need additional healing to forgive.

Perhaps another explanation is to answer our prayers. Often when our loved one dies we pray for their assistance for one reason or another. Maybe we are asking if we made the right decisions, or if the family is in some type of disharmony and how to fix the problem, or maybe we just need to know they made it through okay. It could be almost any reason for which we offer up a prayer. In these cases, it is mostly spirits that have gone through the light following the renewal process that make a connection.

Again, this connection could be made through mediums, our own dreams or a meditative state. Some suggest that these departed spirits who are from the light now have access to our life charts and wish to help guide us through challenging or confusing times. However, they are not able to share with us that which is contained in our charts or what is also known as the Akashic Records or Book of Life.

In other instances, it may be an earthbound spirit; an ethereal form that made a decision not to cross through to the tunnel and light. In this ethereal form, they are able to maintain many of their earthly qualities, such as their personality, addictions, desires, hurts, and just about anything else you can think of. And now, because they are partially crossed over, they in turn can sense the hurt, pain, grief, anger, or whatever emotions we as humans display, only in a more intense manner, of those they love.

Many of you probably already know that earthbound spirits need energy to maintain their existence and they often derive this from humans with whom they have a connection to. It could be family members, friends or even people that may have moved into their old house following a death. Most don't mean to do any harm, and wish to try to put things right, or help a loved one through the difficult period of grieving. But because they feel their loved ones' grief so intently, they direct more of their emotion onto the individual, creating a never-ending source of distressing emotional energy that constantly moves between the loved one and the spirit energy around them.

Sometimes, this earthbound spirit connection may cause illness in the loved one or drive them towards more addictive activities that the spirit energy used when they were in human form. In these times, it's necessary to seek out help that is metaphysical in nature in order to disassociate oneself with the energy that has connected to an individual and encourage that spirit energy to go through the light. This is especially important if the spirit energy believes they have some reason or right to be there and begin to engage in haunting or ghost-like activities.

Many mediums that have written about spirits in the ethereal state, whether earthbound or in the renewal stage, often report that the spirit looks as they did in life! They are able to identify tattoos, scars, missing limbs, etc. It seems also, that for those that have passed through into the light following the stage of renewal, that these are lighter energy sources that may appear younger than they did at the time of their death; for example, an older person may look as they did when they were around 30 years of age.

It is also important to convey that any communication with a spirit must be done with some caution in mind. I know from experience that psychics, mediums and seers can tell you anything they think you want to hear or what they interpret as the message. This message can get all tangled up and/or confused by their own belief system and worldview, creating distress or anxiety in the client, while that was not the intent of the message from spirit. Also, some spirits are just not spiritually advanced enough to give advice and are known as low-level spirits or guides; this runs its own risk of creating anxiety or confusion for individuals seeking a spirit connection.

Spirits from the light recognize and live in love and clearly understand their limitations on what they can share with a loved one as it may interfere with that individual's free will. So, if you do choose to seek out a psychic or medium, please do your research and find someone that meets your spiritual needs in an upright and transparent manner. No person has a right to step into your vibrational energy without your explicit invitation, so beware of those who do.

This leads me to *Guides*. Guides can be both Angelic and Spirit. In this section, I will primarily focus on *Spirit Guides*; however, first let me provide a distinction between the two.

First, research seems to indicate that we have one major *Spirit Guide* that assists us through our entire life on this earth plane and that this guide has at one time lived at least one human lifetime on the earth plane. As our *Spirit Guide*, their role is to help guide us along our path to achieve the spiritual growth we had determined prior to our incarnation or birth. The spiritual growth we seek was important enough that we made the hard decision to live another lifetime on this earth plane. Our *Spirit Guide* also chose to help in achieving our spiritual fulfillment.

Second, but no less important, is our *Angelic Guide*. This guide from the Angelic Realm is of the Highest Order and also is with us our entire life. Their role is to act as a gatekeeper and together with our *Spirit Guide* coordinate other universal energies to assist, guide, or protect us in whatever means necessary for our spiritual journey. They have never lived a human life, so know only love. It is for this reason that our *Spirit Guide* is required to assist us through the real life challenges of the earth plane as they have lived at least once and experienced human emotions and thus have a clearer understanding of how best to guide us through. Our Angelic Guide is with us when we are born and throughout our life. Then, after the death of our physical body, they assist us in our safe return. This gatekeeper is often referred to as our *Guardian Angel*.

As I mentioned in an earlier chapter, we have with us at our birth as many angels from the Angelic Realm as we require for our journey. They are around us always and await our acknowledgement to be of service and to serve God in their service to humankind. Your Guardian Angel will bring to your assistance angelic guides of different orders to assist in balancing your mind, body and spirit, and will often lead you to individuals on the earth plane to share knowledge of various sources when you are ready. Be grateful and appreciative in your daily exchange with your angels, for they ask nothing in return and are as close to God as any creation in this universe will ever be.

Spirit Guides promise to help keep us on our path during our incarnation, but remember that free will reigns once we incarnate, so their jobs can be quite challenging. They know and understand the direction we need to take to attain our spiritual goals for this lifetime, but they are unable to tell us. So, they harness the energy of the angels and the spirits connected to us (loved ones that have crossed over) to nudge us when needed. This nudging can take numerous forms such as a thought that happens to enter your mind and causes you to take action, such as taking a different route to work and bypass an accident, a craving for a certain food that leads to a serendipitous meeting, an off-the-cuff comment from a friend that leads you to seek medical treatment, or a pamphlet handed to you that turns out to be the exact education program you were interested in exploring. I could go on and on, but I think all of you reading this know in your heart that you have experienced this nudging at some point in your life.

Our *Spirit Guide* is also able to bring forward other guides that may have promised to help us on our journey. A particular guide, in a previous incarnation, may have worked or excelled in the area in which we now require assistance. For instance, a guide with expertise in writing may have been brought forward to help me in writing *Heaven's Wait* and now this book. I had no previous experience in writing or publishing a book, yet I was able to do it in two weeks. I truly believe there was divine guidance that assisted me on some level, not only in the mechanics of writing my books, but also in providing me the strength, courage and fortitude to complete the task.

I also know that as I write, guidance is continual. I get a feeling when a word is not correct or when a particular topic has not been fully explained. Just yesterday, my computer shut down and restarted as I began a new paragraph. I was about three or four sentences in when the computer went off. I had been struggling with a new topic, but felt I was finally on track after 10 – 15 minutes of working it out in my head. I was upset that the computer shut down and I thought I had lost almost a page of my work. However, most of the work was recovered except for the final sentence of the paragraph I had just written, but when I reviewed the sentence again I realized the topic matter was too speculative for my spiritual level. Another day, I knew I was already tired from a full day of writing, but I had a number of words in my head that I wanted to complete that day and so persisted in writing for an additional two or three hours. When I reviewed my work the next morning, I had to delete all I wrote the previous evening because it was clearly not written from the heart as it reeked of self-pity.

Spirit Guides also need appreciation for their constant watch. Their protection of us is never ending during our earthly incarnation. They will petition for our needs and never leave our side, regardless of our circumstances. But as I mentioned earlier, sometimes their influence is of little help, and this is never more evident than when we choose to turn away from the light and live instead in darkness, consumed by our own physical and material desires, with little regard for our purpose in this life. In these times, all they can do is wait and hope for an opening, a blink or a slight chance you might take notice, and shift your gaze in their direction. It's in this time that we willingly take hold of the hand that guides us.

I leave you here on this topic and hope you enjoyed reading my perspective on the world of angels, guides and spirits, as I discovered through the many inspiring books I have studied. Though there is much more written about our spiritual journey when we cross over, I could not possibly give each book and/or author their due justice as each presents a viewpoint from a unique perspective. I will await my own experiences and insights that I believe will be forthcoming though my own guides for the purpose of enlightenment and spiritual growth. Until then, I am grateful and thankful to the many authors who have written on this topic and had the courage to share their knowledge and teachings that were so lovingly communicated from their spirit guides.

If there is one thing I know for certain it is that our life has a very specific purpose, both in this world and the world of spirit. A clue or a spark to ignite our search is all we need. The next time you say you are bored, or that nothing good is on television, why not instead download a book or get one from your local library. Select one that connects with you in some way; you never know, it could be the one that changes your life!

10

TAKING FLIGHT

Oh my God, where am I? I struggled to pinpoint something familiar, but the room was dark. I quickly lifted myself from a sleeping position, trying to understand where I was. It was so dark! I looked furtively around, seeking anything that could help me understand this strange place. I felt disoriented and for a moment, alarmed. Slowly the realization came to me that I was at my sister's home and in her guest bedroom. She had curtains that blocked out the light and during the night, the room became pitch black. *Oh yeah*, I thought, and relieved, I laid back onto the pillows. I smiled to myself at the silliness of my alarm, but then the dream that had startled me awake quickly came back to me.

Paula, watch! I heard a female voice around me, but I couldn't see who said it. I looked at a woman lying in a bed and then I heard the voice again, *she is the Queen and you must witness her death*. I looked closely at the sick woman, her breathing was laboured. The voice spoke again and said, *you must witness her death and sign her death certificate*. I walked over to a large ornate wooden table and reached down to pick up a pen and sign the death certificate. *I'll just sign this now*, I thought, *I don't need to wait*. But then, *No, Paula, both you and your husband need to witness her death and sign the death certificate together*, the female voice said. I put the pen down and walked over to the Queen again. I thought, *this is freaking me out, but it shouldn't take too long.* I stood there waiting, then I heard the voice again say, *don't let her drink that!* But it was too late, the Queen drank some coffee and started to dance around. I followed the Queen. She went to a disco. She was dancing around, enjoying herself immensely. But when the coffee wore off, I had to find a way to get her back into the palace. I hid her in my long dress and got her back to her bed, but she still hadn't died. I continued to watch her closely and then woke up suddenly, unaware of my surroundings.

It was two days after my book launch for *Heaven's Wait* at the end of September, 2014. I had hosted the launch at the Membertou Trade and Convention Centre located in the community where I had grown up. The Membertou Band Council had graciously sponsored the event and I was happy to be home with my sisters and brothers, extended family and friends. In addition, my book was now available for purchase at the Petroglyps Gift Shop, which was part of the new Heritage Park the community had recently built. It felt wonderful to be helped out in this manner.

I felt a surge of confidence rise in me with the support of the community and I was ready to finally share my story. A weight had been lifted off my shoulders as I shared the details of my spiritual journey, and the unfortunate experience I had with the Aboriginal traditional healer. I released a lot of angst and no longer felt like the experience was holding me hostage. I finally knew I had a right to tell my story and share the impact it had on me without the feelings of shame and embarrassment I had previously associated with the experience. Once again, my family, friends and community helped me heal and for that I am eternally grateful.

As I contemplated the dream a few days later, I finally understood its meaning. I knew that I was the Queen lying in the bed and I had to witness the death of the old Paula, the one that lived through her ego alone. My husband also had to say goodbye to that old Paula as she was the one that he met and unintentionally nurtured throughout our marriage. We had to both sign the death certificate, so it was important not to re-energize that ego-driven Paula, and let her die a natural death.

When I first met my husband, he used to tease me and call me the Queen of Charlotte Street. In Sydney, where we met and where my reserve (Membertou) is located, there is a street named *Charlotte Street* and it is here where many of the bars are located. When I was single I of course used to frequent these bars quite regularly and my husband teased me, saying they would miss their queen when I left. It was all in fun, but the association came through in my dream.

I thought at the time of the dream, and that I was ready to sign the death certificate. I spoke with my husband about the dream and the meaning it may have held for him as well. He said he was ready to say goodbye to the old Paula and obviously I thought I was too, but as things go, there is always more to the story and more to be released. I was close to saying goodbye to that Queen, but not quite yet!

I sat listening to the messages being given to the people around me. "May I come to you", I was asked. "Yes of course", I replied. I was in attendance at a Spiritualist Church in Brantford and messages from *spirit* are a normal part of that service. "I see a lot of papers around you, is that correct" she asked me. "Yes, I have researched quite a bit" I replied. "They're telling me that you need to write; are you writing a book!" she asked. "I have already written a book," I replied. "No, they're saying it's about all the papers around you," she said.

A few other details were provided, but my mind was not focused on a book. I thought perhaps the message was for someone else near me, I had even mentioned to my friend that I thought perhaps the message was for her as she was seated in front of me at the time. This was sometime in November 2014.

I was just getting started with promoting *Heaven's Wait* and I had no desire to write another book so soon. I had booked a few events and was busy trying to make some sales. I was aware I would continue writing, of this I was absolutely certain. I even confirmed this to people when they asked if I was going to write another book; however, I needed to get the word out about this book first. I was concerned about jumping to write a new book when I still had so much to do with H*eaven's Wait*.

I set this thought aside and busied myself in my work. I was focused on the upcoming Christmas shopping opportunities and joined in with the many other small businesses that relied on Christmas events to boost their sales. At one such event, I was seated across the way from an individual that approached me half-way through the day. Sales had been steady up until that time, but things were slowing a little, so he wandered over to my booth.

I could see him waiting out of the corner of my eye as I talked with other people interested in hearing about the background of my book. Then, as soon as the area cleared, he came forward. He leaned over my table as I remained seated, and then it started. He was intent on his assertions that I must admit I was a born-again Christian based on the brief description I gave him of my book. He began to quote passages from the Bible and said he was a "Minister", so he should know! After about 10 minutes, I very politely said to him that there are many different perspectives and means in which we come to know God and we should perhaps leave it at that; he had his beliefs and I had mine. "We are individuals, we come to our awareness when it is our time", I said. I extended my hand to him as a sign that I was not in any way offended by his assertions, and respected his right to express his beliefs, but I was now ending the discussion. He turned away without shaking my hand.

Truth be told, I was a little shaken. His intimidation was overwhelming and I felt like a deer caught in the headlights. I texted my husband and let him know what happened, and realized that the feelings I had were the same ones I had experienced when with the healer. I didn't like this one bit and for a moment, I felt as if I had lost my voice and my confidence. My husband gave me some reassurance and helped me understand that this person was nothing more than a bully who was intent on getting me into a discussion on religion in order to seek an opportunity to assert his own beliefs by undermining mine. "This is the reason people turn their backs on religion" my husband said, "Now go out there and sell some books!" Following this brief encounter, book sales picked up and I barely had time for a break the rest of the day.

For a few days, I replayed the event over in my head. *Could I have said something different*, I thought; *or perhaps defended my beliefs a little more ardently*, I reasoned. Then, I realized this is about our individual faith and what exists in our own heart. Faith in God cannot be coerced nor can it be beaten into us; it is a love that is unbroken, a promise that we belong and that we are part of something so much greater, and we will never have the words to explain it. Divinity is absolute and no person that is of this world has the authority to dispute, alter, or undermine our direct connection to God.

I sipped my coffee, listening to the people around me in the food court at the mall. My husband and I decided to meet up and do a little Christmas shopping for the boys while they were in school. As we chatted, he casually mentioned that he had noticed a slight change in my optimism about promoting my book. "The aggressiveness of that guy is still affecting you, isn't it" he stated. "A little," I replied. "I don't think I defended myself enough" I said. "You don't need to defend yourself against a bully" he replied. "That person thought you were an easy target and you handled yourself just fine."

We finished up our coffee and made our way to our cars. I was going on to the school to get the boys. "Everything is going to be fine" he said, "remember what you always tell me…there is a reason for everything!" I smiled and got into my car. *At least he listens*, I thought.

As I drove to the school, a familiar feeling washed over me and I could sense a need to write. I found a parking spot in front of the school and went into the memo app on my phone.

Then it started, *what is this?* I thought.

First there was an image, a book cover. I quickly jotted down the details of the image that formed. Then, the following words came:

Beneath your wings I sit, scared to be noticed,
If I just sit quietly, no one will ask what I know,
No one will challenge my words, my messages of faith,
I can go back to anonymity, back beneath your wings,
I am shown my own wings and that I must fly,
That I must share your words, your messages of love, healing and light,
Out from beneath your wings, I must now take flight.

Through this, I was given the title of my new book, *Out From Beneath Your Wings*, to be completed in January 2015. *Okay, I got my marching orders, no more messing around*, I thought.

Not long afterwards, I started writing; however, we soon ran into the Christmas holiday season and the boys were home from school. I chose not to write during their holiday break and picked up again when they returned to school. As I finished writing about the more difficult stories from my youth, I experienced emotional release in laughter and sometimes tears; and, once again, I faced my dreams.

In this dream, I stood watching my husband. A friend was standing to the left, but I couldn't see this friend. It is this friend that led us to a room located down a hallway. In this room there was a closed coffin. I walked up to it and ran my hand across it, feeling the softness of the wood. The coffin seemed like it was on a display mount that was designed to slowly spin so each angle could be seen. Then, the friend told us to run. I grabbed my husband's hand and together we started to run towards the exit, but it was a long hallway. We had to lock each door as we passed through until we were at the end and a padlock was put into this final lock.

I knew instantly, that this dream was connected to the dream I had at my sister's house in September. The Queen had died. With the release of the emotions that still held me captive from my youth, I was finally able to say goodbye to that old Paula, the one that was ruled by her ego. She died with the writing of this book and the embarrassment and shame of my past actions was laid to rest.

11

CONCEPTS FOR LIVING

"*I know it's not much, but it's the best I can do, my gift is my song –yeah --and this one's for you -- And you can tell everybody that this is your song, it may be quite simple but, now that it's done -- I hope you don't mind, I hope you don't mind, that I put down in words-- How wonderful life is while you're in the world...*" Elton John, Your Song.

This song entered my mind and I cried for the feelings it evoked about my husband, Mark; his incredible love and support during our years of marriage and the joy he has brought to such a broken soul. Never once did he walk out on me in anger or frustration because of the emotional baggage I brought into our marriage. He stayed and helped me through each crisis, including one of the biggest tests of our marriage during which our relationship was called into question numerous times by the healer. We withstood, not only as a couple, but as parents committed to providing the best care possible for our boys, Nathaniel and Bradley. Mark's strength, patience, and courage continue to grow and I am awed by his love and innate spiritual connection. This dedication is Your Song, my love, and I hope you don't mind!

Our soul can never really be broken; it is a figure of speech meant to convey a fractured or unstable emotional state. This emotional state is of the physical plane (our physical incarnation or life on earth), whereas the soul is of the spirit world; it is connected to our original "state of being" and is protected at all times.

However, though the soul may never be broken, we can go dark when we turn away from God and God's Light and choose instead to live only to satisfy our physical and material desires. It is always our choice and our choice alone whether to live in light or in varying degrees of darkness. For example, with our eyes closed tightly, it is very dark; but if we relax our eyes while they are still closed, there are some shades that begin to appear. Then, if we try to roll our eyes upwards when they are still closed, even more light shades appear. However, if we just simply choose to open our eyes there is light and we become aware of our surroundings and what was once dark is now illuminated.

What exactly is illuminated? I believe that what is illuminated is our actions and reactions that have prevented us from taking any significant steps towards our growth. We are able to see for the first time the role we play in our life circumstance and how each choice we have made through free will, sets an action into play. Then, when this action is set into play, we further engage with reactions to the actions we have just set into motion. For example, in my youth, I made a choice to not pay my rent. The landlord decided to take action to collect the rent as a result of the action I put into play. I then reacted to the landlord's actions by avoiding the landlord. The landlord reacted to my avoidance action by leaving a very public eviction notice on my door. I now made a choice to "burn" the landlord and not pay any rent and leave without paying. Even further, whenever I was provided the platform, I would talk smack about the landlord, saying what a complete jerk he/she was and that I hoped something bad happened to him/her. (If social media existed 25-30 years ago, this rant probably would have been posted on Facebook and it would have provided only one side of the story…mine!) In a sense, I blamed the landlord for my current state of affairs and my then homeless state. Although the decision was mine and mine alone to not pay the rent, in my immature mind the landlord was always the one that was the jerk who evicted me.

This lesson in responsibility for actions and reactions will continue until we recognize our part in setting these actions into play. As I mentioned, some of the reactions could be things like justifying the actions we took or defending our actions, even when we know they have created hurtful, painful or unsavory consequences. Unfortunately, when the lesson is presented, yet we choose to ignore it, it often repeats.

In opening our eyes, we choose to take responsibility and stop hiding in darkness where we can quietly "stoke the flame" of the injustices we feel were committed against us. Not that we shift blame and punish ourselves relentlessly, but we release the experience and the feelings associated with each of these experiences. What exactly are these feelings? Let's go back to my situation with the landlord. First, I felt embarrassed for not being able to pay my rent. Then, fear kicked in because I realized I would not have a place to live and may end up on the street. In addition, anger manifested towards the landlord for what I consider to be unreasonable interference in my life. Finally, stress overwhelmed me because I realized my worst nightmare of homelessness was upon me. Throw unworthiness in the mix and we have a potent cocktail that seeped into every cell of my body, beginning to consume all that is healthy.

So through this one action, we now have a slight contamination in our cellular structure. But take this same lesson and set it before us multiple times and we continue to engage in the same actions and have the same reactions, then the cells in our body are now fighting for survival. The cells begin to tell us that they don't feel so well.

Anger, shame, guilt, embarrassment, fear, stress, unworthiness and many more feelings neatly store up in the cells; layer upon layer. Soon, feeling tired becomes a normal state. What's our reaction going to be next time? Probably the same because now we have become lazy and complicit and use phrases like "what's the use?" or "I deserve it" and "that always happens, what made me think this time would be any different!"

Our will has become weak and we have allowed our lessons to define us, one by one. There is no thought given to what the lesson may have taught us. We are yet incapable of creating a balance sheet that identifies our gains, losses and current state of affairs. These lessons are meant to assist us in fortifying our strengths and help us bolster areas in which we are weak. There should be no losses at the end of the day as we pull from each experience the good to fortify, and the not so good, to reveal our hidden weaknesses.

How do we do this? We do this by breaking down each lesson until a life principle is revealed. What are some of these life principles? Life principles are things such as forgiveness, compassion, gratitude, humility, generosity, expectation, intention, tolerance, moderation, acceptance, and so on. Let's review our example again about my situation with the landlord to reflect some of these principles.

Principle of expectation: There was an agreement between myself and the landlord, which was paying rent in exchange for a place to live. The *expectation* on behalf of the landlord was that I would pay the rent and the *expectation* on behalf of me was that the landlord would provide a safe, up-to-code rental unit. But I breached this *expectation* and created an imbalance. Additionally, along with the breach, I had created an additional *expectation* that the landlord would "help out" or "give me a break," but this additional *expectation* was unreasonable and was never part of our agreement. The landlord had nothing to do with my financial situation or lack of ability to pay my rent.

My own actions led to the landlord's reactions, which in turn led me to experience feelings of anger, frustration, shame, embarrassment, and stress. I did not properly manage the *principle of expectations* nor did I understand it at the time. This principle often comes into play when we rely on others to maintain our sense of security, happiness, motivation, self-worth, self-respect, and so on. Just as the landlord wasn't responsible for my living situation, others in our lives are not responsible for these either. This stops when we are no longer infants. Even children have the capability of creating their own happiness; each one of us worries about boredom and takes steps to ensure boredom is never felt. We have every right to expect to be happy, safe and secure in all things; but, it is also our responsibility to set out intentions to help us realize our own expectations and to live our lives in balance.

If I had learned to recognize the *principle of expectation*, I would have had a clear path to learn another important lesson, the *principle of intention*. This principle can take the form of honouring my own self with the *intention* to maintain a certain standard of living that no longer involved making bad choices which prevented me from paying my rent. For instance, I could have put forward the *intention* to adhere to a budget that ensured my living expenses were first taken care of before more frivolous or less desirable spending depleted my funds. This may have taken some time to work through and develop discipline, but acknowledging the *principle of intention* and taking steps to balance my life account would have likely stopped the lesson from being repeated or lessened its effect.

We now have reviewed a couple of principles based on my example with the landlord, but I would like to extend this just a little more to include some of the remaining principles outlined earlier: humility, generosity, moderation, forgiveness, gratitude, tolerance, and compassion. Remember, these are not all the principles we must learn in our life, so I would advise reading more on this topic to gain a more thorough understanding of all the life principles.

The following example is a lesson to highlight the *principle of humility*. Let's say you have purchased a vehicle even though it was beyond your financial means. In purchasing the vehicle you stretched your budget to the point where there was absolutely no wiggle room and perhaps even incurred a minor deficit each month. But you loved the car and really felt you deserved it! This need or desire to have what is technically beyond our means is how *humility* presents itself. Often times the ego does not want to wait for a better time, and we think we are losing out because we see so many other people achieve success and we desire the same benefit. The *principle of humility* presents itself in situations in which we want the same or better than what your friend, co-worker, family member or anyone else has that we believe we not only deserve, but deserve better. Then, we take steps like overextending ourselves with credit card debt, a mortgage we can't afford, or a car we can't finance and in doing so leave ourselves with no recourse should an emergency situation arise. Things like a tire blowout, a leaky roof, a death in the family, or an accident have the ability to strain us, sometimes beyond hope. It is only through recognizing humility and embracing its lesson that freedom can be embraced.

The *principle of compassion* presents itself often throughout our lifetime. *Do unto others as you would have them do unto you.* This is one of the easiest ways to balance our life account. We find opportunities every single day in which to show *compassion* to another soul. It could be a hug when someone is distressed, the care of a loved one that is ill, a lift into town to pick up a prescription, the purchase of a few small items for someone in need, a few bucks for gas to help someone make it to school or work, the offer of child care to a struggling single parent, the loving care of the elderly and children, kind words, a call to someone who might be lonely, a hot meal, a warm coat, and on and on it goes. I could fill several pages with examples of *compassion* and how these little acts of kindness fill our hearts and all those we serve in their time of need.

The *principle of generosity* states that *it is better to give than to receive*. This principle of generosity extends into all aspects of our lives and is often linked with the principle of compassion; you recognize a need and it inspires you to give. This generosity can take the form of time, money, a friendly gesture, a helping hand like returning a shopping cart to the corral for a person struggling to load their groceries with children in tow. The point is that you give and do not expect anything in return. You give because it makes your heart swell with kindness towards another. It is not the same as generously loaning money which you expect to be repaid, or generously providing space for a meeting in the hopes of getting a few people to buy your product.

The *principle of moderation* provides us the opportunity to learn balance. It keeps us from straying into the undesirable actions of fanaticism. For example, a woman, I met long ago had a belief that if she consumed a lot of carrots she would be healthy and be able to fend off all type of illnesses. However, this over consumption of carrots turned her skin a weird colour orange. Her friends were too embarrassed to tell her that she didn't look normal. She was an esthetician and I'm sure her skin colour didn't go unnoticed by her clientele. In her attempt to live a healthy life, she didn't consider that even healthy foods require moderation and a healthy balance is necessary to sustain optimal health. This could apply to other matters as well that have potential for fanaticism, such as political views, societal issues, work, sports, recreation, etc.

The *principle of forgiveness* is about taking away the influence another has over our emotional state. This also includes forgiveness for oneself. It doesn't mean we need to go around telling everyone we forgive them for their actions that hurt us; some won't even know that they hurt or caused us to suffer. Instead, it's giving ourselves permission to let our heart release the impact another person's actions have had on us. Sometimes, it helps to perform a little ceremony. We can write down on a piece of paper how the actions of another caused us emotional distress and express our forgiveness for each action. Then, after we're done, we can light the paper on fire, releasing ourselves from the emotions. (Please do this in a fire-safe manner, preferably outdoors.) This doesn't mean we need to be buddy-buddy with the person, but it means we are no longer impacted in one way or another by that person's presence or lack there-of. Additionally, this little ceremony can be done for our own actions that may have created emotional distress in others or for those we wish to seek forgiveness from, especially when we no longer have a connection due to the passage of time or if they are no longer of this world.

The *principle of gratitude* is also one we can use every day to balance our life account. It's simple— be grateful for life. Be grateful for this incredible opportunity we have to give thanks for the many people, things and opportunities we have and the many choices available to us. Think about it – I'm sure most of you have something to give thanks for today. When I ask people if they are grateful for what they have in their lives, many are, but their desire for want is far greater. So I ask again, if you can live someone else's fantastic life for 10 days, would you do it knowing that the payment for that experience is to live another person's life for 20 days that is full of dire poverty and absolute despair! It appears that most realize the comfort of their life situation and can immediately find something or someone for which to express gratitude.

The *principle of tolerance* is the recognition that we are all souls created for the same purpose, which is spiritual growth. There is no one person greater than or less than we are, but there are situations and actions that are good and not so good and which warrant varying responses to appreciate the *principle of tolerance*. For example, someone you love has been on the receiving end of your generous nature since falling into a personal crisis a few months earlier. You have listened for months to their angst and assisted them in every way possible. You love them and really care, so you set aside your own personal needs to accommodate theirs. However, your tolerance level for their whining is diminishing and the stress is beginning to affect your health. They, on the other hand, recognize that your tolerance level is wavering and create more problems. Suddenly, they have undiagnosed aches and pains that leave them bedridden or their addiction issues increase. You think to yourself, *I would really want someone to help me if I was in need*, so you do nothing. Finally, your stress level is so high that your own work and health start to decline. Yet, you receive little assistance from the individual you were trying to help because they have no sense of the stress they are creating.

In these cases, the relationship is no longer soul to soul and the *principle of tolerance* has been satisfied on your part and you must take note of this, or else it will be repeated in behaviour referred to as enabler/rescuer. It is time to release the individual who has put all their energy into trying to get your sympathy so they don't have to make changes. They do not view life soul to soul; they view life as if they are owed something and this you cannot change.

These principles are available for a more thorough review in many resource materials and they vary by identification and purpose. Some use them to explain business practices, spiritual practices, healing practices and so on. However, these principles have an original source and this original source is the **Universal Spiritual Laws**.

So begin your ledger and start managing your life account. Then, each time you are at a loss for which direction to take, you can refer to this ledger and see clearly what a particular decision resulted in and the principles that were noted. Did this decision strengthen your character traits or did you accidently reveal another weakness! What did you learn from this weakness? Remember, at the end of the day, your life account should balance; even mistakes can be taken apart and sorted into different columns. This is not to justify your actions, but just to point out that you took notice.

12

LIVING IN HARMONY

There are many Universal Spiritual Laws, ranging from the most basic level to higher levels as our spiritual awareness develops. They are as follows: **Basic Laws of Life, Laws of Creation, Laws of Higher Awareness**, and **Laws of Higher Frequency**. It is more often than not that we need more than one incarnation (life) on this earth plane to achieve the understanding and application of each of these Universal Spiritual Laws, especially when we feel "we have done enough" or we don't fulfill or even understand our Life Purpose.

I won't review each of them because that would take a lot of time, but there are numerous resources available on the internet, and in bookstores and libraries to research at your leisure. However, I feel it is important to, at the very least, highlight the first level, which includes the **Basic Laws of Life**: *Attraction, Request, Resistance, Reflection, Projection and Attachment*. I will use my own life experience to explain the meanings, so please do your own research to get a deeper and more detailed understanding of each of the Spiritual Laws. You will be happy you did!

THE SPIRITUAL LAW OF ATTRACTION

I have attracted good to me, but I have also attracted bad, depending on my state of mind. Some of the positive things are good health, strong body, creative abilities, financial resources, spiritual guidance, a loving family, a beautiful home, and inner peace, to name a few. Some of the bad I have attracted to me are the healer, a lack of work, emotional upheaval, accidents, negative people, self-pity, anger, and on it goes. So how does the Spiritual Law of Attraction work? Basically, we attract to us what we send out.

If we want to stay poor, we just keep thinking we are poor by never showing gratitude for what we have. If we want to stay overweight, we just keep thinking our self-identity or happiness depend on being thin. If we want to keep attracting negative people and situations into our life, we just keep posting our rants, turmoil, vanity, judgements, and any other negative behaviour on social media or through any other forms of communication; this applies to our thoughts as well. The Law of Attraction guarantees that we will receive what we put out – because it has nowhere else to go, and the Universe will not hold it or cleanse it for us. It has to go back to its origin.

Yes, this sounds harsh. But we are here to learn. How can we begin to understand love when we are caught up in our physical and material environment and making negative comments about anyone or anything that happens to come across our path! This includes our self, too! Creating too much negative output is like walking around with a big black cloud over our head. We all know someone that continually faces challenges, and this could even be you. This black cloud has the energy to pull undesirable consequences to us, and I for one have had enough. These consequences can come to us in the form of a slip/fall, a stiff neck, sore knee or hip, upset stomach or any other ailment, a car accident, betrayal, an argument, physical altercation, relationship breakdown, job loss, a negative or harmful person, and so on.

However, this law will always try to bring us back to balance, regardless of our debt. At any time, we have the power to shift the Spiritual Law of Attraction in our favour.

It takes time to shift our thinking and to pull back a negative thought we were about to say, post, or to complain about whether that complaint was valid or not; but, that's okay. Awareness is the first step to making positive change. Little by little we can make a difference. This difference will be felt by our children, spouse, mother, father, sister, brother, friend and whomever else is in our life. All of a sudden we won't be that negative pulse moving from point A to point B, with people ducking for cover when we are near; and don't think this doesn't happen.

With these small changes, over time we begin to attract different people and resources to our life. For example, our newfound confidence may attract stronger, more helpful people to our life to help us get organized and set positive goals. On the flip side, negative people will no longer be drawn to our energy because they no longer connect with us—we have raised our energy to a higher level and they don't feel comfortable at our new level. It's like they're looking at the sun and it's too bright.

THE SPIRITUAL LAW OF REQUEST

As I mentioned in the earlier chapter about angels, we are in a position to ask for divine assistance and guidance at any time in our lives. These requests cannot be demanded like a petulant child when things are not going our way or, damn it...we want proof! These requests often come when we're ready and prepared to accept and share in the responsibility of transforming our way of thinking, living and being. The *Spiritual Law of Request* ensures connection to all that we need for our growth and spiritual development, but it often does not come exactly when we request it; more often than not, it comes in divine right time, when our angels, guides and teachers recognize we are ready to receive. In addition, just because we asked for something or made a request it doesn't mean it will automatically be fulfilled now or later. Our particular request just sometimes doesn't fit with our path or purpose for this lifetime.

Often what happens and what happened to me is that one day I simply felt a need to know why, or how, or what good all my experiences were for me. In doing this, we sometimes may feel this is a passing thought, but that one little inquiry in our mind may allow a little light to shine through and the angels hear what they are so longing to hear, a request for knowledge. In this instant, we have made it known to the universal energies that we are ready, then somehow, something or someone comes across our path that provides us a little inspiration, and we want to know more.

The day my request was heard, I knew in my heart I couldn't go on living in self-pity and suppressed anger towards the healer, my jobless state, my financial woes and my childhood traumas and poverty. I was beginning to feel the need to run and this was impacting my relationship with my husband. I felt off balance and thought a move would solve all our problems. My husband and I argued that day as I stated to him that I wanted to move. I was fighting against myself like you wouldn't believe. Battles raged in my head, and if I could have beaten the crap out of myself, I would have! I absolutely, positively hated being me. I needed to get out of the house. I drove towards town, ranting in the car like some type of lunatic. I can only imagine what the drivers next to me were thinking. But in all this ranting, was my genuine request to know "why?"

I didn't go to the library because I thought I wanted a book, I went there because it was one of the few places I could think to go that didn't cost money. It was a place I could relax until I had calmed down. I couldn't go back home yet, not until I was thinking straight. One thing I knew was that hurtful comments cannot be taken back! I walked around the library, looking at nothing in particular. I then pulled out a few books that were grouped together and flipped through the pages. *These look interesting*, I thought. My mood started to change. I sat down and began to read. After an hour, feeling lighter than I had in some time, I decided to head home. I talked to my husband and reassured him that I was fine and any thoughts of moving were dismissed.

That day, my request to know "why" was heard. It may have come from a state of anger, but it was genuine and heartfelt. I needed a helping hand to guide me to find answers and it was given. This helping hand came in the form of books written by authors who shared their unique perspective of their own traumas and spiritual experiences and this allowed me to shape my own healing journey. It gave me the strength to endure the process and the confidence to ask for additional help when needed.

Just to clarify, requests are different from prayers. Prayers are sent to receive a personal blessing or to offer a blessing on behalf of a loved one, or someone you know, a community, even the general state of the world; these are always positively received by the Universe.

We all have heard the phrase "Ask and Ye Shall Receive." This promise is the *Spiritual Law of Request*. This process of asking and giving thanks is part of our spiritual growth. It provides us with the knowledge that we are more than just physical beings, and that we are part of something greater and more infinite than we have the ability to describe or ever experience in our physical form. In turn, we are asked to get on with living, to get on with growing and to make our lives more than just routine. Every day we have a choice to open a new gift and see what surprises lie in wait or watch and see what others receive and begrudge that person's gift and light. Every day, I choose light.

THE SPIRITUAL LAW OF RESISTANCE

We have already examined the Spiritual Law of Attraction and the *Spiritual Law of Resistance* is similar, but based on a slightly different concept. This law focuses on our thoughts and speech and the way we use words like "don't", "won't"," can't", "never", etc. In each of these thoughts and words, we are resisting the very thing or quality we hope to gain. For instance, I don't' ever want to date a jerk like so and so again! The next month, you meet a person; but, before you realize it – and perhaps months later you again realize the person is exactly like your previous bad relationships! Your thoughts and words have attracted exactly what you didn't want.

The *Spiritual Law of Resistance* is more than a little frustrating to get our heads around because we have used these phrases every day in our lives from the time we were children; I don't want that, I won't go, I can't do my homework! It is our second nature to express our opinion, wants and desires in this manner. However, after saying it from this negative perspective so many times, all that we hear and all that we put out to the universe is "so and so," and this is what is brought to us. The phrase "don't want" and "do want" get muddled in the exchange. A need to more clearly express your desire is needed. This is also the case with illness, work, children, and so on.

Last year, I attended an event at which a woman, who was close to my age, shared her story about her cancer diagnosis. Prior to the time of her cancer diagnosis, she was a self-proclaimed health nut and ate a purely vegan diet and was obsessed with reading resource materials related to cancer and the prevention of cancer. After all, she didn't want to get cancer and was going to do everything in her power to prevent it from happening to her. Guess what, she did get cancer and she received a very dire diagnosis. In her retelling of her story, she shared her near-death experience and miraculous healing she received in that near-death experience. She also spoke about what had been shared with her in that time when she left her body and she was in the spirit world. Her story is remarkable and is one shared by many who have journeyed beyond. However, she acknowledged that her very obsession with "not" getting cancer actually attracted it to her. She resisted good health from her life by using words like "I don't want cancer," or "I never want to get cancer," and so on.

So if we are not to use words like don't, can't, won't or never, what words should we use? It's more than changing the words we use; it's also in the thoughts we have and the way we allow them to manifest and give them power over us.

In my own transformation, I have incorporated suggestions from authors who have written on this topic. I now use phrases that cut through the resistance. These new phrases are ones that are in the present tense and are not dependent on future output. I now accept that "I am!" In using this phrase I acknowledge that it has happened; I am happy, I am fulfilled, I am debt-free, I am a successful author, I am loving, I am loved, and I am loveable.

In addition, I adopted the phrase "I have". I have a healthy and happy family, I have a successful business, I have a healthy body, I have resources through which I can fulfill my life purpose, I have friends that love and support me. Sure it's easy to slip back into the old way of thinking, but as time goes by, we recognize immediately our slip-ups and are able to set things moving forward once again.

THE SPIRITUAL LAW OF REFLECTION

A few years ago, I met a little girl that I had almost an instant dislike towards. I chastised myself, however, because she was just a kid and did nothing that warranted my intense feeling of dislike. As I watched her, I thought she was too fussy and she talked incessantly about how hot and sticky she felt. She cringed at doing kid stuff or getting even a bit dirty. I found her to be quite annoying. Why was she annoying? I realized it was because she was just like me!

Often we don't like what we see in others because it's what resides in us or how we behave. I'm sure I have annoyed more than a few people throughout my life by being fussy and self-centered. I didn't clue into this right away, but as I discussed it with my husband, he pointed out the similarities; even alluding to the way I was still complaining about it, after the fact. This is the *Spiritual Law of Reflection* and it helps mirror behaviours in oneself that need development.

Another way it can reflect is through symbolism that may come to us in dreams or circumstances in our life. When I first started my healing journey, many of my dreams featured a water source such as a swimming pool, rain, a lake, or the ocean. In the case of the swimming pool, I would float with people or debris all around me. Later it was just me in the swimming pool, swimming leisurely back and forth. But then I was out of the water source and watched others frolic in the water. Water reflects us and can reflect our image back to us. However, water is also capable of cleansing, and in this case, I had a lot of deep emotional hurts that needed to be cleansed and the water reflected this back to me.

In a series of other dreams, I walked along a road. But throughout the months in which these dreams occurred, I went from walking in combat-type boots along a paved road, to cowboy boots along a dirt road, to moccasins on a dirt road, and finally, to bare feet on a dirt foot path. The earth reflects growth and our connection to the growth. My feet were now bare and I was able to feel our connection with all life and receive the amazing healing energy provided by Mother Earth.

I also had numbers reflected back to me time and again. It started with 11:11 and moved on from there to 222 or 333 or 444, 555 and so on. For a time, I would wake up at 3:33 each night. Then, I would receive messages or notices that were 11:44 or 744 and many other series of numbers. I would see license plates, signs, clocks and other objects with certain numbers displayed. After months of noticing this pattern, I finally started to research some of the numbers. I was happy to learn I wasn't going crazy or that I wasn't paranoid. It was only the Universe reflecting back to me my own promise to serve and the awakening I was about to undergo, if I chose to embrace it.

So take note of what is being reflected back to you. Study the four elements (water, earth, fire, air) and their meaning, especially if they appear in your dreams. Think about little things that may be recurring themes in your dream state or life; what do you think they are trying to reflect back to you? For example, in our dreams, cars represent our physical body; but are you driving, or is someone else in the driver's seat. What is the state of the car? Is it in bad shape, scratched or dented? This may reflect back to us that we need to take better care of ourselves and perhaps even a tune-up is in order!

PAULA SEVESTRE

THE SPIRITUAL LAW OF PROJECTION

When I was with the healer, he would announce at least once a week that I needed to be careful not to associate with certain people because they practiced bad medicine. I know now that he was projecting his true evil intentions onto others, and in so doing, denying that what he was doing was wrong. This is how the *Spiritual Law of Projection* provides us insight into another's true intentions or inner-most feelings.

I often did this with my own children. I didn't want my children to view my mother in a casket because I thought it might lead them to have nightmares or fear associated with that viewing. But it was my own fear that I had projected onto them and I rationalized in my mind that it was in their best interest. After all, I didn't want them to suffer the same fate that I did as a result of the many viewings I went to when I was a child growing up on the reserve. At that time, it was normal for kids to walk in and out of homes, where a body was being waked. However, I realize now that it wasn't really the viewings that created the fear; it was the ghost stories we all told later or listened to with rapt attention when the adults entertained us with their own scary stories.

Another way I projected my fears onto the boys was at the amusement park. Since I was afraid of heights, I tried to prevent the boys from experiencing rides I thought might scare them. They were fearless; it was me that was afraid. Fortunately, my husband pushed through and overrode my objections and encouraged the boys to try out the rides in their age/size category. However, as I watched, my stomach did flip flops so badly I often couldn't help but look away. The funny thing is, as they grew we needed to accompany them on a lot of the bigger rides, so I can now get on all the rollercoasters, but my eyes still remain closed most of the time!

The Spiritual Law of Projection opens our eyes to our true inner feelings. These can be fear, like I outlined above or can be anger, hostility, mistrust, unfaithfulness, and so on. When we feel that people are out to get us, may deceive us, or cheat on us, this is our own true feeling being projected outwards then reflected back to us. So now, whomever we project our feelings onto, we now think they are out to get us, will cheat on us or will deceive us.

But then, as you know by now, there is always a flipside. As we begin to clear through a lot of the emotional baggage we carry, the negative projections are lessened or are no longer there at all. Now when we talk with someone, they seem happy, light and energetic. Our own way of viewing life has changed, so now we are projecting this change and our new lightness. This is why happy people attract other happy people, they/we project brightness and light, and it no longer hurts our eyes.

THE SPIRITUAL LAW OF ATTACHMENT

By now, I think most of you realize the extent of my healing journey. In this journey, my attachment, to people who may have hurt me or whom I may have hurt, or attachment to emotions and things needed to be severed. It wasn't easy. There were a few that needed constant pruning until I felt ready to sever the attachment. This severing process was required to prepare me to understand and accept the Spiritual Law of Attachment.

When we associate a "need" with a person, place or object, then we have an investment in keeping that person, place or object in our lives. In our minds, it becomes associated and labeled as property.

In labeling our need, we now have assigned emotions to it and have formed an attachment to it. For some, this attachment can be their spouse, children, friends, house, job, car, household items, furniture, jewelry, and so on. The reason I include children is that we can place on them the burden of our own dreams and desires and become tied to their successes or failures. In these cases, the attachment is to live out our own dreams through the child in order to build up our own self-worth and this is not fair to the child. This is the very meaning of the *Spiritual Law of Attachment*, self-worth tied to a need.

My self-worth was tied to many things. Some ties were more tangled than others and even still some were chains. I didn't grow up in a household that had much money, especially not credit cards. So when I married, my access to credit cards was finally realized. But it was a constant battle between me and my husband. He was extremely financially astute. Me, I had an astute sense of where the sales were! But, he managed to rein me in early in our relationship, though not without underlying resentment on my part. You see, to me, the credit cards were like unused cash…it's there, why not spend it!

There were times when I would push just enough to get my way and we would use the credit cards to book a vacation or buy a piece of furniture I wanted, but this type of spending had an emotional toll on my husband. The stress of buying what he knew we couldn't afford played on his need for security. To me, it just meant I was able to get my own way and I gave no thought to paying the debt; after all, my husband looked after all the financial affairs.

But eventually, the *Spiritual Law of Attachment* comes beckoning. This was one of the first things that the healer had me sever during the release work, but it was done in a manner that created fear. I had to give up the credit cards or else I would cause my husband's death. So I did, but like everything else with the healer, the lesson didn't stick because it was fear-based. It wasn't until my own healing journey that I was able to understand and appreciate that I tied my self-worth to my ability to purchase things or travel at will, thus giving the appearance of wealth.

We do this with many people and things in our life. We say things like "I'd die if I lost my phone" or "I'd die if my husband/boyfriend left me," or even "I'd die of embarrassment if someone ruins my wedding." In many cases, we are so tied to our attachments that the only way for us to learn the *Spiritual Law of Attachment* is through loss. Once the loss occurs, we realize we didn't die. However, many hold resentments over this loss and form new emotional entanglements to this loss. So, the opportunity to learn a lesson is missed, and the lesson needs repeating.

I live comfortably, and have things that are considered extra or frivolous, but I know that I can live without them. I also know my husband is with me because he loves me. He no longer feels the need to give in to my demands in the fear that I would leave him. He has stood up for himself, and in no uncertain terms stated that while he would be unhappy if I left, he would manage just fine without me. In turn, my own need to continually test his loyalty has dissolved and together, our need to hold to each other as if our lives depended on it has been severed. Today, we are each our own individuals and on our own path, but we now journey together in love, respect and honour, neither beholden by need.

13

ENDINGS AND BEGINNINGS

Sometimes, we don't see what is buried deep in our unconscious. For me, it was my own prejudice and racist attitudes towards the Caucasian race. I was often appalled when people spoke badly about who we, as First Nation Peoples, often referred to as "white" people. I didn't like to blame the "white" people for all my life's follies, but really I did and I resented them for many things. This is why I reacted so indignantly when the healer spoke badly about white people and blamed them for many of our problems. The healer was reflecting what I thought, and I didn't like the mirror image I was shown, so I projected my deep-rooted feelings back to the healer. It was his problem, not mine.

You see, almost every time I failed, fell, and embarrassed myself through my own inappropriate actions, it usually involved a person from the Caucasian race. However, in my case, they were only a part in a play I was directing. I continually attracted to myself people I not only deep down disliked, but also mistrusted and gave them all leading roles in my play. Then, when the play didn't go according to plan, I blamed the actors for ruining it. I took no part in my role as director, writer, and producer.

The Universal Spiritual Laws are there for a purpose and they will reveal themselves when we are ready to accept personal responsibility for our own spiritual growth. This means that we can make our lives as easy or as difficult as we choose, by accepting or not accepting the Spiritual Laws and living according to their principles.

Over time, I have come to see people not by their race, but their soul. I realize we have chosen many souls to play a part in the plays that we direct throughout our lifetime. When we gain experience as a director, we understand that to have a successful production, we must work together as directors, actors, stage hands, producers, writers, promotors, etc., for the optimum success of the production. Being able to pull from each member of the cast that which inspires day in and day out, is an indication that we have accepted and acknowledged that many contributions are necessary for the successful outcome of each of the productions we undertake in life.

So, with this in mind, why not open our casting call to all; there are many souls to fulfill a role and at any point in our life, we don't know who may play the leading role in our successful production.

A long time ago, I made a promise to myself that I would travel the world. I was very young when I made this promise and, at that time, the world mainly meant places like Toronto, Boston, New York, Maine or other places people from the reserve had traveled to. I remember sitting in a little park in Sydney called Wentworth Park. Me, and a few of the kids from the reserve often walked to the park to hang out. We used to walk on the railroad tracks to get there, and it was here I dreamt of far places. *Where do they go...*I wondered, as I walked the rail, occasionally slipping and falling on the sharp rocks that lay on either side. At times, we would try to hitch a ride on the train as it went by, but I was never fast enough to grab the ladder.

I remembered this promise just this evening. I had been asked before to consider what my childhood dream had been because therein lies the ties to our life purpose. To me, I thought I had no such aspirations and felt it was my lack of worldliness that caused me to be so uninspired. But I did have dreams. I just put them somewhere unseen until it was safe to bring them forward. The time for my dreams is now, and they are part of my spiritual journey.

I have taken my soul on a wild journey through this life, but it was worth it. Most of the spiraling and extreme experiences in my twenties only lasted about 18 months, but they had lasting effects. I look upon many of these experiences as a lesson in humility. Considering all the weaknesses in my character and my abysmal past, I am humbled by the Grace that has restored my faith in love and in God. I present these stories, not to defend myself, my actions, or my past, but to breathe a little easier and to crawl out from the dirty blanket that I had been suffocating beneath. I lived in fear of my past for too long and in that fear, my ego was able to hold me captive --the healer was able to hold me captive. *No more*, I thought, *now I am free!*

When I reflect on the beauty of knowing my true self and the confidence that brings, I feel like I can do almost anything. I can write ten more books, if that is my purpose. I feel a love that fills me and I must raise my arms to release it to the Universe because it feels too good to keep it to myself. I send to all of you blessings of joy, peace and love. Until we meet again, I wish you thanks in my Mi'kmaq language, *Wela'leig*.

AFTERWORD

This very powerful message was passed on to be shared with the world titled, *A very POWERFUL message from an Angel*; a message on YouTube by Michael New, December 22, 2013. I encourage you to view it at http://youtu.be/TDvJ7DK9Vck.

I dreamed I met an Angel – An Angel of God.
Not sure what to say...I asked "do you have time for a question?"

The Angel said, "I don't have any time...all I have is now."
I smiled and asked, "What amazes you most about humans?"

The Angel Replied...
"You long for Peace...and are at war with yourself."
"You seek freedom...and you are already free."
"You look for love...and you are love itself."
"You are afraid to open your heart...and your heart is always open."
"You fear Death...and you are eternal life."

The Angel held my hand and we were silent for a while.

AFTERWORD

Then the Angel looked deep into my eyes...and whispered these secrets.

"When you stop the war inside...you are The Peace outside."
"When you fully open to your Fear...you can see fear is simply Energy."
"When you meet death fully...you will see you are The Life."
"When you are naked to yourself...you are free to be yourself."
"Look deep with your Heart...and you will see you are Love."
"Forgive yourself so completely...your very presence Forgives."
"Love this moment so fully...You are Free as Freedom itself."
"Love yourself so deeply...when you see another...you see God."

Overwhelmed with Love...I whispered "I am so deeply Grateful."

"Is there anything else you'd like to say before you go?"

The Angel Smiled
"All I have is Now...and Now is Always Here."
"Peace is Alive...Alive within You."
"You are Silence Supreme."
"This silence is...Peace on Earth."
"This is the End...and the Beginning."

Peace

Thank you for walking this journey with me.
Paula
Light from Creator

www.ingramcontent.com/pod-product-compliance
Lightning Source LLC
Chambersburg PA
CBHW071803080526
44589CB00012B/664